BEATS, BOHEMIANS
AND INTELLECTUALS

BEATS, BOHEMIANS AND INTELLECTUALS

JIM BURNS

Edited, with an introduction by John Freeman

TRENT EDITIONS

Published by Trent Editions, 2000

Trent Editions
Department of English and Media Studies
The Nottingham Trent University
Clifton Lane
Nottingham NG11 8NS

Printed in Great Britain by Goaters Limited, Nottingham
ISBN 0 905 488 57 1

Contents

ACKNOWLEDGEMENTS   7

FOREWORD   9

INTRODUCTION   11

BEATS, BOHEMIANS AND INTELLECTUALS   21

    THE AMERICAN INFLUENCE   23
    CHILDREN OF FANTASY   30
    ROBERT MCALMON   40
    ERSKINE CALDWELL   47
    KENNETH FEARING   56
    EDWIN ROLFE   65
    KENNETH PATCHEN   72
    BEAT ROOTS   82
    GARY SNYDER   87
    LEW WELCH   105
    BEAT WOMEN   116
    ALLEN GINSBERG   129
    LORD BUCKLEY   137
    JOHN MONTGOMERY   146
    MIGRANT   155
    SATIS   160
    CHARLES BUKOWSKI   168
    ALFRED KAZIN   176
    IRVING HOWE   189
    GREENWICH VILLAGE   201
    HENRY ROTH   208
    ISAAC ROSENFELD   217
    SEYMOUR KRIM   227
    INDEX   235

Acknowledgements

The essays in this book originally appeared in the following publications:

The American Influence: *New Society*, London, 7th December 1967
Children of Fantasy: *Palantir* 13, Preston, 1979
Robert McAlmon: *Tangent* 1, New Malden, 1976
Erskine Caldwell: *London Magazine*, London, June/July 1996
Kenneth Fearing: *Prop* 1, Bolton, 1996
Edwin Rolfe: *The Wide Skirt* 28, Penistone, 1996
Kenneth Patchen: *Beat Scene* 15, Coventry, 1993
Beat Roots: *Beat Dreams & Plymouth Sounds*, Plymouth, 1987
Gary Snyder: *Beat Scene* 22, Coventry, 1995
Lew Welch: *Comstock Lode* 8, London, 1981
Beat Women: *Beat Scene* 16, Coventry, 1993
Allen Ginsberg: *Beat Scene* 10, Coventry, 1990
Lord Buckley: *Beat Scene* 19, Coventry, 1994
John Montgomery: *The Kerouac Connection* 24, Glasgow, 1992
Migrant: *Ambit* 27, London 1966
Satis: *Stand* Volume 39 Number 3, Newcastle, 1998
Charles Bukowski: *Beat Scene* 20, Coventry, 1994
Alfred Kazin: *The Penniless Press* 2, Preston, 1996
Irving Howe: *The Penniless Press* 1, Preston, 1995
Greenwich Village: *Beat Scene* 23, Coventry, 1995
Henry Roth: *The Penniless Press* 3, Preston, 1996
Isaac Rosenfeld: *The Penniless Press* 4, Preston, 1997
Seymour Krim: *Stand* 12: 4, Newcastle, 1971

The editor wishes to thank Roy Fisher, Edwin Morgan and John Lucas for writing in support of this publication; Stephen Knight, Acting Head of the School of English, Communication and Philosophy at Cardiff

ACKNOWLEDGEMENTS

University, for authorising payment for the retyping of the essays, and for general support; Anna Wigley, especially, for doing the typing and a great deal more; Dean Burnett and Dawn Harrington for much technical advice and help; and the University of Cardiff for the allocation of a semester's study leave to complete the editorial work. Final thanks to Jim Burns himself for his ever-prompt and friendly collaboration, and his patience.

Foreword

When I first started writing and publishing in the early 1960s I wanted to do more than get a few poems in magazines and then see them collected in a slim volume. There were things that I was interested in, and it seemed logical to write about them, so from the beginning I produced articles and reviews for publications like The Guardian, Jazz Journal, New Society, Tribune and a host of little magazines. I didn't think of them as destined for book publication. They were write for immediate use and I moved on to other matters once I'd done them. As the years progressed I did write more substantial essays, though the impulse behind them was what it had always been – to occupy myself with what interested me and to draw attention to writers I thought unfairly neglected or forgotten. But, again, I wasn't necessarily thinking of these pieces as eventually meant to be in between the covers of a book. Other people – John Freeman, John Lucas, Alan Dent (editor of the Penniless Press) – began to suggest that what I'd been doing over the years had a continuity and cohesion that would enable the best pieces to stand together as a part-record, at least, of my interests (some would say obsessions) and as a chart of areas of intellectual activity too often overlooked in this country. I'm grateful to them for their encouragement. And I'm grateful to all the editors who gave me space in their magazines to enjoy myself by writing what I wanted to write.

Jim Burns

Introduction

The essays in this book are concerned with American literature, culture and society in the twentieth century, and to some extent with their reception and influence in Britain. They are a selection from a much larger number of articles Jim Burns has published on these and related topics in various journals over a period of more than thirty years, though the majority of the pieces included here were written in the last decade.

The different contexts in which the essays first appeared, together with the natural evolution of a writer's outlook and manner over many years, inevitably occasion some variations in style. It is equally true, however, that the whole collection is characterised by an unfussy straightforwardness, together with a thorough knowledge of his material, which are the hallmarks of all Burns's prose.

Most of the essays focus on individual novelists, poets, and critics: but there are common themes running through the collection, beyond the fact that many of the writers examined are associated, more or less closely, with groups such as the Beats, the poets of the San Francisco Renaissance, and the New York Intellectuals. Among these themes is the social and political background, of which the essays taken together form a coherent picture. Several of the writers discussed experienced the Depression, with its poverty and radicalisation, had more or less uneasy relations with the Communist Party, and suffered from the McCarthyite persecution of the fifties. Others stayed clear of political involvements, but most had firsthand knowledge, reflected in their writing, of the hardships and often (not always) the loyalties of working-class life: though, as Burns remarks, class differences have often been less important in America than in Britain.

In his essay on Isaac Rosenfeld, Burns quotes a tribute by Theodore Solotaroff:

> Like many of the young writers who came out of the Depression,
> [Rosenfeld] had learned, as he says, "through political activity, to admire
> the vigour which a social orientation will impart to thought," and from
> the start his criticism was given vitality and point by his consciousness
> of what a given book was saying – implicitly and unconsciously as well
> as explicitly – about the times, about us.

This quotation could well stand as a summary of Burns's own aims
and achievements as a critic, provided one adds at once that he also
admires Alfred Kazin and his significantly titled autobiography, *Writing
Was Everything*. It is good writing that interest Burns, like Kazin, first
and foremost, and that provides the focus for his essays.

The Beats, and the bohemians of Greenwich Village and the
expatriate community of inter-war Paris, are seen in this book as
reacting, like the radicals and socialists, against the grey conformity of
much American culture: and some of the Beats and bohemians
themselves have been radicals and socialists. They are examined
sympathetically but not uncritically, and the self-indulgent and
destructive tendencies that sometimes limited their achievements are
noted. But they are not condemned for their commitment to art, beauty
and pleasure. As Burns notes in an essay on Greenwich Village:

> Strike leaders and union organisers mingled with the Villagers, partly
> because they provided a sympathetic audience (and a useful one in
> terms of publicity), and partly because, for many people, the dream
> was then of 'Bread and Roses', i.e. a socialism which would not only
> abolish poverty and injustice, but would also usher in a new era in
> which the 'good things of life' would be available to all. And both
> bohemians and political activists saw the arts as being foremost among
> those good things.

The social awareness running through these essays, and the social
conscience that Burns shares with many of his authors, is not a matter
of simple sloganising or us-and-them attitudes. Erskine Caldwell, for
example, is shown in his fiction and reportage as depicting poor Southern
whites as often racist and violent: no idealisation of the proletariat here.
And several New York intellectuals are shown to have found it

increasingly difficult to identify with political groups and ideologies, even while retaining a strong loyalty to the ethos of the (typically) hard-pressed, working-class immigrants of their parents' generation.

Some of the essays touch on jazz culture, which has been predominantly a Black culture, and Burns, who has been for many years jazz editor of *Beat Scene*, has written scores of articles about jazz and the jazz milieu. For reasons of space all these articles (and others on writers, magazines, painters and booksellers) have been omitted. It is hoped that a selection of the jazz articles may appear in a separate volume.

Radicals, working-class writers, bohemians, Beats and Blacks: most of the American writers and other artists Burns has written about can be included in one or more of these categories, and they are all to some extent 'outsiders'. That there is much good writing outside the orbit of 'establishment' publishing, publicising, and literary history, which never attains the currency and more or less classic status of (say) Faulkner and Hemingway, is an implicit and sometimes explicit part of Burns's critical agenda. There are essays here on writers such as Kazin, Caldwell, and Gary Snyder, and an interview with Allen Ginsberg, all of whom are far from unknown: but of these perhaps only Ginsberg is something like a household name in this country, and Caldwell, the only one who has had a mass readership, has, Burns argues, never had the critical recognition that was his due. Again, when Burns writes about Charles Bukowski, he deals with the early poetry and not the later, more publicised prose work or Bukowsi's reputation as a larger-than-life boozer, womaniser and gambler.

More typical of Burns's subjects in their status are novelists like Henry Roth and poets like Kenneth Fearing and Lew Welch, or unclassifiable but lively figures such as Seymour Krim and the delightful 'Lord' Buckley. In the survey articles on Greenwich Village and on the women writers associated with the Beats, but also in other articles describing the social and intellectual milieu of the writers under discussion, a host of even less well known writers make brief appearances, usually with an economical characterisation that leaves the reader with some sense of the nature and quality of their work.

Famous names such as James Joyce, William Carlos Williams, and Saul Bellow do appear because of their influence on, and interaction with, the other writers: but Burns appears to feel no need to add more systematically to the considerable critical writing already devoted to them. It is, I think, significant that Burns has never written a full-length article on Jack Kerouac, though he quotes him frequently in articles on other Beats: but Kerouac, even more than Ginsberg, has had plenty of attention from other writers (and readers). There is, it is true, a substantial article on Kerouac and jazz, and perhaps he will write one day about Charlie Parker and literature: but to date there is no substantial piece about Parker among Burns's copious writings on jazz, though his long-established devotion to him is clear. His early and abiding attachment to American cinema notwithstanding, Burns's criticism is a one-man crusade against the star system in literature: he is interested in the whole picture, to which the bit players and technical staff also make essential contributions. (Why stop there? he might ask, thinking of the whole social and economic world supporting, reflected in, and subsequently affected by any major production.)

This crusade on behalf of the forgotten has had repercussions in America as well as in Britain: anyone who seeks out the anthologies of writing by Beat women mentioned in a note at the end of Burns's article on the subject will find Richard Peabody, the editor of *A Different Beat: Writings by Women of the Beat Generation*, acknowledging that some of its inclusions are directly inspired by Burns's piece.

Given their deviation from any beaten track, these essays will constitute for many readers, as they did for me, an invitation to a voyage of discovery. I hope such readers will find, as I did, that they gain a clear sense of the nature and achievement of the work produced by the writers discussed, a desire to read more of it, and a greater insight into the world in which they lived.

Burns is always aware of the importance of the channels by which writers reach readers, and the crucial role played by small presses and little magazines. Many such presses and magazines appear in these pages, and two chapters are devoted to significant though short-lived magazines, *Migrant* and *Satis*, which helped to mediate American writing to a British audience and put British and American writers in touch.

Most of the essays are objective in the sense that they address any reader who is, or might become, interested in the topics discussed. But the first (and earliest) essay, 'The American influence', is a more personal account of Burns's own developing interest in American literature, its origins in his early enthusiasm for jazz, and its relation to his social background and his career as a poet. Since this article appeared in 1967 Burns has published many volumes of poetry, more articles and reviews than even he could probably count, and edited two magazines, *Move* and *Palantir*, which printed poetry, fiction, reviews and articles by both British and American writers.

Move ran from 1964 to 1968 and produced eight issues, plus a supplement, *Thirteen American Poets*, published in November 1966. *Palantir* ran from 1976 to 1983, with Burns taking over the editorship – initially as a temporary measure! – from the third issue to the twenty-third and last. *Palantir* was, in my view, one of the most interesting and important little magazines of its time: but the contribution of the more short-lived *Move* may have been even more important, since it appeared at a time when there were very few other outlets in Britain for American poetry or the British poetry that was in sympathy with it.

If you pick up a recent issue of a British literary magazine like *Ambit, The Penniless Press, The Wide Skirt* or *Prop*, there is a good chance you will find one or more, possibly several, reviews of recent British and American poetry, and a full-length article – sometimes two – by Jim Burns. Between 1965 and 1984 Burns wrote regular columns, one on little magazines and another on small presses, for *Tribune*. 'They were', he says, 'the only regular columns (outside the little mags themselves), and having them in *Tribune* meant that it was a chance to bring stuff to the attention of non-specialist readers', – readers, one might add, whose political views would be broadly similar to Burns's own. Burns has probably done more for the health of our little magazine culture, such an essential part of a flourishing literary life, than any other single person; and he has probably also reviewed more contemporary poets than anyone else living, an important service for readers interested in finding their way among the large quantities of poetry books now published.

The magazines I've mentioned and many others are also likely to carry some of Burns's poems, and despite his valuable work as a critic and editor, it is as a poet that Burns is, and deserves to be, bestknown. This is not the place for an extensive consideration of Burns's poems, and I have written about them elsewhere:[1] but it is right to remark that the reader of the poems will find the essays illuminating, and vice versa. As a poet, Burns's style, or styles, owe more to American influences than British ones, though his idiom and observations are as authentically local as William Carlos Williams could desire. Themes, events, and names which crop up in the essays appear also in the poems. Burns's awareness of the social matrix of personal experience, and his loyalty to the disadvantaged and to egalitarian ideals combined with an unsentimental realism, align his poetry with the work of the novelists and critics as well as the poets who appear in this book.

Though an interest in Burns the poet is not a necessary qualification for reading the essays with pleasure and profit, an awareness of the persona projected by the poems will alert the reader to the roots in personal experience which nourish many of the perceptions and reflections in the essays. When, for example, Burns remarks that any balance-sheet of the achievements and failures of Greenwich Village should include its inspirational effect on artists and writers who never lived there, we can guess that he is one such himself. Similarly, when Irving Howe wonders how to explain to a younger generation of 'intellectuals of Left or Right [attacking] unionism' the ways in which, in the New York of the thirties, 'the garment unions were an essential part of the immigrant life, helping to ease its hardships and giving our people a fragment of dignity', we know that Burns knows how he feels. A further quotation from Howe is followed by a quiet hint of Burns's empathy:

We need not overvalue the immigrant Jewish experience in order to
feel a lasting gratitude for having been part of it. A sense of natural
piety towards one's origins can live side by side with a spirit of critical
detachment. We take pleasure in having been related to those self
educated workers, those sustaining women, those almost-forgotten
writers and speakers devoted to excitements of controversy and thought.

'It was a personal note,' comments Burns, 'and yet could apply to the
feelings of many people reflecting on their roots.' Similar sentiments can
be found in his poems, such as 'Village Life' from his recent collection,
Confessions of an Old Believer (Redbeck Press, Bradford, 1996):

> so the talk turns to parents,
> and Philip Larkin is quoted,
> naturally, and everyone nods wisely,
> though it never struck me as smart,
> and I always liked my mum and dad,
> and thought they did the best they could,
> in the circumstances,
> which included the Depression,
> the Second World War,
> and the resurgence of Conservatism.

Like Irving Howe, Alfred Kazin strikes a chord with Burns when he
speaks of encountering among the students at Black Mountain College,
in its pre-Olson/Creeley period, some 'vagrant idealists a decade before
hippiedom who flopped on the college steps and wanted to live with
us Thoreau's life of the spirit.' Burns finds in this remark 'something
of the puritanism of the autodidact, the man who had few advantages
and had to obtain his education the hard way in public libraries and
by systematic reading.' Burns himself is essentially an autodidact, having
left school at sixteen to work in factories, offices and the army: and
these essays give a good indication of his 'systematic reading' – though
it extends well beyond the subjects of this book. (It ought to be added
that, following a spell of unemployment in middle age, Burns did
eventually take a university degree: but whatever he may have gained
from the experience, by that time his reading and writing habits, and
his interests and outlook, had already been long established.)

In fact, Burns is as well-read, and as intelligently informed, as anyone I have ever encountered, and has the priceless independence of mind, originality and integrity, as well as the inexhaustible appetite for books, that sometimes distinguish the self-taught. As for puritanism, Burns is certainly no prude, but he does value hard work, self-reliance and self-discipline, responsibility and seriousness: and other comments in the essays (and some of the poems, too) indicate that he shares, in the light of these values, Kazin's implied rejection of 'hippiedom' and a great deal of what is conveyed by reference to 'the sixties'. Puritanism of this sort, with a political edge, is evident in Burns's poem 'Change' from the collection *Fred Engels in Woolworth's* (Oasis Books, London, 1975):

> Don't blame the elderly,
> some of them at least tried
> a General Strike. What have
> you done? Don't look for the
> easy way. There isn't one.
> Don't let them make your bed
> for you. Rumpling the blankets
> won't alter anything. Get
> rid of the bed and sleep
> on the floor. It's uncomfortable,
> but it's the only way. Nothing
> worthwhile comes easy. Live
> by yourself or with a few others,
> and state your own terms. Work
> at it. It's the only way.
> Think about what you haven't
> done yourself. Change.

Even later in life than taking a university degree, Burns visited America for the first time, and several poems in the same recent collection as 'Village Life' refer to that experience. One of them, 'Autumn in New York', might stand as the final link offered here between Burns the poet and Burns the critic. It might be taken, perhaps, as an epigraph to the essays, except for the fact that in the essays the America of the recent past, which the poet finds only as a memory in the modern city, is recreated in all its vitality and immediacy. But the poem, like the essays, is a testament to Burns's lifelong fascination with America, and his willing exposure to its influence:

> I wonder what I thought I'd find in New York?
> Old communists speaking in Union Square,
> Jack Kerouac on Macdougal Street,
> Bird at the Jazz Corner of the World,
> Franz Kline sitting in the Cedar Street Tavern?
>
> Forty years of books and music and paintings
> drifting around in my head,
> I knew the place so well
> a stranger asked me for directions,
> and I told him which turnings to take.
>
> But nothing remained of what I'd gone to see.
> Wanting time to stand still,
> forgetting all the lessons of history,
> I think I expected to find myself in the city,
> and instead met someone who was lost.

*

When I showed him a draft of this introduction, Jim wrote to me:

> I think the influence of Kenneth Rexroth might need to be acknowledged in terms of his work as an essayist and reviewer (and, of course, his example as an autodidact). Rexroth wrote about all kinds of things – jazz, poetry, politics, utopian communities, painting, urban problems, religion, other writers (not only poets but novelists, etc.). So, he was an example for me to follow in some ways. And he'd always been politically engaged, in one way or another. His poetry was important to me, too.
> I suppose it's curious that I didn't write much about Rexroth – a shortish article for *Beat Scene* years ago, and a couple of reviews of his books – but he was always a presence in my thinking.

John Freeman

Footnote

1. 'Jim Burns's Poems', *The Cambridge Quarterly*, 6:3, Cambridge, 1975, 258-267; 'War, Class War, History and Narrative in the Poetry of Jim Burns', *Poetry Wales*, Volume 31:3, Bridgend, 1996, 25-28; 'Jim Burns, *Confessions of an Old Believer*', *Tears in the Fence*, 19, 77-78, Blandford Forum, 1997.

BEATS, BOHEMIANS AND INTELLECTUALS

THE AMERICAN INFLUENCE, 1967

L ooking through some of my poems recently, an acquaintance remarked that the influence seemed predominantly American. He was surprised, and perhaps a little perturbed, when I told him I didn't think it could be anything else.

Now he wasn't just talking about the technical aspect of writing poems – although that did come into it – but more about the fact that the references, attitudes and some of the language all reflected a more than passing knowledge of Americana; and this despite the fact that I've never been to the United States. I think he was of the opinion that I'd deliberately used, say, the name of Custer instead of Cromwell, as a kind of concession to the current taste for pop culture. But as I pointed out, Cromwell may have had a battle at Preston, where I live, but I can't recall that when we were kids we ever fought it over again. We did, however, die regularly around Custer's 7th Cavalry flag.

That was just one example, and my acquaintance went on to point out others, like the obscure bandleaders (Claude Thornhill, Boyd Raeburn) and film stars (Joanne Dru).

My companion's objections to my happy acceptance of 'cultural isolation' centred on the fact that he thought I'd wilfully denied my heritage, and so lost the benefits I could have gained from a realisation of where my roots really are. It's difficult not to be sarcastic with people who lecture me about my 'heritage' and 'roots' but I restrained myself, and tried to think about the matter objectively. I couldn't see that he was right then, and on reflection I still can't.

Growing up, as I did, in the working-class area of a medium-sized northern industrial town, the chances to come into contact with 'culture' (in the normal, not 'pop,' sense of the word) were few and far between.

Agreed, the library was open to everyone, but it seemed to me to have been designed mainly for the middle-class. The whole atmosphere of the place, and the attitude of those who ran it, was enough to frighten off any inarticulate youngster in shabby clothes. Not only that, but the idea of books — of the arts, in fact — was something which, whilst not completely alien, was disconcerting. I suspect that this was partly because of the slow-dying — it's far from gone yet — attitude amongst working-class people that good music, books, and so on, were not for the likes of them.

Oh yes, it was permissible to read books, provided they were textbooks connected with your work, or popular fiction. I've often read of the working-class communities in which a respect for the arts is instilled into children, but it certainly didn't work that way in the part of Lancashire I lived in.

At the same time that I felt this alienation from middle-class culture, I also had a yearning for something I could identify with. A few books did come into the house — mostly Sunday school prizes and the like — and the radio was, of course, available. It was radio which was responsible for the start of the American influence. Obviously, if I couldn't get to grips with the prevailing established culture, and the pop culture was unsatisfactory (the thought of those variety shows on BBC radio's 'Light Programme ' still sends embarrassed shivers down my spine), then I had either to give up, or turn elsewhere.

My mother and father may have doffed their headgear to culture each Sunday by listening to Albert Sandler and the Palm Court Orchestra. But my own tastes — usually indulged in later when my father had gone to bed, and my mother, a more tolerant person, allowed me to fiddle around with the radio — ran to AFN, or the various foreign stations playing American jazz records. The taste for jazz was not only a means of satisfying my appetite for something relatively 'serious,' but also gave me a kind of underground culture to identify with, one which hadn't yet been taken over by the middle-class.

My initial liking was for the 'modern' jazz (bebop) of the late 1940s, which had certain intellectual implications. This, plus the cinema-going normal in those pre-television days, was a major factor in my

'Americanisation.' I suppose the image of America – a not unattractive one even after Hollywood had finished with it – was more interesting than the reality of Lancashire. I also honestly thought that America, despite being 2,000 miles away, was closer to me in spirit than, say, the Home Counties, where I envisaged a middle-class culture which was an expansion of the local one.

I read magazines and papers, and saw films (as few as possible, British productions being anathema to me in those days), all produced in the south, and they often seemed to be talking about a country which, for all it meant to me, could have been even farther away than the United States. And not only that, they talked about it in a language which, in many ways, had less in common with my manner of speech than had American. On reflection, this may just have been self-delusion, but it appeared to be true then, and this period was a formative one for me. It's perhaps significant that many of the first English 'little magazines' to make contact with, and publish, young American writers of the Black Mountain/William Carlos Williams school of thought were based in the provinces.

The American poet, Gilbert Sorrentino, once said that

> The chances are that a young man who, in 1945, didn't 'dig Dizzy,' would never in 1955 read Charles Olson. Bop, for me, was the entrance into the general world of culture, although at the time, I wouldn't have believed it. When I was 14, culture meant going to the opera and doing your homework every night.

There was a time lag in the impact of Dizzy Gillespie's trumpet in this country, and my own interest in bebop didn't really get under way until 1950; but Sorrentino's thesis nonetheless holds true for me. I don't think I would have read Charles Olson in 1958 or 1959 had I not become involved with bop some eight or nine years before. Other people I know have confirmed similar experiences. The American poets, Kenneth Patchen and Kenneth Rexroth, both came into my world through the pages of jazz magazines, but I don't recall ever reading about any English poets.

Had I gone through the middle-class mill – i.e. grown up in a house where 'culture' was encouraged, been taught the standard manner of speech and so on – I doubt whether I would have ever heard of Olson or Rexroth, or written much myself for that matter. Had I come across Carlos Williams I would probably have been at variance with his use of language and his ideas on technique. I think this is what would have happened had I even remained working-class in my background, but gone chasing after middle-class ideas of culture.

As it is, Williams's *Paterson* says more to me than any English poem, with the exception of a few poets whose interests lie in the same direction as mine. What it boils down to is that Williams, despite his obvious interest in the American experience, can see the application of the experience to the individual situation, whereas most English poets are social beings caught in the web of their habits.

Paradoxically, my interest in American writers has led me back to neglected English poets (Basil Bunting, for example, whose work first became known to me from references in an American magazine), and some European ones. The point is that the Americans, in the tradition of the modern movement, are international in their scope and appeal, and I doubt that I'd have become very familiar with Céline, Artaud, Jarry, Cendrars and others, had I not first of all been interested in contemporary American literature. Agreed, it's possible to get to these writers without having to go via America, but I found it easier to get their work in American publications than through the local library.

But, to revert to my deepening involvement with a sort of 'underground', I remember that in 1954 when I went to Germany the pattern continued as before. I didn't listen to BFN, I tuned in to AFN, where at least the announcers sounded friendly, and not patronising. BFN seemed to be nothing but relays of the Light Programme, or a few BFN-produced shows which for mediocrity even the Light couldn't beat. They didn't play as many pop discs on AFN; they did play a fair amount of jazz; and they also didn't presume that the audience was made up of semi-morons. It was on AFN that I first heard Carl Orff's *Carmina Burana*.

In the church army hut one could get a few magazines (like *Reveille*) and paperbacks (Agatha Christie). But the German shops had plenty of American books. I read Faulkner, Hemingway, Caldwell, Mailer, Capote, Dos Passos, Scott Fitzgerald, not to mention a horde of minor writers and some nineteenth-century classics.

By the standards of an intellectual I was probably pretty middle-class in my tastes, but by middle-class standards I was out on a limb. I got an idea of my position from the reaction of two other people. One, a National Service private who had a degree in literature, looked through my small library and found it of interest, though I could tell he wasn't madly enthusiastic about my leanings. The other, a National Service officer, whose father owned a factory in Wales, glanced at some of my books during an inspection, then gave me an odd look.

Later, back home in England, the Beat writers, as their work filtered through, seemed more interesting than the Angry Young Men, most of whom were fairly middle-class in their habits and attitudes. Admittedly, it could be argued that Allen Ginsberg was too; but class didn't seem as important to the Americans, and they also appeared alive to people as individuals.

On the other hand, Amis (no, I'll be honest, I never did get past the first few pages of *Lucky Jim* because it was almost like reading science fiction so far as its relation to my situation went), Wain, Braine and the others seemed to create cardboard figures to fit into set scenes, most of which were foreign to me. I wasn't even moved by Braine's account of a man from my type of background struggling to make good, because it didn't occur to me to try and make it into the local middle-class society. As for the English poets, well they were, with a few exceptions, still wrapped in the womb of Oxford, Cambridge, London; and their work showed it, especially in the way they used language.

As I gradually got drawn into writing, I found that the Americans I admired – and the few Englishmen connected with those provincial magazines I mentioned earlier – were interested in writing for its own sake, not because it was a social activity. Since those days I've published in various places, but have always remained outside the English literary scene in many ways, preferring to keep in touch with American and Canadian writers by mail, rather than meet most of my own countrymen.

I suppose I am, in a way, an exile in my own country. I don't take any part in the activities of the town where I live, and my main reason for staying here is that it is relatively quiet, and I can do what I want to do, see my few friends, and bring up my family. I don't feel part of the English scene. My first book of poems was published in New York (by a poet/publisher who saw some of my poems, and liked them – I wonder if that would happen here?). In fact, I can't honestly say I feel very much a part of English life in general. I'm probably in a position similar to the American expatriates in Paris in the 1920s, moving around the area I know best, ignored by most of the locals, and in touch with a few literary acquaintances by mail, and a few local friends because of our interest in jazz and drink.

I've sometimes thought that maybe people of my generation (I am 31 now) are in a kind of no man's land, not relating to the periods before 1945 or since 1955. The values of people from similar backgrounds to myself were formed between 1945 and 1955, and consequently we missed out on the patriotism of the war years, and the insularity and confidence of the past ten or twelve years. Today's teenagers don't look to the USA – for films, music, clothes style – as much as we did, and their parochialism seems strange to me. For better, or for worse, the United States provided most of my entertainment and culture. So my friends, acquaintances and readers will just have to live with the fact that I mention Custer instead of Cromwell, and Boyd Raeburn instead of Ted Heath.

Note

This piece was written over thirty years ago and has dated in the sense that some of the facts have changed. I have been to the United States, and I have been far more involved in literary activity in this country as a magazine editor, poet, literary journalist, and odd-job man on the fringes of the academic world. But I still stand by much of what it says about the influence of American music, films, writing, etc. And my interest continues, as I hope the essays in this book will show.

CHILDREN OF FANTASY, 1979

Children of Fantasy: The First Rebels of Greenwich Village by Robert E. Humphrey. John Wiley & Sons, Baffins Lane, Chichester, West Sussex.

The development of Greenwich Village as a bohemian centre has more than a little to do with its physical layout, so it's of interest to consider, if only briefly, what gave the area a distinctive character. The mid-nineteenth century saw New York expanding on a large scale with the city authorities attempting to impose some form of standardisation in the shape of a gridiron pattern of streets. When they looked at Greenwich Village –and it had existed as a village in its own right for some time – they were faced with the fact that it housed a lot of people, and to knock down all the buildings that lined its winding streets would be an almost impossible task. So, the rest of New York developed to order and left behind the Village. It soon became a haven for various immigrant groups hunting for relatively cheap housing. The Irish arrived in the 1850s, the Blacks after the Civil War, and the Italians in the 1890s. By the beginning of the twentieth century Greenwich Village was largely a low-rent area with a population made up of second-generation Irish and recently-arrived Italians. The Blacks had mostly moved on. There were, of course, representatives of other nationalities scattered around the Village, but the Irish and Italians predominated.

There was a tradition of artists and writers living in the Village as far back as the mid-nineteenth century, and others used the area, and its restaurants and bars, because of the relaxed atmosphere compared to the rest of New York. Those used to the layout and atmosphere of European cities especially found the Village to their liking. But although small pockets of bohemians existed, and occasional attempts were made to push the idea of an American Bohemia, there was no overall sense of an actual community. Greenwich Village was not then a name synonymous with poetry and music and painting. The writers and artists themselves lived in groups which rarely mingled, and – perhaps of more importance – there wasn't a widespread awareness of bohemianism amongst the general public, despite the fuss that had greeted the publication of Du Maurier's *Trilby* in the 1890s. But around 1910 or so a trend became obvious. There was an almost conscious movement of talented people into Greenwich Village. Along with the writers and artists came a flood of teachers, social workers, journalists, political activists, and others whose interests complemented those of the creative types. To be fair, some social workers and journalists were already there, working to alleviate and expose the conditions in which the poor immigrants lived. And the influx of bohemians didn't necessarily make their work any easier. Rents tended to rise, and families were evicted so that landlords could cater for the bohemians (mostly from the middle-class, of course) who were anxious to have studios and garrets.

It's essential to bear in mind that, during the period we're concerned with (roughly 1910 to 1920), art and politics, or at least social concerns, were linked in many people's thoughts. And even when someone wasn't convinced that socialism or anarchism had the answers to all the ills of society he or she often wanted to argue his or her point of view with those who were. Many of the most active Villagers contributed to magazines which advocated left-wing solutions to social and economic problems, and some even went so far as to participate in strikes and similar activities. Strike leaders and union organisers mingled with the Villagers, partly because they provided a sympathetic audience (and a useful one in terms of publicity), and partly because, for many people, the dream was then of 'Bread and Roses,' i.e. a socialism which would not only abolish poverty and injustice, but would also usher in a new era in which the 'good things of life' would be available to all. And both bohemians and political activists saw the arts as being foremost among the good things.

Cheap accommodation was obviously a determining factor in inducing the first bohemians to move to the Village, and fashion no doubt also played its part. But one has to take into account the effects of the general urbanisation of the United States. Although it was the twenties before the urban population outstripped that of the rural areas the pattern had been set before then, and once the westward expansion had reached its limits there was, in a sense, nowhere to go but the towns and cities. The growth of urban centres, the increase in industrialisation, and the spread of a new middle class, meant that there was an increased demand for higher education, and for books, magazines, music, paintings, and so on. The sons and daughters of the middle class found that they had the time, money and education to indulge in what were, by the standards of the settlers, often seemingly impractical occupations. They were also anxious to break away from the drabness and conformity of many of the new towns and cities. Urbanisation provided the surplus funds whereby a number of people could survive on odd jobs connected with journalism, music, painting, and teaching. It was an ideal climate for bohemianism. New York was not the only city which eventually produced a bohemia. Chicago, for example, had a vigorous, productive artistic community in which writers, artists, and political activists mixed. Kenneth Rexroth's *An Autobiographical Novel* gives a lively, evocative picture of Chicago's 'Red Bohemia,' as it was called.

If economic matters, and fashionable impulses, determined many Villagers' reasons for their arrival it can't be denied that artistic ones were also important. There was, it seems, something in the air. The famous magazine *Poetry* was founded in Chicago, and poets like Robinson Jeffers, Ezra Pound, Vachel Lindsay, and Edna St. Vincent Millay were active. Another famous magazine, *The Little Review*, was born in 1914. In 1913 the Armory Show in New York introduced the work of Matisse, Picasso, and many others to American audiences. Marcel Duchamp's 'Nude Descending a Staircase' became the sensation of the exhibition, arousing extreme responses among both bohemians and bourgeoisie. Isadora Duncan was moving the young with her expressive dancing. Women's Rights, too, were a subject for debate, and the anarchist Emma Goldman was a well-known figure in the Village. On the political front the interest in socialism was demonstrated by the fact that membership of the Socialist Party boomed, and E.V. Debs, its candidate in the Presidential election, got almost one million votes. In addition, the I.W.W. (Industrial Workers of the World) was at its peak and leading a wave of strikes that caught the attention of the nation. It appeared as if the stage was being set for radical changes throughout society, and Hutchins Hapgood was moved to suggest that perhaps the artistic and political unrest of the period had a common foundation. Both artists and workers wanted, in his view, to 'loosen up the old forms and traditions.' He may well have been right about some artists and some workers, but it's more than probable that the majority of people in both groups were less interested in radical change than in altering their own personal situations to their own satisfaction.

A major point to consider in connection with the various activities I've referred to is that America did not enter the First World War until 1917. The events in Europe had their effect, of course, but anti-war sentiment, and sometimes a sense of isolation, combined to sustain a situation where radical change seemed possible. This mood did begin to falter after 1914, but it only really collapsed in 1917 when it became obvious that the Government was prepared to take extreme measures against dissidents, and the population in general was caught up in the war hysteria and not prepared to tolerate anyone dissenting from it. The I.W.W. was harassed by state and federal authorities (though, as an organisation, it never actually took an anti-war stance) and over one hundred of its leading lights eventually placed on mass trial for alleged subversive activities. And, in the Village, *The Masses*, one of the most influential of the left-artistic publications, found itself under attack, with its editors arrested and accused of 'conspiracy against the Government' and 'interfering with conscription.' Among the editors were Max Eastman, Floyd Dell, and John Reed, all of them (with Hutchins Hapgood and George Cram Cook) dealt with in detail in *Children of Fantasy*.

Eastman, at that time militantly left-wing, swung to the right later in life, and became a fervent anti-communist and a highly-paid writer for the *Reader's Digest*. But when he was editing *The Masses*, and its successor *The Liberator*, he championed the Bolshevik cause, as well as speaking out in favour of the working-class, women's suffrage, and other radical concerns. He also led a lively sex life, and displayed a tendency to take to ideas or movements which seemed to offer total solutions to mankind's problems. The concept of the techniques of social control – whether derived from Freud or Marx – appealed to him strongly. Like many other intellectuals, Eastman doesn't seem to have really liked the mass of people all that much, especially when they lived in a manner he didn't care for. So 'the scientific control of mass behaviour' seemed to him of value. In a way this kind of attitude possibly pointed towards his later conservatism. So far as writing was concerned he was very much a populariser, a man who could take involved political and social theories and simplify them into books and magazine articles for wider consumption. There is nothing basically wrong with that, of course, unless one gets the theories wrong. An unkind comment about Eastman was that he was 'the Frank Harris of socialism, an inspired amateur from the moment a girl friend explained Marx to him in three easy lessons,' but he could be fairly astute at times. *Children of Fantasy* is only concerned with Eastman's career prior to the twenties – a recent biography, *The Last Romantic* by William L. O'Neill, tells the full story – and consequently his later writings are only occasionally referred to. But books like *Love and Revolution* and *Great Companions* are still worth looking at.

Floyd Dell, like Eastman, had an early vision that the triumph of socialism would lead to 'a pastoral idyll where love and freedom flourished.' On a more practical level he moved through Chicago's Bohemia between 1909 and 1913, and then went on to Greenwich Village where he worked on *The Masses* and produced stories, plays, and journalism. Again like Eastman, he favoured psychoanalysis, loved more than a few women, and eventually lost interest in radical ideas. He also took to enthusing over the joys of married life, parenthood, and domesticity, much to the disgust of fellow-Villagers who had once followed his teachings on the subject of 'free love.' A neat satirist of the time may have hit the target when he suggested that behind such a switch of beliefs lay the philosophy that, when you've shocked people by campaigning against it, the only unconventional thing left to do is get married. On the whole Dell was certainly less interesting than Eastman, and his literary achievements reflect this fact. Little of his work now stands up to close inspection, although *Love in Greenwich Village* and *Moon Calf* may be of interest to social or literary historians. One suspects that had he not been a denizen of the Village during a publicised period Dell would be virtually forgotten.

Hutchins Hapgood and George Cram Cook are probably even more obscure figures. Cook's claim to fame rests primarily on the fact that he founded the Provincetown Players, a theatrical group which flourished in New York between 1916 and 1922. Most of the Players were Villagers, and their acting talents variable, but they were the first to stage Eugene O'Neill's plays. Like Eastman and Dell, Cook was a dreamer, though in his case his flights of fancy ran to comparisons with Ancient Greece rather than notions of future socialist utopias. He was also a bohemian in the easiest-understood sense of the word, and booze, women, scattered writings, and failed schemes were the hallmarks of his life. Still, he did drum up the enthusiasm to get the Provincetown Players going even if many of the plays they performed were mediocre. They were written by Villagers, about Villagers, for Villagers, and were soon forgotten by everyone but the Villagers. But Cook did have the intelligence to recognise that O'Neill was in a different class, and although his association with the playwright later foundered he played an important part in making his name known to the wider public. Cook went to live in Greece in the twenties, battling with his bottle problem and attempting to live like a Greek peasant. He died there in 1924.

That many of the villagers lived fairly locked-in lives is evident from *Children of Fantasy*. Floyd Dell and George Cram Cook had been associated in Chicago and Hutchins Hapgood also spent some time there. For a period he shared ideas and women with Terry Carlin, an anarchist who provided the basis for the character of Larry Slade in Eugene O'Neill's *The Iceman Cometh*. Hapgood, though never as politically motivated as some other Villagers, had a fixation about the various low-life types, ranging from criminals to anarchists and the less respectable elements of the working-class. His idealistic notions about such people often broke down when he came into close contact with them – criminals turned out to be vain and frivolous. Terry Carlin sometimes seemed merely perverse rather than idealistically motivated in his anarchism, and the lumpen proletariat were suspicious and resentful of well-meaning slummers like Hapgood. One of his books – *Types from City Streets*, published in 1910 – is a neat summary of most of his preoccupations. It ranges over boxers, criminals, bohemians, grass-roots politicians, anarchists, prostitutes and other 'street people' in an easy-to-read style which has a surface appearance of intellectual concern, but which is actually fairly shallow and steers clear of commitment by evoking an attitude of detachment.

Like the other Villagers Hapgood had his share of sexual adventures, one of them with Mabel Dodge, a lady probably best known for her links with D.H. Lawrence when he was in Taos, New Mexico. For a time her home in New York (just on the fringes of the Village) was a regular meeting place for assorted radicals, bohemians, intellectuals, writers, and artists, the idea being to throw together disparate types and then see what happened. When something did happen Mabel Dodge was delighted. In effect, all ideas, causes, movements, etc. were in existence only to provide entertainment for her guests and to add to her reputation as a hostess. And there's no doubt that her salon did attract many talented people from all walks of life. One of them was John Reed, still remembered today for his classic account of the Bolshevik Revolution, *Ten Days that Shook the World*. Reed was very much an all-American boy, educated at Harvard, personally attractive, and with a flair for vivid journalism that took him to cover strikes, revolutions, and the war in Europe. He also put himself on the side of radicals and workers – though it's frankly doubtful if he ever had a deep understanding of political or economic ideas – and generally roughed it more than most Greenwich Village left-wingers. He died in

Russia in October 1920, a victim of a typhus epidemic, after various adventures that had demonstrated his dedication to the Revolution. As Robert Humphrey says,

> Reed burned his bridges, sacrificing money, praise, and security for poverty, and the vicissitudes of a radical career. No one else in the Village could make that claim and no one else paid so high a price.

Summing up the lives of his five Villagers, Humphrey comments:

> The careers of Hutchins Hapgood, George Cram Cook, John Reed, Max Eastman, and Floyd Dell demonstrate the successes and failures common to those who experimented with a Bohemian life-style. In reaction to painful childhood and adolescent experiences, Villagers evolved a romantic outlook that became the hallmark of their rebelliousness. Finding conventional society monotonous and oppressive, they sought a community where they might escape conformity in the company of other idealists. The appealing vision of a playground unfettered by respectability lured them to Greenwich Village. They anticipated that Bohemia would provide a setting where potential might be realised and life made more exciting.

He points out that few, if any bohemians had specific plans for realising their ideals, and that sustained endeavour on behalf of radical causes was frequently beyond them. When the demands of political activity grew too onerous they went back to their garrets and studios, and wrote, painted, drank, and made love. But their dabbling in politics, as well as their involved personal lives, limited their capacity to achieve anything artistically too, according to Humphrey. In other words, they were playing at everything – art, politics, personal relations – and consequently rarely succeeded at anything.

Humphrey may have a point, and certainly one could draw up a long list of writers who served their time in the Village without producing anything of great value. One could also draw up a list of non-Villagers who did write good books. But I'm not sure what this kind of comparison ever proves. One could probably also prove that important writers did live in, or frequent Greenwich Village. A much more interesting angle to explore is that the five bohemians inspected by Humphrey were, at bottom, old-fashioned in their approach to the arts. Most of their own writing was well within a 19th Century tradition, and none of them broke any new ground. George Cram Cook had the sense to acknowledge Eugene O'Neill's talents, but it was his only important indication of sympathy for genuinely new writing. John Reed was a good reporter, but his poems were little more than doggerel. Hutchins Hapgood gave an indication of his feelings when he called one of his books *A Victorian in the Modern World*. Max Eastman and Floyd Dell wrote very conventional novels. The real artistic innovations of the 20th century hardly affected any of these people.

Humphrey also makes play of the fact that, despite their attacks on social conventions within society in general, the bohemians erected barriers of their own. These applied not only to outsiders, but were also designed to maintain a hierarchy within bohemia itself. In addition, they didn't always practise what they preached in sexual matters. Some of those advocating 'free love' in print were less enthusiastic when their particular partners wanted to dabble at it. Male bohemians were notoriously hypocritical, expecting their women to tolerate their affairs but asking for fidelity in return. None of this seems strange. Human nature doesn't alter because people leave their home town and talk a lot about freedom.

Generally, Humphrey's aim seems to be to deny claims made in other books that the Village was a centre in which art, politics, and bohemianism combined to create a cultural renaissance. He largely does so by pointing to the failures and inconsistencies in the careers of the people he deals with. That most of their work hasn't survived is easy to prove. But then, most books don't survive, and that includes those written by academics as well as bohemians. It really is almost impossible to draw any definite conclusions from surveys of bohemianism. Who is to say whether or not things would have been different had Greenwich Village not existed? Many of the Villagers may have failed, but had they not gone to New York they might not have written or painted at all. Is it so bad that they tried to create something? Give flowers to the rebels failed, as the old anarchist saying has it. The major changes in the arts were often brought about by people who weren't bohemians, or at least chose not to live in places like the Village. And shifts in social and economic matters were determined by forces beyond the control of a handful of Villagers. But the bohemians, for all their faults, added something to society and the arts. They took their chances, made their mistakes, but usually played the game their own way. Their hearts were in the right place, even if their heads were too often in the clouds.

Adrift Among Geniuses: Robert McAlmon, Writer and Publisher of the Twenties by Sandford J. Smoller. The Pennsylvania State University Press.

In a recent radio programme devoted to Caresse and Harry Crosby ('The Gossamer Bridge', Radio 3, July 6th, 1975) mention was made of the various writers known to the romantic expatriate couple and, in some cases, published in their Black Sun Press/Crosby Continental Editions series. One name missing from the programme, however, was that of Robert McAlmon, himself an influential publisher of the twenties, associate of Joyce, Hemingway, Stein, Ford, and others, and a writer whose collection of stories, *The Indefinite Huntress*, was issued by Crosby Continental Editions in 1932. This neglect of McAlmon was not untypical, because even now, when much of the expatriate experience has been examined in detail, he remains a largely unknown quantity, especially in this country.

McAlmon was born in Kansas in 1896, and spent much of his childhood in South Dakota, which he described as 'a wild and dreary plains state.' He seems to have led a fairly normal life until the age of sixteen, in that he did the kind of things most people of his age would do at the time, but, from sixteen onwards, his days were marked by one dominant characteristic – restlessness. On leaving school he worked at a variety of jobs, drifted around the Midwest, tried university life, did a stint in the services, sampled Chicago's bohemia, and finally ended up in Greenwich Village in 1920. He had published a few poems in *Poetry* and elsewhere, and soon got to know William Carlos Williams,

Lola Ridge, Marianne Moore, and many others. With Williams he started the magazine *Contact* which, in its brief lifetime, published Pound, Wallace Stevens, Kay Boyle, and Marsden Hartley, to mention only a few names.

It was in New York, too, that he met Winifred Ellerman (better known in the literary world under her pen-name, Bryher), an event that probably had traumatic effects on his life, but which did lead to his moving to Europe. He soon knew just about everyone who was anyone in the world of the artistic avant-garde, and he also published stories and poems in *transition, This Quarter, The Exile* and *The Transatlantic Review*, magazines that were the meeting places for many of the later great names of twentieth century literature. McAlmon's reputation stood high in those days, and it was generally expected that he would produce some significant work. But the impatience, the restlessness, the bitterness that scarred his personality, and his heavy drinking, played havoc with his plans, and his writing often lacked care and form. He couldn't be bothered with revision, and James Joyce's suggestion for a title for the first book of stories – *A Hasty Bunch* – published by McAlmon's own Contact Press, aptly sums up the effect of much of his work. I would guess that once he'd sketched out an idea he lost interest in developing it, and his energies were then devoted to something else.

His story, 'An Illiterate but Interesting Woman,' is perhaps typical in this respect, and its very title is almost a reference to McAlmon's fascination with the off-beat. The woman of the story is rich and travels around, partying, having affairs, marrying, divorcing, making money, spending it, and generally leading a hedonistic life which, with its variety of experience, could provide many writers with material for a lengthy story, if not a novel. McAlmon, however, packs an outline of her activities into four pages (2,000 words at the outside) and leaves it at that. It is immensely readable, and McAlmon thankfully steers clear of any moral conclusions, but the reader never gets near to knowing what makes the woman the way she is. In a sense it is like an extended anecdote, and its main attribute is the manner in which it catches the rhythm of its character's life, and the tone of the period. And that's maybe what intrigued McAlmon more than well-rounded story-telling and analysis.

Although he published in many of the significant magazines and anthologies of the twenties and early thirties, McAlmon could never find a major publisher in the USA willing to handle his work. He brought out his own novels, stories and poems in his Contact Editions series, something he was derided for in certain quarters, but he also published Hemingway, Stein, Joyce, Williams, Mary Butts, and many others. As the twenties ran out, and the bulk of the expatriates returned home, McAlmon continued to drift – Germany, Spain, Mexico, England, and occasionally the United States. He drank and wrote as steadily as he drifted, although little of his work appeared in magazines after the early thirties. A collection of his poems, *Not Alone Lost*, was published by New Directions in 1937, and his memoirs of the twenties, *Being Geniuses Together*, came out in London from Secker and Warburg in 1938.

By 1941 he was back in the USA, a sick and dispirited man. The hard living of the previous two decades had taken its toll on his health, and financial problems forced him to accept a job in his brother's surgical goods store. In 1951 he gave up work, and the final years of his life (he died in 1956) were spent tinkering with manuscripts, writing letters to old friends, making plans for a projected long work, and occasionally railing against the state of a world that gave a Nobel Prize to a Hemingway, and yet couldn't find space for a book or two of McAlmon's. He had tried, unsuccessfully, all through the forties to place collections of stories, and his autobiography, with various American publishers, and it must have seemed that the odds were totally stacked against him. The ironic thing is that, had he lived a few years longer, he would probably have been rediscovered. The post-1955 upsurge of the non-establishment writers created a fair amount of interest in their ancestors from the twenties and thirties, and I feel sure that McAlmon's lively stories, at least, would have found favour with the enthusiasts of the Beat movement.

McAlmon's reputation suffered after the activity of the twenties partly because he didn't adjust to the demands of the thirties and forties, partly because of the enemies he made. Many of the people he'd helped – Hemingway, for example – repaid him with snide remarks and worse, though to be honest it must be admitted that McAlmon could be difficult to get along with. But this is no reason for his writing to be neglected. It had a great deal of vigour, and it was usually honest. Hemingway's *The Sun Also Rises* is often considered the classic description of the expatriates, but I would suggest that McAlmon's stories are a more reliable source of information as regards the general atmosphere of the period. There are three, in particular, which offer views of expatriate life, and each points to McAlmon's involvement with a wide variety of people: 'It's All Very Complicated' tells the story of a lesbian who, bored with women, seduces Sam, a newcomer to Paris, and then discards him when she decides that girls are better anyway; in 'The Highly-Prized Pyjamas' another newcomer to the scene has a brief affair with a French prostitute, much to the amusement of her acquaintances; and 'In-Between Ladies' describes a group of wealthy, middle-aged women who hang around the bars, hunting for the good-looking young men. McAlmon is in all the stories, functioning as a kind of detached observer, and yet he never moralises, nor is he unkind about the characters he meets. Occasionally, he mocks slightly, and he is almost always ironic, but the reader never feels that he is attempting to sit in judgement on the people he describes.

If McAlmon didn't judge his characters, he didn't romanticise them either, as witness 'Evening on the Riviera, The Playground of the World,' a story set among the rich and their cronies. In it McAlmon offers a more down-to-earth portrait of them than did Scott Fitzgerald in *Tender is the Night* (another little-known story from this period – Dorothy Parker's 'The Cradle of Civilization' – complements McAlmon's, and contradicts Scott Fitzgerald, in its cryptic view of the attitudes of the playboy set), though again he lets the reader draw his own conclusions. If the characters are condemned, they are condemned in their own words, and not in added comments from the writer.

In his novels and stories McAlmon covered most of the ground worked by other writers of the time. Sinclair Lewis's *Babbit* and *Main Street* shredded the small-town values of the American Middle-West, but McAlmon, although fully aware of the limitations of life in that area, attempted to show his people as more varied, more able to assert their own individuality, than Lewis's satire allowed. And the three Berlin stories in *Distinguished Air (Grim Fairy Tales)* probably offer as direct a view of aspects of life in the then wide-open city as we're likely to find in the fiction of the period. The title story is a deliberately flat account of a night spent visiting the bars, dance-halls, etc., drinking, taking drugs, meeting and observing the addicts and sexual deviants of all kinds, and generally wallowing in the sordid. The story is formless, other than in the way it follows the events of the night, but McAlmon's honesty invariably stopped him shaping his work in the manner of a slick novelist. One of the other stories, 'Miss Knight', is probably McAlmon's finest single piece of writing, and is a superb description of a flamboyant homosexual. The rhythm of the piece perfectly captures the tone of the man's gestures, his constant histrionics, and his exaggerated mode of speech. It is a vignette, and it is true that it doesn't attempt to go deeper than the surface, but it sustains its drive and, as with most of McAlmon's work, doesn't ring false in its sense of period and place.

It will perhaps seem that McAlmon concentrated exclusively on the deviants, the oddballs, and the eccentrics, but this wasn't so. A story like 'Machine Age Romance' shows him in a quieter, more reflective mood, and fully capable of observing and understanding the everyday and ordinary. And, as mentioned earlier, he wrote extensively about his boyhood, and his integrity always impelled him to set down things as he had known them. His work seems flat because of this – there are no rigged climaxes, no characters one can't accept as true-to-life – but it is completely honest in its portrayal of day-to-day events. The same can be said of *Post-Adolescence*, the novel in which he dealt with his early experiences in Greenwich Village. The literature of Bohemia is prone to exaggerations, with its stereotyped eccentrics and romanticised situations, but McAlmon again prefers to set down his material without frills. For all its faults (and some clumsy writing was amongst them) the novel has a vitality that probably resulted from its being written when McAlmon was still fascinated by what were then to him lively and interesting people with fresh and exciting ideas to talk about.

Besides novels and stories McAlmon also produced a little criticism – the pieces he wrote on Gertrude Stein and James Joyce were his most significant efforts in this line – and a fair amount of poetry, including one or two attempts at long works. A handful of his poems – 'The Crow Becomes Discursive' (from *Not Alone Lost*) and 'How Variously in France' (printed in *The Little Review*, Autumn-Winter, 1924/25), to mention just a couple – deserve to be reprinted, if only in anthologies. But his main achievement was, I think, in the field of the short story, and sufficient material of a worthwhile nature exists to produce an excellent collection. The Paris and Berlin stories are particularly interesting in this connection. Whether a publisher could be found for such a book is, of course, another matter.

I've attempted to give a brief outline of McAlmon's life and writings, and anyone interested in going further into either subject is referred to Sanford J. Smoller's valuable book. He's done his work well, although there are a few omissions in the useful bibliography of McAlmon's published items. It is time that McAlmon was given a little of the credit he deserves as both writer and publisher, and Smoller's well-documented account should help to open a few eyes to this fascinating man.

Note

Smoller's book is the first proper biography of McAlmon to be published. However, Robert E. Knoll's monograph, *Robert McAlmon: Expatriate Publisher and Writer* was published by the University of Nebraska Press in 1959. They also brought out *McAlmon and the Lost Generation: A Self Portrait* (1962), a selection from the autobiography, novels, and stories, edited by Knoll. *Being Geniuses Together* was reprinted in 1969 in a revised version which also included Kay Boyle's memoirs of the twenties. It was published here by Michael Joseph in 1970.

Since this piece was written *A Hasty Bunch* has been reprinted by Southern Illinois University Press in 1977, and the long poem *North America: Continent of Conjecture* by Dark Child Press in 1983. The University of New Mexico Press has published *Village: As It Happened Through A Fifteen Year Period* (1990), *Post-Adolescence: A Selection of Short Fiction* (1991) and *Miss Knight and Others* (1992).

Erskine Caldwell, 1996

In the 1950s, when I was a young soldier in Germany, Erskine Caldwell's books were easy to find amongst the American paperbacks that most local bookshops stocked. And when I was out of the army, and back in England, Pan and Four Square editions of Caldwell's work were always in the paperback racks in newsagents and elsewhere. The covers more often than not showed a dishevelled couple frolicking in a rural setting and highlighted that he was also the author of *Tobacco Road* and *God's Little Acre*.

What was interesting was that, although Caldwell seemed to be a contemporary of Hemingway, Faulkner, and Steinbeck, he certainly didn't attract the same sort of critical attention. It was easy to find essays about the other three, but little about Caldwell existed in surveys of American fiction, and the few references were usually less than enthusiastic. He was, they sometimes grudgingly admitted, a good storyteller, and few of the critics seem to have understood Otis Ferguson's astute comment that:

> A good story is the easiest thing to read there is, and the damnedest thing to write; and while there are many writers who can take a day off now and then and do a story, there are very few story-writers. Erskine Caldwell is one of those rare birds.

Of course, what also worked against Caldwell was his popularity with general readers. That, and the fact that some of his books, notably *God's Little Acre* and *Tobacco Road*, had a reputation for being mildly pornographic. Caldwell had fallen foul of censorship laws more than once but not too many literary critics rallied in his support. An obituary in *The Times* when he died in 1987 referred sniffily to his later work as 'a stream of sensationalist, semi-pornographic potboilers,' and one suspects that Caldwell's success in selling books – eighty million copies of his novels and other publications had sold world-wide in forty-three languages – was seen as somehow indicative of a lack of quality in his writing. It's true that large sales are not usually a guarantee of literary worth, but in Caldwell's case there would appear to be a case for placing the best of his work alongside that of other leading twentieth-century American writers.

Caldwell was born in Georgia in 1903, the son of a Presbyterian minister whose work kept him on the move and so gave the youngster an opportunity to see the life of the South in some detail. Later in life he wrote:

> The experience of living for six months or a year or sometimes longer in one Southern state after another, in cities and small towns and countrysides, and being exposed to numerous varieties of Protestant sects which were Calvinist in doctrine and fundamentalist in practice proved to be of more value than the intermittent and frequently-curtailed secular education I received during the first seventeen years of my life.

The varied nature of his experiences continued after his seventeenth year, with odd jobs, broken stints in higher education, newspaper work, and in 1928 a decision to give himself five years in which to establish a career as a writer. He began sending his work to little magazines, and when asked about this many years later, he said:

> Everybody in those days either wrote for a little magazine or tried to edit a little magazine. There were dozens of them, dozens of them. That's how I started getting published. There happened to be a magazine in Paris called transition that did it. That was the first one. That was the only way to get published in those hard times.

Several other little magazines, *Pagany*, *blues*, *Front*, and the 1929 anthology, *New American Caravan*, also provided outlets for Caldwell's stories, setting him alongside writers like Louis Zukofsky, Kenneth Rexroth, and William Carlos Williams. But Caldwell never really saw himself as a member of the literary avant-garde, and the little magazines were merely a way to break into print, though he always spoke warmly of what they had done for him and what he had learned from some of the other writers in their pages. As well as contributing to magazines, he placed two short, early novels, *The Bastard* and *Poor Fool*, with small presses. Caldwell's writing was not experimental in any deliberate sense, but appeared to be trying to break new ground with its downbeat subject-matter and forceful story-telling, and was of interest to editors with an eye for radicalism of both style and content.

He soon began to break into a wider world of publishing when some of his stories were accepted by *Scribner's*, then a leading magazine. And a contract from Scribner's publishing house soon followed. Unusually, it was for a collection of stories, something which publishers preferred to restrict to authors who had already established a reputation with a novel or two. But the famous editor, Maxwell Perkins, had seen the promise in Caldwell's work, and so *American Earth* appeared in 1931. It was not a good time for an unknown writer to attempt to claim the high ground, and the book sold only a few hundred copies. Caldwell was still faced with the problems of earning a living and again turned to a variety of jobs to provide him with an income. He never complained about this. 'It made me live with people,' he once said, 'and I got to know them. I learned how to write from living...not from books.'

This indifference towards books, or at least the learning to be gained from them, was fairly typical of Caldwell. He never claimed to be widely read, and said: 'I've never been much of a reader – not because I don't like to read, but because I'd rather write than read.' And he recalled that there were few, if any, books other than the Bible around the house when he was growing up, and that, when he did attend school or college, he was always more interested in economics and sociology than in literature. When asked, he confessed that he had read few classics, American or otherwise, and that included Mark Twain. He had learned his trade writing journalism, and his reading, when it occurred, was largely limited to a few contemporaries. Even then, he said he'd read only one novel by William Faulkner, a writer he was often linked to because of their Southern origins. It's difficult to know just how serious Caldwell was when he talked like this. In interviews over the years he was quite forthcoming about other writers, and clearly knew their work. But he seems to have enjoyed playing the role of the bluff, no-nonsense tradesman, especially in front of academics and professional literary critics.

The stories in *American Earth* included several which pointed to Caldwell's use of the bizarre in comic form, as in 'Midsummer Passion,' where a middle-aged farmer finds some female underclothing and, catching a neighbour's wife unawares, tries to dress her in it. The setting, the garden patch outside the neighbour's house, and the reaction of the wife, who finally pulls on the garment herself and then simply tidies up the man and sends him on his way, highlight the almost ludicrous nature of the story, though Caldwell's skill as a story-writer enables it to hold the reader's attention and establish its own truth. Caldwell never claimed to write social-realism, though some of his work came close to it, and always insisted that fiction was not meant to represent reality directly. 'All fictional characters are created from the materials of human experience,' he said, 'but rarely are they replicas of living persons.'

At the same time, however, he insisted that his work always had a basis in reality. When questioned about the use of violence in his stories, he said:

> Well, it is a violent country. I've seen a man beat a mule to death because the sun was hot and he was tired and tense, sick of the endless sameness of his life. I've been in a barnyard at the end of the day in the cotton fields when the boss came over to ask why a mule was lame. A Negro explained that the mule had stepped in a rabbit hole. The boss beat the Negro unconscious – knowing the Negro couldn't fight back. I've been an unwilling witness at a number of lynchings.

So, in the story, 'Savannah River Payday,' two white sawmill workers travel into town with the body of a Negro killed in an accident. On the way they try to remove the corpse's gold teeth with a monkey wrench, attempt to rape a black woman working in the fields but only manage to injure each other, and finally abandon the body while they get drunk and attack a bystander who comments on their pool-playing. When stories like this were first published some critics tried to categorise Caldwell as a proletarian writer, but if he was he certainly didn't portray workers who were influenced by collective sentiments, intent on any sort of revolution, or even likely to be made better by a change in their economic circumstances. Caldwell's characters were ignorant, racist, and opportunist, and had a frightening taste for violence.

If *American Earth* didn't sell well it at least had the effect of giving Caldwell some minor status in the literary world, and it led to the publication of his novel, *Tobacco Road*, in 1932. As with many of the short stories, it portrayed a world where people lacked both economic and spiritual opportunities, and where moral virtues were virtually unknown. Occasionally, one of the characters might strive for something different. A twelve-year-old girl, pushed into marriage with a man much older, is taken to task by her father because she won't go to bed with her husband. The father assumes that the man simply wants sexual satisfaction, but he does have at least a vague notion that there could be more to a relationship than that. The husband wants his wife to talk to him, to 'ask him if his back were sore, and when he was going to get his hair cut, and when it was going to rain again.' He is, of course, seen as deranged by the other characters because he can even think in those terms.

It shouldn't be assumed that *Tobacco Road* was an immediate success. Maxwell Perkins had been enthusiastic about it, but other voices at Scribner's worried about questions of good taste in a book that broached some uncomfortable truths, albeit sometimes in a grotesque manner, about the lives of poor whites in the South. And the effects of the depression were being felt in publishing. It was only when Caldwell's next novel, *God's Little Acre*, appeared in 1933 and was attacked as obscene that he achieved national fame. A year later, Jack Kirkland's stage adaptation of *Tobacco Road* opened on Broadway and was such a hit that it ran for seven-and-a-half years, and provided Caldwell with the financial support he needed to carry on with his writing.

He was, at that time, not only producing fiction, but also travelling around America and reporting on social conditions in factories and on farms. He offered a generally left-wing viewpoint, though his politics were idiosyncratic at best. He was contemptuous of the so-called radicals he met during a brief sojourn in Hollywood, and refused to accept advice from Mike Gold, the commissar on literary matters for the American Communist Party. Caldwell sometimes called himself a communist, and he agreed that something needed to be done about the economic circumstances of many of his fellow-countrymen, but his Presbyterian background possibly inclined him to think that not every problem was simply a material one. Stories such as 'Saturday Afternoon' (a harsh account of a lynching which the white participants treat almost as a Saturday afternoon outing) were praised in *New Masses* and other left-wing publications, but Caldwell was generally too individual in his approach to be seen as useful to the Party line. It's interesting to note how his treatment of the well-documented strike at Gastonia, North Carolina, in 1929 differed from that of several other novelists who used it as the background for their books. Mary Heaton Vorse's *Strike!*, Grace Lumpkin's *To Make My Bread*, Myra Page's *The Gathering Storm*, and at least three others, use the strike in a fairly straightforward way. In *God's Little Acre*, it is there, but is hardly the key to how the characters behave. Indeed, Caldwell's picture of factory life is less than realistic. In one curious passage he writes:

> All day long there was a quiet stillness about the ivy-walled mill. The machinery did not hum so loudly when the girls operated it. The men made the mill hum with noise when they worked there. But when evening came the doors were flung open and the girls ran out screaming in laughter. When they reached the street they ran back to the ivy-covered walls and pressed their bodies against it and touched it with their lips. The men who had been standing idly before it all day long came and dragged them home and beat them unmercifully for their infidelity.

It wasn't quite what Communist Party intellectuals expected of a writer supposedly linked to the working-class, and although the urban sections of *God's Little Acre* do utilise many of the characteristics of proletarian novels they are never simply factual descriptions of factory life and its problems. One always has the feeling that Caldwell is digging deeper than the economic surface and is looking for a reason for the spiritual malaise that affects his characters. As he pointed out much later, 'I never fell out with the Marxist critics because I was never in their camp to begin with.'

Caldwell never looked back once his reputation had been established by *Tobacco Road* and *God's Little Acre*. He spent some time in Hollywood, toured the South and wrote newspaper articles about his experiences, and was in Europe in the late 1930s. During the war he visited Russia, again went to Hollywood, and saw his popularity continue to rise as the novels and short stories poured from his pen. But his critical reputation slumped as his sales rose. It was said that he was writing far too much, and that his work was variable in quality. There is some truth in both suggestions. But Caldwell had never been the kind of writer who refines his work. He simply continued to write stories, some of which were better told than others. *Georgia Boy*, which appeared in 1943, was amongst his best work, though political correctness might now affect judgement of it. The characters it portrays – a poor, white Southern family and their feckless black farmhand – are dealt with humorously and with some sympathy, the white father being just as unreliable as the black worker. Caldwell always thought it one of his best books, and it has a charm and gentleness not often found in his novels.

By the 1960s Caldwell's interest in fiction was slowing down, and he turned to autobiography and travel writing. *Deep South*, in which he retraced his early wanderings as a preacher's son and compared what he saw then to what he found in the South fifty years later, is vibrant journalism and points to his skill as a writer always intent on keeping the reader interested. He knew that he had not sustained the quality of his early novels and stories, but he thought that he at least ought to be recognised for what they had achieved.

There is, in Caldwell's *Call It Experience*, one of his autobiographical works, an amusing account of how he incurred the wrath of more-sensitive authors when he held a book-signing session in a drug store, with people queuing to buy the 25 cents paperback edition of one of his books. Caldwell claimed that Walter Van Tilburg Clark told him how other writers at a conference they were attending thought he had 'brought disrepute to the profession of authorship' by taking part in such an undignified scheme. It was typical of Caldwell that he told this story with glee. He had little time for people who thought that writing was something produced only for consideration by other writers or academics, and he was always pleased when ordinary men and women stopped him in the street to say how much they had enjoyed his books. I don't think this liking for popular acceptance contradicts his need for some sort of critical acknowledgement. Caldwell knew that he was, at his best, a good writer, and he thought, not without some justification, that snobbishness was partly responsible for his neglect by the critics.

Little of his work has been in print in recent years, though it's still relatively easy to find second-hand copies of his novels and short-story collections in bookshop basements and on market-stalls. And one or two university presses in the United States have started to re-issue some of his books. Caldwell would no doubt be amused by the attention he is receiving a decade after his death. He ought to be remembered, if only for a handful of novels (*Tobacco Road, God's Little Acre, Georgia Boy, Tragic Ground,* and *Trouble in July*), the fascinating *Deep South*, and perhaps most of all, the wonderful short stories. There were around 150 of them, and some are clearly better than others, but the collection, *Jackpot*, which was published in England in 1950, is probably one of the best of its kind by an American writer. There are stories in it to haunt the imagination, such as 'Masses of Men,' which captures the human casualties of the depression in a few bleak pages, and the raw 'Blue Boy,' in which a retarded Negro is made to perform for a party of supposedly sophisticated whites. But Caldwell could also be gentle, as in 'The Strawberry Season,' a story about growing up, and his sense of the tragic possibilities of everyday life is brilliantly demonstrated in

'Wild Flowers,' which he considered one of his best short stories. Erskine Caldwell was a story-writer, as Otis Ferguson said, and good stories are always worth reading, and re-reading.

Note

There are two useful biographies of Caldwell. Harvey L. Klevar's *Erskine Caldwell: A Biography* was published by The University of Tennessee Press, Knoxville, in 1993, and Dan B. Miller's *Erskine Caldwell: The Journey from Tobacco Road* by Alfred A. Knopf, New York, in 1995. *Conversations with Erskine Caldwell*, edited by Edwin T. Arnold, was published by the University Press of Mississippi, Jackson, in 1988.

KENNETH FEARING, 1996

Kenneth Fearing may be known to most contemporary readers, if he is known at all, as the author of *The Big Clock*, a classic crime novel which is regularly reprinted and has been used as the basis for two successful Hollywood films. He may also be known to readers of American literature for a handful of poems which appear in anthologies. One of them, 'Dirge', is a sardonic study of an executive type on the way down, and its vivid language, in tune with the cadences and colloquialisms of the street, still has power. It works rather like Arthur Miller's great play, *Death of a Salesman*, in that it has both a political and personal impact, and it consequently transcends any limitations that might stem from it having been written during a certain period when specific social circumstances were in evidence. And, in any case, events have easily demonstrated that what were once thought of as thirties concerns are just as relevant today. When Fearing produced much of his best poetry he took the headlines of the day and shaped them to present a picture of a society on the verge of breakdown, but he didn't wave a political flag, nor did he offer glib political solutions, and he looked at the individual casualties rather than the mass effects when constructing a critique of the social situation. It might be true to say that, as with any good poet, his was a personal and not a party version of what was happening in the world around him.

Fearing was born in 1902, his father a successful Chicago lawyer whose family background went back to the early days of American society and his mother a member of a well-established Jewish family. But the marriage failed shortly after he was born, and he grew up theoretically spending equal time with each parent but, in practice, living with the Fearings most of all. He was said to have loved his father and tolerated his mother. One thing was certain: Fearing had a fairly comfortable upbringing in material terms, hardly wanting for anything and attending good schools and, eventually, the University of Wisconsin. His academic career perhaps indicated the way he would live in the future, with productive spells mixed with periods of lethargy and inactivity. He felt that he wanted to be a poet and he moved to New York in 1924, his plan being to work as a journalist to earn money whilst writing poetry as his 'serious' occupation. His early work was formally structured and dealt with what might be called obvious poetic subjects, such as death, nature, and war. The language of the poems was elegant, but slightly hackneyed. 'Villanelle of Marvellous Winds' begins:

> Patient are the winds that blow
> Around the crannies of the town,
> And gather and spend the drifting snow.

The poems from this period (roughly prior to 1926, though as with any young poet he was probably veering between styles, so a clean break with tradition is not evident) are not without interest, and they do occasionally point to his essentially pessimistic and sceptical state of mind. From around the mid-1920s, though, he does appear to have aimed for something different, and a poem called 'St. Agnes' Eve' makes a move towards the language and subject-matter of his later work:

> The settings include a fly-specked Monday evening,
> A cigar store with stagnant windows,
> Two crooked streets;
> The characters: six policemen and Louie Glatz.
> Subways rumble and mutter a remote portent
> As Louie Glatz holds up the cigar store and backs out with $14.92.

There isn't the flexibility of expression, nor the complete ease with the colloquial of the later poems, and a phrase such as 'Subways rumble and mutter a remote portent' still searches for the 'poetic' in a formal way, but generally speaking the poem does point to a quickly changing tone in Fearing's work.

Between arriving in New York in 1924 and publishing his first book in 1929, Fearing placed over forty poems in magazines, a quarter of them in *New Masses*, a left-wing publication which was later heavily controlled by the Communist Party but still operated a relatively open policy in the 1920s. That he published regularly in *New Masses*, to which he also contributed articles and reviews, says something about his general social and political views, though Fearing was never easy to place when it came to such matters. *Angel Arms*, his first collection of poetry, has been seen by some literary historians as a pioneer work of proletarian writing, but it is, if anything, broader and darker than that hard-to-define description suggests. Fearing does not offer a message from a proletarian point of view, nor does he celebrate proletarian values. A poem such as 'Cultural Notes' seems to be laughing at all sides instead of taking one, and its language, though of the everyday, avoids the supposed plain speech of what was soon to be known as proletarian poetry:

> After the performance Maurice Epstein, 29,
>   tuberculosis, stoker on the S.S. Tarboy,
> rose to his feet and shouted,
> "He's crazy, them artists are all crazy,
> I can prove it by Max Nordau. They poison
>   the minds of young girls."
> Otto Svoboda, 500 Avenue A, butcher, Pole,
>   husband, philosopher, argued in
>   rebuttal,
> "Shut your trap, you.
> The question is, does the symphony fit in
>   with Karl Marx?"

What is fascinating about Fearing – and this is true of other left-wing American poets – is that he clearly saw no contradiction about using the techniques of literary modernism to express radical ideas. There are still English readers who see 1930s left-wing poetry as largely represented by the formalities of Auden and his followers, but this viewpoint represents only part of the story. And if we look to America, where the class divisions that bedeviled English poetry were nowhere near as influential, the range of work on offer is far more interesting and exciting. The work of poets like Fearing, Sol Funaroff, and Herman Spector, reflected a wider awareness of the possibilities of the poem, and even Michael Gold, cultural commissar for the American Communist Party and, when the Party line required it, a staunch opponent of modernism, wrote poems that went outside the usual forms.

Some of Fearing's poems, such as 'Denouement', can be taken as almost explicitly Marxist in what they say, but it would be impossible to apply a Marxist label to everything he wrote in the late 1920s and the 1930s. The fact that he was highlighting the chaos, and illustrating the injustices, of the Depression doesn't in itself make Fearing a Marxist. He had a local tradition of protest to draw on, something true of other American poets who, because of their appearance in left-wing publications, were often assumed to be communists. But the social situation simply drew them to people and magazines sharing their anger. Fearing always denied having been a party member, though the FBI claimed to have evidence that he was, and when, in the 1950s, he made an appearance before an investigating body and was asked if he belonged to the Communist Party, he replied, in typically quirky fashion, 'Not yet.' A late 1930s poem, the cryptic 'Q & A', possibly sums up how he really felt about political, and all other, theories. There are questions, it says, but the answers

> Will not be found in Matthew, Mark, Luke,
>   or John,
> Nor Blackstone, nor Gray's, nor Dun &
>   Bradstreet, nor Freud, nor Marx,
> Nor the sage of the evening news, nor the
>   corner astrologist, nor in any poet

People who knew Fearing in the 1930s recalled that he could be as satirical and questioning about communists as he was about other types, and he is portrayed as such in Albert Halper's 1933 novel, *Union Square*, where he is described as 'making sport of the communists again.' Fearing appears under the name of Jason Wheeler, 'ex-poet and ex-communist, pot-boiler writer for the cheap sex-story magazines and former student of world affairs', and his heavy drinking, a factor in his life from his student days, is also noted.

He had written pulp fiction, as Halper says, and the lack of income from his poetry caused him to turn to novels as a means of earning a living. His output of poetry slowed down and the poems he did write were less overtly political. They also turned away in part from the more extreme forms of modernist dislocation of language and structure. But Fearing never was consistent in these things. When he published a *Collected Poems* in 1940 he stated:

> I think that poetry must be understandable. Everything in this volume has been written with the intention that its meaning should disclose itself at ordinary reading tempo.

Some critics thought he was being deliberately perverse in saying this, some of his 1930s poems needing more than one reading to realise their full meaning, and even then not necessarily giving it all up. Fearing could be oblique about his subject matter. But it may have been that Fearing was merely saying that the content of his poems was clear enough. They didn't rely on references outside the images of the day as found in newspapers, movies, advertisements, and popular songs, and he disliked poetry which made 'recondite allusions' and lent itself to academic analysis. His friend, the poet Carl Rakosi, said:

> Fearing's language, which is what you would have heard in a newsroom in the Middle West in the 1930s, plain and ordinary, has a cadence, a music of its own, not borrowed from any English or French literary models or any other, that's distinctively American.

And Kenneth Rexroth, in a typically idiosyncratic but accurate insight, commented:

No-one else so completely immersed himself in the lingo of mass culture. ... Kenneth Fearing didn't think like an advertising copywriter. He thought like the advertising copy itself, or at least like a taxi driver reading a billboard while fighting traffic.

There were only a limited number of poems after the mid-1940s and Fearing was busy writing novels and other prose. In addition, he had severe problems with alcoholism, his drinking almost spiralling out of control when the success of *The Big Clock*, published in 1946 and soon snapped up by Hollywood, brought him the kind of money that many writers would use to guarantee their future security. Fearing spent it quickly and had to turn to writing short stories for pulp publications to earn more. In addition, by the mid-1950s, he had to take a job writing reports and publicity releases for the Muscular Dystrophy Association. The poems he did complete were less adventurous than his 1930s work, and there is evidence of a waning of interest in modernist techniques which paralleled a waning of involvement with left-wing politics. This isn't to say that the poems lacked a cutting edge when it came to commenting on contemporary matters. The post-war paranoia and the increasing suspicion, in Fearing's mind, of the power of the State and its bureaucracy, were sharply dealt with in 'Decision', which has a Kafkaesque flavour:

> Do not be dismayed, be at ease, the
>   assistant secretary will see you now,
> Here and finally the right man, the
>   assistant in the soft, thick, blue-
>   carpeted room with the deep leather
>   chairs at the proper end of the right
>   marble hall,
> The authoritative man with those powerful
>   but delicate photo-electric eyes,
> Perception like radar, a calculator mind –

And the late poem, 'Family Album', can be read as a statement about McCarthyism and its effects. Fearing had, in the introduction to his *New and Selected Poems*, published by Indiana University Press in 1956, talked about a kind of conspiracy in which the whole society was involved and which was directed against the individual, and M.L. Rosenthal, reviewing the book in *The Nation*, summarised his views:

> In Fearing's writing, the 'enemy' gradually becomes the Mob, official and unofficial, that thrives on the regimentation of individual thought and feeling through the ever-greater control of the avenues of communication. Its triumph, he says, is being brought about by 'the revolution that calls itself the Investigation'. ... the same types in all countries employing the Investigation and the mechanical media of information for the same ends; the system proliferates, is perhaps too pervasive for individuals to handle.

And he quoted a few lines from 'Hold the Wire':

> If the doorbell rings, and we think we were
>   followed here; or if the doorbell should
>   ring but we are not sure –
> How can we decide?

Poems such as this were not just a reflection of a personal paranoia, because in 1950s America 'the Investigation' was very much a fact of life for some people, and Fearing could also see how the modern world and its technology could be a threat to individual freedom. He had, in a sense, moved beyond political comments that could be linked to certain social conditions, as in some of his 1930s poems, to a general suspicion of capitalist society, whatever material benefits it might be said to have brought. Robert M. Ryley, in his introduction to Fearing's *Complete Poems*, gets it right when he refers to the poet's 'sickened abhorrence of the Yahooness that everyone else seems to revel in and take for granted.'

There was, too, a personal despair in Fearing's later poems (to be accurate, it had always been there, though not necessarily as clearly stated), and he was a master at the art of describing it in a few words. A poem called '4 A.M.' reads like a word picture that Edward Hopper might have painted:

And here we are, four lost and forgotten
    customers in this place that surely will
    never again be found,
Sitting, at ten-foot intervals, along this lost
    and forgotten bar
(Wishing the space were further still, for we
    are still too close for comfort),

And another poem, 'American Rhapsody (5)', has a bleakness that is almost frightening in its intensity:

Then the doorbell rings. Then Peg drops in.
    And Bill. And Jane. And Doc.
And first you talk, and smoke, and hear the
    news and have a drink. Then you walk
    down the stairs.
And you dine, then, and go to a show after
    that, perhaps, and after that a night
    spot, and after that come home
    again, and climb the stairs again, and
    again go to bed.

It all seems so simple, even typical, but that repetition of 'again' highlights the quiet despair that is felt in relation to what is, on the face of it, a not-unpleasant routine.

Fearing had been a heavy drinker and smoker all his life, and had never looked after himself, with the result that he was in bad health towards the end of the 1950s. He died in hospital on 26th June 1961.

I've tried in this short piece to say something about Kenneth Fearing's life and work, though I'm conscious that I've really only skimmed the surface of his skills. He has been for too long linked to the 1930s, and whilst he can be seen as a major poet of that period his best work moves beyond it and offers a response to the twentieth century generally, as well as to human experience in the broad sense. And it would seem to me that his poems can provide younger poets with lessons about how to deal with the modern world. Fearing's use of technique and language can still be seen as provocative and his ideas worth considering.

Note

Fearing's *Complete Poems*, edited and with an extremely useful introduction by Robert M. Ryley, was published by the University of Maine, Orono, Maine 04469-5752, in 1994.

EDWIN ROLFE, 1996

Some years ago, collecting books and magazines with material about the Spanish Civil War, I came across the name of Edwin Rolfe, an American writer and volunteer in the International Brigades. A pamphlet, *Salud! Poems, stories and sketches of Spain by American Writers*, published in 1938, had a contribution by Rolfe, alongside work by Kenneth Rexroth, Kenneth Fearing, Sol Funaroff, Norman Rosten, and others. And somewhere along the way I luckily found a copy of Rolfe's *The Lincoln Battalion*, originally published in 1939 and providing a history of American involvement in Spain. Some of his poems could also be found in various anthologies of left-wing writing.

It was a fact, though, that until comparatively recently little of Rolfe's poetry was easily available, nor was much written about him. I doubt whether many people in this country had even heard of him, and the situation wasn't much better in the United States, where the McCarthy era had the effect of suppressing interest in poets with left-wing sympathies. And Rolfe's early death in 1954 may also have contributed to the neglect that was his lot. Poets slip from sight all the time, of course, and many deserve to, but Edwin Rolfe's work has a power which allows it to transcend the limitations of time and place which often affect political poets. At the same time it can provide a marvellous account of what it was like to be alive and involved in the turbulent events of the thirties, forties, and fifties. As Cary Nelson wrote in the introduction to the recently published *Collected Poems*:

> It gives people for the first time a comprehensive view of one of the more inventive political poets of the Great Depression, of the writer Americans who fought in the Spanish Civil War regard as their poet laureate, and of a writer who used poetry as a weapon against the reactionary politics that dominated the United States in the 1950s.

From what has been said, it will be obvious that Rolfe was a committed left-winger. He was a member of the American Communist Party, a fact that was to affect his life in the late 1940s and early 1950s, and the tendency has been to regard anyone with that kind of political belief as either a naive and gullible fool or a Stalinist stooge. We look back easily from our lofty vantage point and dismiss the strivings of the 1930s as deluded and we prefer, instead, to pick up on the doubt and cynicism of other poets as more to our taste. It's interesting, I think, that some younger British poets have discovered the work of Weldon Kees, a good poet but with a vision that asks and expects little or no political commitment, or at least prefers a sombre view of life in place of it.

I don't want to offer a lengthy account of Rolfe's life, but a few details may help to place him in context. He was born in 1909 in Philadelphia, his parents Russian Jewish immigrants. They were active in politics and trade union work. The family moved to New York in 1915 and Rolfe was already publishing as a writer and cartoonist when he was a teenager. He appeared in *The Daily Worker*, joined the Young Communist League, and got to know people like Michael Gold and Joseph Freeman, both leading lights in Communist literary circles. Rolfe's poems were published in radical magazines, and 'Asbestos,' from 1928, is a good example of his combination of formal technique and contemporary language and concerns:

> Knowing (as John did) nothing of the way
> men act when men are roused from lethargy,
> and having nothing (as John had) to say
> of those he saw were starving just as he
>
> starved, John was like a workhorse. Day by day
> he saw his sweat cement the granite tower
> (the edifice his bone had built), to stay
> listless as ever, older every hour.

He spent some time at an experimental college in Wisconsin, reportedly quit the Communist Party because 'it demanded too blind and rigid a loyalty,' and did a series of odd jobs to stay alive. At the same time he was publishing poems in magazines with names like *Front* and *The Left*, but he was also interested in areas of the literary scene which firmly flew the modernist flag. Some critics have tried to make out that left-wing poets in the 1930s often opposed modernist experiments, but this certainly wasn't true of the United States. Rolfe may have been on the Left and he worked for *New Masses*, but he also contributed to *Pagany* and *Contempo*, little magazines which were not linked to literary communism. An overlooked world of radical and experimental activity is evoked by the names of these publications, with Rolfe alongside William Carlos Williams, Basil Bunting, Gertrude Stein, and many others.

But Rolfe's heart was firmly on the Left and he re-joined the Communist Party in 1931, working for *The Daily Worker*, writing for *New Masses*, and participating in the early days of *Partisan Review*. He was one of four young, radical poets (Rolfe, Herman Spector, Sol Funaroff, Joseph Kalar) included in a collection, *We Gather Strength*, published in 1933. By the time the Spanish Civil War started in 1936 he had established himself in Left literary groups, and was politically committed enough to feel that it was essential to volunteer for service in Spain. He was there from June 1937 to December 1938, working as editor of the English-language edition of *Volunteer for Liberty*, the journal of the International Brigades, but also seeing active service at the front, despite the ill-health which dogged him for much of his life.

When he returned to New York early in 1939, Rolfe worked for TASS, the Russian news agency, and was then called up for service in the US army. He was treated with suspicion, being regarded as a 'premature anti-fascist,' and eventually discharged because of his health problems, but a number of first-rate poems were written during this period, among them the beautiful 'First Love', which looks back to his time in Spain. Like many Spanish Civil War veterans, Rolfe saw the experience as a high-point in his life, a time when idealism was expressed in concrete terms and a genuine comradeship existed between many of the men who had often sacrificed a great deal to fight for the Spanish Republic:

> Again I am summoned to the eternal field
> green with the blood still fresh at the roots of flowers,
> green through the dust-rimmed memory of faces
> that moved among the trees there for the last time
> before the final shock, the glazed eye, the hasty mound.
> But why are my thoughts in another country?
> Why do I always return to the sunken road through corroded hills,
> with the Moorish castle's shadow casting ruins over my shoulder
> and the black-smocked girl approaching, her hands laden with grapes?

Rolfe went to California in the mid-1940s, partly because his wife had been offered a job there, but also because he thought he might be able to get some work in the film industry. Left-wing writer friends, like Albert Maltz and Clifford Odets, had established themselves in Hollywood, but Rolfe found that it was a struggle to survive. His health continued to bother him (he had a heart attack in 1944), and he was primarily a poet, not a prose writer or playwright. He did pick up a few writing assignments, including the verse commentary to a short film, *Muscle Beach*, which has become something of a cult classic and still shows in specialist cinemas, and he collaborated on a crime novel, *The Glass Room*, with Lester Fuller. Film-makers expressed interest in this book and Humphrey Bogart and Lauren Bacall were lined up to star in a screen version, but the project was dropped, possibly because both Rolfe and Fuller were known communists. The anti-communist hysteria which would soon sweep America was then building up and writers in Hollywood were among the earliest targets for investigators.

Poems by Edwin Rolfe continued to appear in magazines, though few editors would take chances with his overtly political work. He was summoned to appear before the House Un-American Activities Committee in 1952, but his doctors were of the opinion that any unnecessary stress would cause another heart attack and the hearing was delayed. The effects of the harassment on his life and work −

Rolfe was named by other people who did appear before the Committee and co-operated with it – were noticeable to his friends, and he died from a heart attack on May 24th, 1954.

He had continued to write poetry and many of his poems from the late 1940s and early 1950s make bitter reference to the anti-Left mood of those days, But he wasn't just concerned to protest against the hounding of radicals. He wanted to point out how the atmosphere was generally polluted when hysteria became the norm, so that everyone was affected:

> The poisoned air befouled the whole decade,
> corrupting even those whose childhood vision
> contained no hint of bomb or nuclear fission,
> backed them against walls, cowering, afraid.

And even the poems which didn't seem to talk directly about politics described a world which wasn't functioning as it should:

> That was the year
> the small birds in their frail and delicate battalions
> committed suicide against the Empire State.

That poem, 'A Poem to Delight my Friends Who Laugh at Science-Fiction,' was one of the few that Rolfe managed to place outside small, left-wing magazines. It appeared in the prestigious *Poetry* and was reprinted in several anthologies. As Cary Nelson puts it: 'He had a few mainstream successes, but only when the analogies with McCarthyism were oblique enough to be missed by many readers.' Nelson also pointed out how the poem is 'easily decontextualised,' meaning that we can, if it suits us, disassociate it from its very real place in the politics of 1950s America, though we reduce its power by doing so. Much of Rolfe's later poetry only found a home in a handful of publications prepared to give space to an acknowledged communist who wasn't apologetic about his past. A scathing piece, written after hearing his one-time friend, Clifford Odets, had recanted and named names, should have appeared in *The Nation*, a liberal magazine, but the editors got cold feet and never used it. Even *California Quarterly*, a radical journal which had used some of Rolfe's political poems, jibbed at the savage, 'Little Ballad for Americans – 1954,' which perhaps seems strange to us but does say a lot about the way things were in the United States at the time:

Brother, brother, best avoid your workmate –
Words planted in affection can spout a field of hate.

Housewife, housewife, never trust your neighbour –
A chance remark may boomerang to five years at hard labour.

Student, student, keep mouth shut and brain spry –
Your best friend Dick Merriwell's employed by the F.B.I.

Lady, lady, make your phone calls frugal –
The chief of all Inquisitors has ruled the wire-tap legal.

Daughter, daughter, learn soon your heart to harden –
They've planted stoolies everywhere; why not in kindergarten?

Lovers, lovers, be careful when you're wed –
The wire-tap grows in living-room, in auto, and in bed.

Give full allegiance only to circuses and bread;
No person's really trustworthy until he's dead.

As I said earlier, Rolfe's poetry has never been well-known, and his political sympathies, which can be viewed as those of the 'Old Left,' no doubt made his work unattractive to a lot of people. But it seems to me that his best poems do a lot more than merely mouth political slogans. There are, in fact, few slogans in his writing, though one is never in any doubt as to where he stands. His honesty simply wouldn't allow him to lapse into slogans, any more than it would allow him to lapse into cheap cynicism. Another fine but equally neglected radical poet, Thomas McGrath, said of Rolfe:

He was a serious poet – that is to say, he did not believe that one could create a whole corpus of work out of little moral or mock-moral allegories concerning birds and animals, or out of the eccentric learning of pedantic uncles. He was always smelling the real sweat of the terrible Now, the terrible Always. Probably all really good poems have that smell.

Note

Edwin Rolfe's poetry is now easily available. The University of Illinois Press published his *Collected Poems* in 1993, in an edition with an informative introduction by Cary Nelson and also including useful notes and a bibliography. There is, also, a splendid *Biographical Essay and Guide to the Rolfe Archive*, edited by Cary Nelson and Jefferson Hendricks, and published by the University of Illinois Press in 1990, which has a great deal of information about Rolfe's contemporaries and so helps the reader to see him in context. Among his friends and associates were poets like Ben Maddow and Norman Rosten, both now virtually unknown but in their day innovative and imaginative. Maddow's long poem, 'The City', appeared in 1940, and was known by the young Allen Ginsberg, who later said that it was an influence on the writing of 'HOWL'. Norman Rosten's long poem, 'The Fourth Decade', once described as 'the major epic poem of the 1930s', was published in a book of that name in 1943. My own second-hand copy was once owned by the Army Welfare Services Libraries and was donated to them by the Book Committee of the British War Relief Society of the United States of America. It bears an additional stamp, 'Books are Weapons in the War of Ideas', which is typical of the time, and has an ironic ring now when one thinks of the way in which many of these radical writers were harassed and blacklisted simply because of their ideas.

When the Beats began to hit the headlines in the 1950s they helped focus attention on some American writers who, despite having been around for many years, were relatively neglected, or at least pushed onto a bohemian fringe that was given a grudging acknowledgement but perhaps wasn't taken too seriously. This attention was welcome, but it occasionally had the effect of making people think that such writers were themselves Beats. It wasn't enough to suggest that they had simply been influential on the Beats, either in terms of their approach to writing or their relationship to the literary establishment. Some journalists wanted to make out that poets and novelists like Paul Bowles, Kenneth Rexroth, Edward Dahlberg, Paul Goodman and Kenneth Patchen were part of the Beat movement. And some readers, one suspects, wanted to believe them, though any kind of familiarity with the work of the people concerned would show that they were definitely not Beats. And all of them made it obvious that, even if they had an interest in what the Beats were doing, they didn't want to be considered one of them. Of course, this didn't stop the Beats paying homage to Bowles, Patchen and others. Their existence outside the framework of the academy or the establishment was a model to be admired. As one critic said of Patchen, his 'long line of avant-garde work, his defiance of academia, and his constant anti-war and anti-materialism values made him an immediate artistic presence and influence on the Beat and later West Coast literary movements.' The fact was, though, that Patchen had created a varied and fascinating body of work long before *Howl* and *On The Road* were published.

KENNETH PATCHEN: BEFORE THE BRAVE   73

Patchen was born in 1911 in Niles, Ohio, and the family moved to nearby Warren when he was four. His father was a steelworker, and Patchen himself worked in a steel mill for a time in order to earn enough money to go to college. He was already writing and publishing poetry, and he did have short stints in college in Wisconsin and Arkansas, where he seems to have made an impression as an athlete as well as a poet. He did not stay long enough to get a degree, nor did he wish to return to the steel mill, which he once described as 'my idea of hell on earth.' Instead, he began to wander around the United States and Canada, working at odd jobs and writing. After a couple of years he settled in Boston, where he met Conrad Aiken, married a young student, and had work published in *Poetry* and *The New Republic*. Later in the 1930s he moved West and tried to earn a living in Hollywood, though seemingly without any great success. He returned to the East Coast in 1939 and eventually settled in Greenwich Village in 1940.

His first book, *Before The Brave*, had been published by Random House in 1936 and was widely reviewed. Because of his working class background, and the strong element of protest in his writing, he was often looked on as a proletarian poet. The 1930s saw the rise in interest in literature which reflected the outrage many people felt about the inadequacies of the capitalist system, and reference to Patchen's early work will turn up a number of poems which refer to poverty and injustice and speak out against both. He had also written in praise of Lenin, and one of his best known poems of the period, 'Joe Hill Listens to the Praying', was published in the Communist magazine, *New Masses*, and anthologised in *Proletarian Literature in the United States*. But it seems evident that Patchen soon had doubts about the possibility of radical change being brought about through mass action on the part of the working class. In his autobiographical story, 'Bury Them in God', two characters who represent the debate about commitment, which was then presumably going on in Patchen's own mind, argue about 'the workers', and one says

> knock all the howling rubbish about "the workers" out of your head.
> Jesus, think of all the poison that's been poured into them! Wake them
> up, for God's sake wake them up! But don't come bleating to me
> about how fine and noble they are ... .

It's reasonable to assume that these were Patchen's thoughts, and that
his future protest writing, while not overlooking the misery and suffering
caused by exploitation, would not find its base in one particular class,
nor in one particular political system.

It was in the 1930s that Patchen began to suffer from the back
trouble which dogged him for the rest of his life. Seemingly caused by
trying to separate the locked bumpers of two cars, it resulted in constant
pain. It was only in 1950 that treatment gave him some temporary
relief. Throughout the late 1930s and the 1940s he had to try to come
to terms with being restricted in his movements, and it was during this
period that he turned to visual graphics as a means of expanding his
artistic world and soon began to produce what were called 'painted
books' and 'picture poems'. But it was a fact that his suffering influenced
his writing, and he was to say:

> I feel that I would be something else if I weren't rigid inside with the
> constant pressure of illness; I would be purer, less inclined to write
> (say) for the sake of being able to show the sick part that it can never
> become all powerful; I could experience more in other artists if I didn't
> have to be concerned so closely with happenings inside myself.

Patchen's prolific imagination, and the need to produce as a kind
of defiance, enabled him to turn out a book each year, many of them
published by New Directions, with whom Patchen had a long
relationship. His novel (or anti-novel, as some have described it) *The
Journal of Albion Moonlight* appeared in 1941, though not from New
Directions. Money for its publication was raised by subscription, with
fellow writers such as William Carlos Williams, e.e. cummings, and
Wallace Stevens happily contributing. Despite his neglect by academic
critics, and his ambivalent relationship with the literary establishment,
Patchen invariably got support from other writers. The novelist Millen

Brand once reminisced about how Kenneth Fearing would scrounge money from him to give to Patchen, 'because he really needed it.' Some people perhaps felt sorry for him, but many also admired his writing, variable though it could be. Paul Goodman reckoned that Patchen had created 'an immense body of work, some of which is obviously good,' and that seems to be a fair summing up.

It would be foolish to pretend that everything he wrote was of equal value or interest. The 1940s found Patchen veering more towards an anarchist position, and it's worth noting that his work was well known to some British writers and readers at this time. Magazines like *Poetry Quarterly*, *The Wind and the Rain*, and *Modern Reading* published his poems, and Grey Walls brought out a collection, *Outlaw of the Lowest Planet* in 1945. Wrey Gardiner, guiding light behind Grey Walls, was an enthusiastic supporter of Patchen's work, and in his autobiography, *The Dark Thorn*, he says,

> I have finished *The Journal of Albion Moonlight*. I feel like becoming a missionary and preaching the Old Testament of Miller and the Gospel according to Patchen. These books have come to me now that I am ready for them.

British poets such as George Barker, Paul Potts, and Nicholas Moore knew and respected Patchen's writings, and the anarchist editor and writer George Woodcock was aware of him, as was Albert McCarthy, the jazz journalist. I mention these people (and there were many others like them) because it's often forgotten that in the 1940s there was an active British literary scene which had contacts with developments in the United States and elsewhere. Too many readers assume that poets like Patchen, Kenneth Rexroth, and William Everson were only known in this country after the rise of the Beats, but that certainly wasn't the case. To think that it was is as ridiculous as thinking that Patchen, and the others, were Beats.

Before leaving this brief aside on Patchen's reception in Britain, it may be of interest to refer to David Gascoyne's introduction to *Outlaw of the Lowest Planet.* Gascoyne, a poet with roots in surrealism, at least in part, described Patchen as 'the lone one-man DADA of contemporary America,' and said:

> What other honest and sincere expression can we give to our reaction to such a situation (the hypocrisy and vulgar falsehoods of society) than a burst of furious, incoherent laughter?

Patchen took issue with this description of his work, and replied,

> Oh, but there are a lot of others! As poets we can reassert our belief in the essential nobility of human beings, our love and humility before the art of poetry itself – for without these we are not poets at all ... we can weep, and our tears will not be those of spoiled children but of men who have serious lives in this world of horror and wonder ... we can kneel, because the Beautiful is kneeling beside us, and the mystery is watching us with its eyes that are the cold flowers of the sky.

In 1950 Patchen and his wife moved to California, living initially in San Francisco and forming friendships with Kenneth Rexroth and, later, Lawrence Ferlinghetti. The interesting thing is that, although Patchen lived in the city and knew its poets, painters, and musicians, he had something of a separate identity. He was not, strictly speaking, a part of the San Francisco Renaissance, in that his work was already formed by the time he arrived on the West Coast and he had his own independent voice. Asked in a 1959 interview about his links to the North Beach Beat movement, he spoke out against the way things had gone:

> Well, I live and have lived for some time about thirty-five miles from San Francisco on the map, but I think further from San Francisco than is imaginable almost in every other way.

Patchen had moved to Palo Alto by this time, hence his saying he lived about thirty five miles from San Francisco. He went on to castigate the beatnik scene, and said,

> What has been demonstrated by these people is that there is an audience for people who are willing to strip in public, put on ladies' hats and

the whole nonsensical pseudo-bohemian bit, and this is not my dish
and it's not the dish of any artist I know, or any writer I admire.

Patchen's move to California coincided with improvements in his
health which enabled him to lead a more active life. City Lights Books
had published *Poems of Humor and Protest* in the Pocket Poets series,
and other books continued to appear. In 1957 he began to work with
jazz groups on the West Coast, pioneering poetry-and-jazz, and he
appeared in the United States and Canada in concert and on record
with the Chamber Jazz Sextet, and also performed with famed bassist,
Charles Mingus. He seems to have given a lot of time and energy to
making the presentation of poetry with jazz something more than a
novelty, and he did gain a certain amount of public acclaim for his
efforts. His interest in jazz generally was indicated by his play, *Don't
Look Now*, which had a jazz background and was staged off-Broadway.

Things appeared to be going well, but fate took a hand and Patchen
had to enter hospital for more surgery. A so-called 'surgery mishap,'
when he slipped from an operating trolley, further damaged his back,
and he was sent home virtually destined to spend the rest of his life
lying down or making only restricted movements. The old American
socialist, Norman Thomas, wrote a moving account of visiting Patchen
around this time:

> But at midmorning his face is grey and the lines at the sides of his
> mouth are deep, his eyes sunken and dark with miserable night
> memories. When he moves it is with so much care and with such
> apprehension. For all his nights are long: all his sleep is troubled. And
> there is nothing much in the day to look forward to except a few
> minutes at a time of work carefully set up and prepared for with
> medication.

Other writers, Kenneth Rexroth and Jonathan Williams among them,
organised benefit readings to help Patchen and his wife, who was also
ill, but either by choice or circumstance he withdrew from contact with
many of his contemporaries. Books of one kind or another continued
to be published, and his art work went on show. And because so many

of those involved in what was referred to as the 'counter-culture' often mentioned Patchen as an influence, or someone to be admired, he did have some continuing literary importance.

He died in 1972, active to the end and mourned by his contemporaries, as well as by a younger audience. Larry R. Smith, a sympathetic critic, said of him,

> Patchen's own influence on contemporary literature should finally be recognised as the embodiment of the committed artist, for he makes a way for the artist of engagement, for the anti-cool, compassionate creator committed to life in an absurd time.

He added that Lawrence Ferlinghetti 'accurately portrays Patchen as an exemplar of the socially engaged and idealistic artist.'

I've already mentioned that Patchen wrote a great deal, and that much of his work can be variable in quality. Kenneth Rexroth expressed some doubts about certain of the poems, and said, 'For my taste, there have always been two fields in which his stuff never quite came off: first, a peculiar topsy-turvy bitter whimsy; second, the sentimental love lyric.' But there may also be some truth in the words of Jack Conroy, a 1930s left-wing novelist who was asked to contribute to a late 1960s tribute to Patchen, and remarked, 'To know Patchen you've got to read him, and read him lots. For it is out of his totality his greatness emerges.' A more detailed exposition of this notion was given by John William Corrington in the 'Homage to Kenneth Patchen' issue of *The Outsider*:

> Strangely enough, Patchen's genius (like that of Faulkner, I think) is not resident in any single work. I cannot name a poem and say, "this is Patchen's essence." I can name 'Gerontion' and say with some certainty that Eliot's best talent is revealed in it. I can suggest that "anyone lived in a pretty how town" goes far toward revealing the substance of cummings. It may be over-simplification to suggest that "I think continually of those who were truly great" serves as a kind of illumination of Spender's finest work, or that 'Musée des Beaux Arts' is a kind of compendium of Auden's brilliance – but I feel that either poem does a much better job of summarising its author's best than would any single specimen of Patchen's poetry. Like Faulkner's

epic fiction, Patchen's poetry is a body, and it will not permit sampling, will not give up the sum of its accomplishment to a casual reading. Possibly this is because, like Faulkner, Patchen knows too much, and no single poem, possibly no single talent, can make much of a dent in the enormity of such inner experience.

This is true enough, and it's partly the reason why I've not quoted from the poems in this piece. To pull a few lines out of context, or even to give the full text of a short poem or two, simply wouldn't be fair to Patchen. There are poems which have individual qualities, and lines and phrases which stay in the mind. The problem may be that it's the kind of poetry which lends itself to personal selection. I happen to share Rexroth's indifference towards some of the whimsical poems and the more sentimental love lyrics. On the other hand, I do like the early poems, particularly those such as 'Joe Hill Listens to the Praying', 'Street Corner College', 'The State of the Nation' and 'Class of 1934', perhaps because they stem from a period when Patchen was directly experiencing the social conditions he attacked. But I would not want to deny the positive qualities to be found in Patchen's later work, and it has to be accepted that the totality is where the essence is to be found.

One final point that needs to be made is that, whatever else may be stated about Patchen's poetry, it is original. Henry Miller said of him, 'A voracious reader, he exposes himself to every influence, even the worst.' And Patchen himself, in a 1967 interview in which he was asked about influences, replied, 'They are as varied, I imagine, as your own, and as difficult to pin down. I would be hard put to say whether I was more influenced by poets or by people in general.' It's possible to point to poems which show the influence of 1930s social writing, to others which take on surrealist colours, and some which simply seem to draw from traditional verses, but in the end all of them are shaped by the Patchen mind and this results in them becoming a part of the whole.

I've mentioned one or two of Patchen's prose works, and it has to be taken into account that he did write several novels, and some short stories and other prose. *The Journal of Albion Moonlight* has gained in reputation over the years, and its aim to provide a record of a time 'when all the codes and ethics which men had lived by for centuries were subjected to the acid test of general war and universal disillusionment' has proved to be prophetic in that it could be said to describe today's situation, as well as that of 1940, which was when the book was written. Patchen in fact described it as 'a journal of the summer of 1940,' but it obviously goes far beyond any conventional notions of what a journal, or novel, comprises. Larry R. Smith commented that 'rejecting the conventional treatments of narration, characterisation, plot, style, and distancing, he creates his own forms to capture the world's madness and to engage us in the essential struggle for meaning and new order.' In the book itself, Patchen says, 'I believe that the revolutions of the future will be concerned with altering the minds of men, with vomiting out all that is insane for his animal.'

The Journal of Albion Moonlight is Patchen's most powerful prose work, and for some readers it is not an easy book to come to terms with. *Memoirs of a Shy Pornographer* is a lighter and more accessible novel, though that isn't to say that it is conventional in structure. Other prose, including *Sleepers Awake* and *They Keep Riding Down All The Time*, might be an acquired taste. It has been suggested that Patchen's longer prose works suffer from the same problems as surrealist novels, none of which could be said to be totally successful. The reader finds it difficult to stay interested in the absence of a formal narrative framework. But Patchen deserves credit for his efforts to break out of that kind of framework. His failures, if they are that, are magnificent. Interestingly, his one attempt at a straightforward novel was unsuccessful. *See You In The Morning*, written on his own admission to earn some money when he badly needed it, was published in condensed form in *Ladies Home Companion* and was meant to cater to popular tastes. Patchen, however, couldn't adapt successfully to the kind of writing required for commercial success. His plot is melodramatic and his dialogue stilted and sentimental. He needed to be his own man before he could produce work of quality, and it's interesting that, over the years, he wouldn't compromise (or couldn't compromise) sufficiently to turn out poems acceptable to the establishment, scripts that Hollywood wanted, or novels that a mass audience might like.

I've tried to give an indication of the range of Patchen's writing, much of which can be easily sampled. New Directions have kept many of his books in print, including the splendid *Collected Poems* which, in its 500 pages, contains most of his best work. Anyone wanting a starting point need look no further than that volume. I've also attempted to say something about Patchen's life, and his links to other writers. Many of the Beats admired him, despite his own insistence that he had nothing in common with them. Allen Ginsberg, reminiscing about his first meeting with Patchen in City Lights Bookshop in 1955, described him as 'a senior survivor of the poetry spiritual wars who'd kept his verse-line open, spontaneous, and his heart in human body.' It's easy to understand why he didn't want to be associated with the worst aspects of the Beat movement, but it's also possible to accept, in retrospect, that Kenneth Patchen was an influence on the Beats, and that some of the best work produced by Beat writers reflected that influence.

BEAT ROOTS, 1987

It's too often assumed that the Beats suddenly appeared in 1956 or 1957, around the time that Ginsberg's 'HOWL' and Kerouac's *On The Road* were first published. But any real study of the movement has to take account of what was happening ten or more years before that. *On The Road* may have been treated as a guide-book by the late-1950s beatniks, but it was actually about the bohemians and hipsters of the 1940s, as a reading of its jazz references will show. Don Byas, George Shearing, Wardell Gray, Dexter Gordon, Slim Gaillard: those are the names of musicians popular in the immediate post-war years. By 1957 it's doubtful if, Shearing apart, many of the younger enthusiasts for Kerouac's work had even heard of them, let alone listened to the records he mentioned.

Likewise, 'HOWL' largely used incidents and personalities from the 1940s scene to illustrate Ginsberg's claim that he'd seen the best minds of his generation destroyed by madness. The poem was, in fact, dedicated to Carl Solomon, and he was one of the younger New York bohemians friendly with Ginsberg and Kerouac in the 40s. And the 'Footnote to HOWL', with its long list of things the poet thought holy, has a give-away section which says, 'Holy the bop apocalypse! Holy the jazzbands marijuana hipsters peace & junk & drums.'

Beat history shows that Kerouac, Ginsberg, Burroughs, and others now dead or forgotten, were friends as early as 1944. They were all, to varying degrees, involved in the 'underground' scene that existed in New York. It wasn't an 'underground' in the 60s sense of flower-power, mass publicity, pop music, and alternative life-styles, but was, rather, a little-known aspect of urban life that took in jazz musicians, junkies, petty criminals, show-business types, hustlers, prostitutes, and the general floaters that any large city can support. Kerouac's *The Town And The City*, published in 1950, long before the Beat idea hit the headlines, has a section which describes that bop/beat 'underground.'

I think it's necessary to understand the mood that stemmed from the mass disruption of the war years. People were uprooted and shipped out to places they'd never seen before. Children were left fatherless. Women had to work in factories. Relationships were disrupted. At the same time there was, as a contrast to the personal dislocation, a kind of forced cohesiveness that came from government pressure to pull together in aid of the war effort. What resulted from that sort of atmosphere was, in many cases, a suspension of belief. People drifted into experiences they might normally have never known. John Clellon Holmes' *Go*, one of the first and certainly most accurate Beat novels, is especially good on this topic. As he says of his characters, 'they could not be insensitive to the wartime chaos in which they had been thrown.'

In this situation, and in some cases seized with doubts about politics, the early Beats intellectualised the mood they were sensing, and developed their theories of alienation and disaffiliation. The confused political angle, reflected in the disaffiliation, isn't one much explored by Beat researchers, but it seems to me worth paying a little attention to it. Holmes has admitted to having been interested in Marxism and, like others in the United States, found his dreams fading as the Cold War set in, the organised Left began to fall apart, and world events brought cynicism instead of hope. There is a highly relevant passage in his memoir of the Beat years, *Nothing More to Declare*:

> The forepart of my brain finally died in 1948, giving birth to an unknown grub, the truth of resurrection being that it actually happens every day. . . . Nuremberg, Wallace, the Cominform, Bongo bongo bongo I don't want to leave the Congo: so many smoky, argumentative afternoons I lived in a pathetic, imaginary pogrom! I think back with amazement, but no regret, on the time when I believed that out of street fights, Delacroix, hectic posters, surplus value, Ernst Toller (all

amounting to nothing but the dim shuffling of refugees towards eternally closed frontiers) an industrial Shangri-La might come, a fine brave world that was also new.

Hideous gobbets of *Daily Worker* prose went down, and somehow stayed down. The International Bookshop was riddled with drafts, and empty of everyone but the voice of Paul Robeson booming "Meadowland." Barley soup scorched the throat in 14th Street radical restaurants: one wore a lumberjack shirt and hurried to make the next show at the Irving Place ... .

There was finally a night in Clarke's Bar when my head was in Czechoslovakia, and Alan Harrington said, "Well, no matter. You were naive to think it was going to be any different."

Another forties Beat, Carl Solomon, when interviewed in later years, recalled being a member of a group called American Youth For Democracy, a typical communist front organisation, and also said that he joined the Communist Political Association, which was the American Communist Party under another name. He soon broke with his communist friends and drifted to Greenwich Village, where he mixed with a circle of people disillusioned with left-wing politics and got interested in avant-garde art and existentialism.

And there was, of course, Allen Ginsberg, born into a politically-inclined family. His father, Louis Ginsberg, was a minor poet whose work appeared in liberal and left-wing magazines in the 1930s, and his mother, as the long poem 'Kaddish' attests, was heavily involved with politics. The fictional portrait of Ginsberg in *The Town And The City* refers to him dreaming of becoming a great labour leader, and Ginsberg's poem, 'America', has ironic asides about Mother Bloor, Scott Nearing, and Israel Amter, names that will be familiar to students of American Communism.

From a literary point of view it's interesting to look at possible influences on Ginsberg's writing. There's a link with Whitman, and Ginsberg himself has spoken of Blake and Christopher Smart, as well as Jewish religious literature. But there may also be a connection with a strain of populist poetry with which, in a house where left and liberal sympathies predominated, he could have come into contact. The long lines, the hortatory tone, can be found in the work of the Communist poet Mike Gold, for example, and if Ginsberg did once dream of being a labour leader then the flamboyant Arturo Giovannitti, a union activist who was also a poet of some note, might not have been unknown to him.

Other Beats, though linked to the movement only in the 1950s, also had more than a passing acquaintance with politics. Gary Snyder grew up in the Pacific North West and was aware of the Wobblies and their struggles and songs. Bob Kaufman had been a union activist in the merchant navy and blacklisted for his left political leanings. And Lawrence Ferlinghetti drew on the anarchist traditions of San Francisco, as well as on his knowledge of European politics. You can even, if you look hard enough, find occasional references to radical politics in Kerouac's books, though he was always a conservative at heart. The point is, I think, that he couldn't have helped coming into contact with those ideas in the 1940s and before. It took the Cold War and the McCarthyism of the 1950s to make them almost unacceptable.

If, as Holmes and Solomon indicated in their separate ways, the post-war period brought disillusionment with politics, it also provided an alternative outlet for their energies. As the poet Robert Creeley once stated, 'This was the time of the whole cult of the hipster, which is a Forties designation, the crew is defined then, the whole thing of being with it.' And Creeley stressed the importance of Charlie Parker, and his 'place in Jack Kerouac's writing.' John Clellon Holmes said of himself and his associates, 'all of us, then, were bop mad,' and Gilbert Sorrentino, not a Beat but a contemporary of many of them, said of the music that 'its adherents formed a cult, which perhaps more than any other force in the intellectual life of our time, brought together young people who were tired of the spurious.'

It does seem that a whole generation of American writers, Beat and otherwise, was influenced by bop. I've indicated that Ginsberg paid homage to the music in 'HOWL' and that Kerouac often mentioned jazz and jazz musicians. He claimed to want to write like a jazz soloist, improvising around the basic theme. Holmes wrote a novel, *The Horn*, that used the jazz life as its central idea, and as the 1950s brought the development of a Beat literary movement, numerous writers – LeRoi Jones, Diane di Prima, Gregory Corso, Dan Propper, and Ted Joans, to mention just a few – produced poems and stories which made reference to their jazz heroes. The jazz beat was at the heart of Beat literature.

It may be that, a love of the music itself apart, what the bop world provided in the late 40s and into the 50s was a kind of refuge for people critical of society but disillusioned with formal political activity. They perhaps used it as a way of also avoiding the restrictions of middle-class life. Someone said of the Beats, when they emerged as a definable movement in the late 50s, that they were 'the only rebellion around,' and there is some truth in that statement. But the 'underground' of bop and Beat bohemianism had managed to survive the age of conformity and mediocrity that many people saw as the 1950s. It was in that 'underground' that Lord Buckley and Lenny Bruce could find an audience, that jazzmen could play what they wanted, and that writers like Kerouac and Ginsberg could struggle to get their work written and into print. It was as valid a radical activity as that of the 30s and 40s for, as Gary Snyder once said, 'Anything that speaks truth is a protest if what's going on around it is not true.'

Gary Snyder's Back Country, 1995

Japhy Ryder was a kid from eastern Oregon brought up in a log cabin deep in the woods with his father and mother and sister, from the beginning a woods boy, an axman, farmer, interested in animals and Indian lore so that when he finally got to college by hook or crook he was already well equipped for his early studies in anthropology and later in Indian myth and in the actual texts of Indian mythology. Finally he learned Chinese and Japanese and became an Oriental scholar and discovered the greatest Dharma Bums of them all, the Zen Lunatics of China and Japan. At the same time, being a Northwest boy with idealistic tendencies, he got interested in old-fashioned I.W.W. anarchism and learned to play the guitar and sing old worker songs to go with his Indian songs and general folksong interests.

That passage from Jack Kerouac's novel, *The Dharma Bums*, is a fictional portrait of Gary Snyder and points to many of the concerns and involvements of his early days. It does leave out one significant factor, and that is Snyder's liking for books. He himself has never played down that aspect of his background, and once said:

My mother was, and is, a very high-strung neurotic person with literary ambitions, and farm life and poverty wore her down. But she got me onto books and poetry at the age of five. When I was seven, I burned my feet badly while burning brush, and for four months couldn't walk. So my folks brought me piles of books from the Seattle Public Library and it was then I really learned to read and from that time on was voracious – I figure that accident changed my life. At the end of four months I had read more books than most kids do by the time they're eighteen. And I didn't stop.

It's important to keep those remarks in mind because they'll help to clear away any misconceptions, if they exist, about Snyder being a kind of home-spun philosopher, busy chopping wood with one hand and writing with the other. He has chopped wood, and done many other manual jobs, but he's also a highly literate and well-educated man. Someone who knew him when he was young recalled how Snyder's mother insisted that he attend the most intellectually demanding school in the area, and that she constantly pushed him to achieve academic excellence.

Snyder was born in San Francisco on May 8th, 1930, but his family moved to the Seattle area in order to escape the worst hardships of the Depression. They got 'a tarpaper shack and an acre of stumpland out north of town,' and Snyder recalled that, 'over the years my father built the place up, fenced it, got another acre, fixed the house, built the barn and got the cows and chickens.' In comparison with other struggling families in thirties America they were able to survive reasonably well, though Snyder later said that they were still very poor. When his father managed to obtain a job the rest of the family were kept busy looking after the farm. But Snyder does not seem to have minded his frugal existence. As he puts it,

> I never felt deprived or annoyed by poverty, which I regarded as a minor obstruction; for it seemed we were always going to the public library to get books, and we always had dozens of books around the house.

He was also interested in what was around him in the natural world, noting that he:

> Was hung up on American Indians and nature all through childhood and hated civilisation for having screwed up the Indians, as described in Ernest Thompson Seton's *The Book of Woodcraft and Indian Lore* ... and for ruining the woods and soil – which I could see was going on all about me.

He continued to develop his interest in these matters even when his parents separated and he was taken by his mother to live in Portland.

His teenage years saw him spending summers in the mountains, where he learned the rudiments of climbing and backpacking.

By the time he entered high-school in 1945 Snyder was writing poetry, though he later claimed not to remember too much about it, other than that it was mostly concerned with nature or youth. He carried on with his trips to the mountains, but also did vacation jobs with a local radio station and worked for United Press as a copy boy. He graduated from high school and entered Reed College on a scholarship in 1947. This was, perhaps, the point at which he began to really respond to poetry and to people of a similar disposition to himself. Reed was an establishment with something of a reputation for radicalism, and Snyder said that he associated with 'still struggling ex-Communist Party professors who had found the last haven, you know, somewhere to teach.' Several Reed academics were investigated for alleged Communist sympathies during this period, and elsewhere in America similar suspicions were directed at those with left-wing tendencies. Business interests proposed blacklists in 1946, Hollywood activists came under fire in 1947 and after, and in 1948 many universities and colleges insisted that staff sign loyalty oaths. The University of California dismissed numerous faculty members for refusing to take the oath, and this pattern was repeated elsewhere. Snyder's comments about Reed need to be seen in the context of this purge of radicals of every persuasion (not only communists were involved) and the general background is relevant to the rise of the Beats as a reaction to the conformity that engulfed American society. And Snyder did not escape being investigated by the FBI when he applied for a passport. One of his fellow-students remembered being visited by agents asking questions about Snyder, and his father, who had moved back to San Francisco, was also contacted by FBI men who wanted to know about his son's politics.

Snyder attended Reed College from 1947 until 1951, graduating with a joint degree in anthropology and literature. He seems to have enjoyed his student experience, despite being short of money:

With scholarships and odd jobs and greatly enjoyed tricks of living on
nothing I made it through college, making it summertime by trail-
crewing and logging and labour jobs. And in the summer of 1948 I
hitched to New York and worked on a ship to South America. I had
to wait until I got the ship and I was broke in New York. For a couple
of days I panhandled for food and slept on park benches, while roaming
through Greenwich Village. I was very Marxist in college, but couldn't
make it with the regular Commie bunch because of my individualist-
bohemian-anarchist tendencies, all much looked down upon.

There is a poem called 'Cartagena' in Snyder's first collection, *Riprap*,
which refers to his experiences in 1948, though it was most likely only
written, or at least completed, ten years later, so it is not a guide to
how he was writing when he was eighteen. Another early poem, 'Out
of the Soil and Rock' which seems to relate to his 1948 visit to New
York can be found in the collection, *Left Out in the Rain*. As for the
desire to work on a ship, Snyder commented:

Going to sea was part of a long growth and extension of my sympathy
and sensibilities outside simply one area and to many classes and kinds
of people and many parts of the world.

During his student years Snyder married a girl named Alison Gass.
It may have been that the marriage had some sort of basis in shared
inclinations towards radical politics, but Snyder's developing interests
in other matters do not appear to have aroused much enthusiasm in
his wife. In his own cryptic words: 'I was married for about six months
and my left-wing wife didn't dig the sudden interest in Oriental
philosophy and Shoshone folk tales.'

Reminiscences by those who knew the couple suggest that they had
little in common and that the marriage surprised their friends. And
Snyder was supposedly on the rebound after being rebuffed by a girl
called Robin. There is a touching record of this in a sequence of poems
in *The Back Country*, where Snyder writes that she 'chose to be free'
but suggested that they might get together again in ten years, and he
wonders if he should have contacted her.

When he left Reed, Snyder went to Indiana University, intending to develop a 'professional scholar's career in anthropology' but soon decided that academic life wasn't what he wanted. He knew that he would have to strike out on his own if he was to mature as a poet and a person. It was during this period that he worked as a timber-scaler on the Warm Springs Indian Reservation, an experience which produced the important long poem, 'The Berry Feast'. His observations of Indian life and customs, together with reading D. T. Suzuki on Zen Buddhism, helped crystallise many of the ideas that had been swimming around in his head, and further persuaded him that academic work was not where he should use his time and energy. He took a deliberate decision to 'drop out,' though I think it needs to be stressed that to do so required a degree of courage and commitment that was on a different level to the 'dropping out' of the 1960s. As Snyder said, 'America was much poorer then than it is now and there wasn't any welfare.' And the social and political climate of the early 1950s meant that anyone not conforming to orthodox notions of success and security was likely to be viewed with suspicion. The McCarthy years did not only affect those with politically deviant beliefs, but also extended to the arts and life-styles outside the norm. No one knew for sure if and when things would change, and none of the future Beat writers could then have known whether or not they would achieve success in the literary world.

Moving to San Francisco in 1952, Snyder worked at various jobs, and shared a room with Philip Whalen, an old friend from Reed College. Whalen also had a North-West background and an interest in Buddhism, though he does not seem to have been as politically aware as Snyder. It's worth reading his work, and that of Lew Welch, another ex-Reed student, alongside Snyder's. All have their own voices, and Welch is probably nearer Snyder than is Whalen, whose poems can often be personal to the point of obscurity, but there are definite links resulting from a common background and philosophy. Welch, it's true, had a different social upbringing, but he gravitated to the West Coast and easily adapted to its moods after meeting Snyder and Whalen at Reed. He went back East for a time, but returned to California when the Beat poets began to gain some recognition.

Whalen and one or two others apart, Snyder knew few people in San Francisco, but he carried on developing his skills as a poet. A painter, Dick Brewer, made arrangements for Snyder to meet the poet Robert Duncan, but the meeting never took place. And an encounter with Kenneth Rexroth, probably the leading San Francisco poet and a man whose interests and ideas were similar to Snyder's, does not appear to have been particularly important, though Snyder did later acknowledge a debt to the older man for his influence as a thinker and writer. Towards the end of 1953 Snyder moved to Berkeley:

> I was living in a little cottage and studying Chinese and Japanese at the university and going up to the woods and mountains in the summer, writing and reading. Intellectually, and in every way, that was a period of great excitement and growth for me – but a solitary period too. I had very few friends and almost no social contacts for three or four years. I was doing nothing but studying and working.

In 1954 he got a job as a forest lookout, but was fired as a security risk on orders from Washington, an incident that relates to my comments about the political atmosphere of the 1950s. Later, he worked for a lumber company in the same area – the lookout job came under Government control so was more susceptible to blacklists – and then as a member of a trail crew in the Yosemite National Park. This was a period when, in many ways, Snyder's poetry began to establish itself as both individual and important. The poems reflected his interests and his everyday involvements, as in the excellent 'The Late Snow & Lumber Strike of the Summer of Fifty-Four' which describes the physical appearance of the country he passes through and also brings in his awareness of social matters. Technically, the poem is deceptively simple, but shows how he had mastered his craft and fashioned a style that was to serve him well over the years. The sharp piling-up of images is typical, as is the manner in which the seemingly fragmentary and accidental have a continuity and relevance enhanced by the way they are placed in the poem. This poem, and others like it, were included in *Riprap*, a small book which was dedicated to a dozen men Snyder had worked with 'in the woods and at sea.'

Snyder's increasing confidence as a poet coincided with the first stirrings of the fifties Beat scene on the West Coast, and he was consequently involved in some of the now almost legendary events of the period. Allen Ginsberg had moved to San Francisco in 1952 and was slowly breaking free of the constraints holding him back both socially and politically. He met Snyder in 1955, and introduced him to Jack Kerouac, who had travelled to California after a visit to Mexico. Philip Whalen, just back from a summer job in the forests, was also there, as were Philip Lamantia and Michael McClure. They were all relatively unknown writers, though Lamantia had appeared in print in surrealist journals in the 1940s. And an older group of poets, including Kenneth Rexroth, Robert Duncan, William Everson, and James Broughton, together with others like Jack Spicer and Lawrence Ferlinghetti, were also around San Francisco. The history of the post-war literary scene in the city is fascinating and covers much more than the work of the Beat poets. It's significant that Rexroth, Duncan, etc., were outside the American literary establishment, and were admired by Snyder, Ginsberg, and the rest, none of whom were writing the kind of work likely to be applauded by academics or New York intellectuals. Ginsberg, who always seems to have had a sense of his own potential, as well as that of his fellow poets, knew that something was about to happen in the 1950s and arranged a poetry reading to feature some of the newer writers.

There are various accounts of the now famous Six Gallery reading on October 13, 1955, but I'll merely quote Snyder's brief version, as given in an interview years later when he was a little hazy about the actual date:

> Somehow a poetry reading was held at the old Six Gallery in the Marina in October or November of 1955 and at that reading Ginsberg read 'Howl' for the first time it had ever been heard in public, and I read some things and Philip Whalen read some things, and it sort of started things going: Michael McClure and Lamantia also read that evening, and Rexroth was a master of ceremonies.

Snyder also recalled that he read 'The Berry Feast', together with some short poems subsequently incorporated into *Myths & Texts*. It may help to set the Beats in context, and point again to the mood of the mid 1950s, if I mention that the Six Gallery had been the only location willing to give a platform to Walter Lowenfels, an old thirties avant-garde poet in Paris (he is in Henry Miller's *Black Spring* under the name Jabberwhorl Cronstadt), who had been an active communist in the forties, and in the fifties was being harassed by the authorities.

Snyder and Ginsberg hitch-hiked north early in 1956, reading at the University of Washington and Reed College, and arguing all the way about their different social outlooks. Some of the events of late 1955 and early 1956 are described in *The Dharma Bums* and John Montgomery's *Kerouac West Coast*, and it would have been understandable had Snyder decided to stay in the San Francisco area as the Beats began to attract attention, and the literary scene generally burst into life with little magazines, anthologies, small press pamphlets, and poetry readings proliferating. But in May 1956 he took advantage of a scholarship offered by the First Zen Institute of America and went to Japan for over a year, living in a Zen temple and studying Japanese. He left Japan in August 1957, and signed on a ship called the *Sappa Creek*, intending to work his way back to San Francisco but actually staying on board for eight months and making trips to Italy, Ceylon, Turkey, and other places. It was, he recalled, a key period in his life, and confirmed his idea that 'intelligence and insight, sensitivity, awareness and brilliance are not limited to educated people.'

I mentioned earlier that *Riprap* was dedicated to some of the men he was with on the ship, and he said that he

> owed them as individuals, as persons, as much as he owed any books. They were real teachers, they were all men of no education, but men of great natural brilliance and life. Some real fuck-ups too, of course. The 'T-2 Tanker Blues' in *Riprap* is about that ship, and the *Sappa Creek* poem is also about that experience.

He did eventually return to San Francisco, and in late 1958 and early 1959 participated in the poetry scene, met old friends, and wrote. A short essay, 'North Beach', in the collection *The Old Ways* partly refers to this period and expresses how close he felt to the area and its artistic and libertarian traditions:

> In the spiritual and political loneliness of America of the fifties you'd hitch a thousand miles to meet a friend. Whatever lives needs a habitat, a proper culture of warmth and moisture to grow. West Coast of those days, San Francisco was the only city; and of San Francisco, North Beach.

His main achievement during this time was completing *Myths & Texts*, a long sequence described by one commentator as written in a 'tough Poundian verse laced with Zen.' This appeared in 1960 and established Snyder as a major figure amongst the new American poets. Divided into three sections – 'Logging,' 'Hunting' and 'Burning' – it combined many of Snyder's interests, ranging from his appreciation of the American North-West, to his knowledge of Indian lore and customs, Zen Buddhism, and his awareness of social and political matters. Snyder's grandfather had been a Wobbly (a member of the I.W.W., the Industrial Workers of the World), and there are a number of references to the history of this organisation and events such as the Everett Massacre of 1916, when a number of Wobblies were killed during a strike. The poem refers to 'Thousands of boys shot and beat up/For wanting a good bed, good pay/decent food', and incorporates conversations with old workers about the hard times they experienced. But if it pays homage to forgotten radicals and their dreams, it also acknowledges that orthodox left-wing theories are not likely to be totally useful in a world threatened with ecological and other problems. *Myths & Texts* is a major poem and perhaps stands midway in Snyder's development as a poet and social theorist.

Returning to Japan in 1959, Snyder married Joanne Kyger, a poet he had met in San Francisco. Apart from six months in India he stayed in Japan until late 1964, studying in Kyoto under a noted Zen Master. There are a large number of poems from these years, not to mention some prose pieces ('A Journey to Rishikesh and Hardwar' in *Earth House Hold*, for example), which document his experiences and the development of his philosophy of life. It's also worth referring to 'Passage Through India' and Joanne Kyger's *The Japan and India Journals* for further details about this period in Snyder's life.

At some point in the early sixties the marriage to Joanne Kyger collapsed. Snyder was back in the United States towards the end of 1964, taught briefly at the University of California, but returned to Japan the following year and remarried, this time to someone called Masa. Poems from this new phase make frequent references to Masa, and to Snyder's son, Kai, and were designed to explore

> The most archaic values on earth ... the fertility of the soil, the magic of animals, the power-vision in solitude, the terrifying initiation and rebirth, the love and ecstasy of the dance, the common work of the tribe.

Many of them were collected in *Regarding Wave*, published in 1970 when Snyder was back in the United States. He had lived in San Francisco for a brief period on his return, but told journalist Bruce Cook that he was planning to move to Sierra County:

> It's just some acres of wilderness I bought with a cabin on it. But I want to get us out there, so we can begin to learn to break the habits of dependency. It's important for me. I think it will mean more consciousness, more awareness. And nothing has more value for the individual than his consciousness, intensifying and refining it.

Snyder has made Sierra County his base since those days, continuing to write both poetry and prose and involving himself in community schemes in an effort to develop his theories about 'the tribe.' Jack Kerouac said that Snyder would most likely end up as a hermit in the tradition of Han Shan, but when this point was raised during an interview, the poet replied:

> But Han Shan didn't live in a community. And another thing that is part of my personal world is erasing some parts of my ego increasingly into the co-operation of the group, and the decision making of the group.

It's relevant to add that Snyder has even involved himself with what might be called establishment organisations in an effort to influence decisions about local matters and gain support for bringing art into the community. He was a member of the California Arts Council and supported the use of public funds for research into Chicano and Native American cultural history. Nor is he averse to employing new methods of production when writing. A piece by Carole Koda, who has been his partner in recent years, described how he was hard at work on a new book and using a computer to write it. The tools of the new are at hand to be used alongside those of the old.

This piece has essentially looked at the facts of Snyder's life, while sketching in some of his ideas and theories. But it may be worth adding a few notes on his beliefs. There is an early essay, 'Buddhist Anarchism', which gives a good outline of his attitudes in 1961, which is around the time he was immersing himself in Zen Buddhism, but hadn't shown any major indications of a need to be seen as a kind of Shaman of the tribe. He later revised the piece for publication in *Earth House Hold*, but the section which follows is essentially the same as in the original:

> The mercy of the West has been social revolution; the mercy of the East has been individual insight into the basic self/void. We need both. They are both contained in the traditional three aspects of the Dharma path: wisdom (prajna), meditation (dhyana), and morality (sila). Wisdom is intuitive knowledge of the mind of love and clarity that lies beneath one's ego-driven anxieties and aggressions. Meditation is going into the mind to see this for yourself – over and over again, until it becomes the mind you live in. Morality is bringing it back out in the way you live, through personal example and responsible action, ultimately towards the true community (sangha) of all beings. This last aspect means, for me, supporting any cultural and economic revolution that moves clearly towards a free, international, classless world. It means using such means as civil disobedience, outspoken criticism, protest, pacifism, voluntary poverty, and even gentle violence if it comes to restraining some impetuous redneck. It means affirming the widest possible spectrum of non-harmful individual behaviour – defending the rights of individuals to smoke hemp, eat peyote, be polygynous, polyandrous or homosexual. Worlds of behaviour long banned by the Judaeo-Capitalist-Marxist West. It means respecting intelligence and

learning, but not as greed or means to personal power. Working on one's own responsibility, but willing to work with a group. Forming the new society within the shell of the old – the I.W.W. slogan of fifty years ago.

The insistence that the various strands of East and West should be intertwined is typical of Snyder, and crops up constantly throughout his poetry and prose. 'Passage to More Than India', an important essay which lifted off from the famous 'Human Be-In' held in San Francisco in 1967, points out how many of the 'new families' are living communally, and then goes on to discuss the concept of the family, with particular reference to Engels's *Origin of the Family, Private Property and the State*, the Peyote and other ceremonies of the Indians, and the historical influence of the Christian heretics – the Ranters, the Brotherhood of Free Love, and the myriad groups which flourished in Europe in the Middle Ages and as late as the seventeenth century. As Snyder makes clear, they were not only concerned with sexual liberation, but believed that it would lead to new forms of society:

> Love begins with the family and its network of erotic and responsible relationships. A slight alteration of family structures will project a different love-and-property outlook through a whole culture ... thus the communism and free love of Christian heresies.

Earth House Hold is an important book in that it brings together work from Snyder's days in the North-West ('Lookout's Journal', dating from 1952) and at sea ('Tanker Notes', from 1957), and links it with more determinedly social and philosophical pieces. Thus one can see a continuity of thought, as well as the development of it. It's easy to understand how a man who, in the early fifties, was expressing an interest in American Indian life should, twenty years later, be working on a programme for a form of tribal organisation. The Indians were, and are, tribal people. Likewise, there is a link between Snyder's approach to the Indian awareness of the question of existence and his dedication to Zen Buddhism. Both have a practical side which ties in with Snyder's down-to-earth view of the need to deal with everyday problems, and yet at the same time have an overall philosophy which can give cohesion to the various experiences seemingly encountered in piecemeal fashion. In this connection it should not be forgotten that Snyder has never tried to deny the facts of his upbringing as a twentieth-century American. Nor has he ever rejected his early involvements with academic learning. In an interview in *The Real Work* he said of his years at Reed College:

> I had some marvellous teachers, I learned how to use a library, I was in an atmosphere that challenged me and pushed me to the utmost, which was just what I needed. They wouldn't tolerate bullshit, made me clean up my prose style, exposed me to all varieties of intellectual positions and gave me a territory in which I could speak out my radical politics and get arguments and augmentations on it. It was an intensive, useful experience.

This leads me towards another side of Snyder which is worth investigating, and that is his position as a 'Westerner,' by which I mean a man born in, and still relating to, the part of the United States referred to as the West. This is not just the West of the movies, of course, with its plains and deserts, but also includes the Pacific Coast states, such as Oregon and Washington. There has been, in recent times, a conscious attempt to show that the West has a definite literary tradition which embraces specific social and philosophical positions. Readers interested in finding out more about this idea could usefully refer to William *Everson's Archetype West: The Pacific Coast as Literary Region*. This contains references to Snyder which are complemented by the poet's own statements in his essay, 'The Incredible Survival of Coyote', based on a talk given to a conference of Western writers:

> But something has happened since World War 2. I can see a little bit how it happened in myself. Our sense of the West is changing from a history of exploitation and westward expansion by white people, into a sense of place ... . Poets who have lived in the West all their lives, teaching in universities, can only speak of the urban world, some of them, and they're not paisanos, you see. Paisanos in the sense of knowing a place. So there is work to be done in the matter of knowing

where you are, the old American quest, which I share with all of you, for an identity, a sense of place. To know the place well means, first and foremost, I think, to know plants, and it means developing a sensitivity, an openness, an awareness of all kinds of weather patterns in nature.

This sense of place adds another dimension to Snyder's amalgam of anarcho-syndicalist theories, communitarian experiments, Zen beliefs, Shamanism, ecological concern, and down-to-earth commitment to finding a way to survive in a hostile world which seems hell-bent on self destruction, in one way or another. This is a heady brew, and it's possible to question parts of it. For example, I find Snyder's concepts of the tribe more than a little naive. In his essay, 'Why Tribe?' he said:

> The revolution has ceased to be an ideological concern. Instead, people are trying it out right now – communism in small communities, new family organisation. A million people in America and another million in England and Europe. A vast underground in Russia, which will come out into the open four or five years hence, is now biding. How do they recognise each other? Not always by beards, long hair, bare feet and beads. The signal is a bright and tender look; calmness and gentleness, freshness and ease of manner. Men, women and children – all of whom together hope to follow the timeless path of love and wisdom, in affectionate company with the sky, wind, clouds, trees, waters, animals and grasses – this is the tribe.

Now that was clearly fine propaganda, and no doubt written on a wave of enthusiasm for the 'alternative society' when it seemed viable and energetic. And it would be unfair to hold it against Snyder because his vision of an uprising in Russia didn't work out. There was an uprising, of course, and the communist state collapsed, but the only 'tribes' to have emerged have been the old nationalities, together with all the hatreds they nurture. In fact, the rise of 'tribalism' generally has led to ethnic cleansing and worse. It's unfortunate that Snyder lowered his intellectual sights in order to get away with some glib preaching, and it inclines me, at least, to wonder whether his sense of history is as strong as his awareness of Eastern religions and related subjects. In other areas, such as his seeming encouragement of drugs experiments in the Sixties, he's been honest enough to admit that it led to a number of personal tragedies. The same has most likely been true of many people who involved themselves in half-baked schemes for communitarian living or supposed sexual liberation. Any historian of communes could have pointed out the pitfalls that have led to the collapse of so many of them. And there is cause to treat theories of sexual liberation with a degree of caution. Historians are now pointing out that, in the nineteenth century, so-called 'free love' was often just a device to exploit people, particularly women, and that the supposed sexual puritanism we often perceive in that era was, in fact, a way of curtailing the excesses of prophets of libertinism.

On the subject of the influence that people like Snyder can have, he himself said: 'I've had people turn up at my door who were half-insane, who told me that I had set them on their path.' And on the question of the 'underground' or 'alternative culture' generally, he remarked: 'You've got to realise that there's an underside to this, that at its bottom is Charlie Manson.' Snyder obviously can't be blamed for what Manson did, but poets, like anyone else, ought to have a sense of responsibility when making statements likely to influence other people's behaviour. It could also be argued that a poet like Snyder, who has always professed to be adopting moral positions against the corruptions of power and the abuses of privilege, has a greater responsibility than most to make sure that what he advocates is tempered with wisdom. Not everyone has the intellectual capacity, or integrity, required to evaluate suggestions made in a context which may appear to lend them more substance than they actually have. And it may also be necessary to be wary of poets when they try to be philosophers or priests.

Which brings me to my final point. Whatever else he's wanted to be – sage, scholar, Shaman, social critic, prophet – it strikes me that Snyder's main achievement is as a poet. That's what he ought to be seen as, with the rest of his writing providing a background to the poetry. The major works, such as *Myths & Texts, Six Sections from Mountains and Rivers Without End*, and *Cold Mountain Poems* (translations from Han Shan), not to mention the best of the first-rate shorter poems he's written, are what he has to be judged by, both now and in the future. The core of his philosophy, without the agit-prop qualities that occasionally affect his prose, is to be found within the poems, where a saner, more considered view of things comes through. But let me finish by quoting a few lines from the *Cold Mountain Poems*. They seem to me to suggest, in a sly way, that both Han Shan and Snyder know that it's not easy to reach the heights they're aiming at (and Cold Mountain is a state of mind, not a place) and that you have to work hard at it:

> Men ask the way to Cold Mountain
> Cold Mountain: there's no through trail.
> In summer, ice doesn't melt
> The rising sun blurs in swirling fog.
> How did I make it?
> My heart's not the same as yours.
> If your heart was like mine
> You'd get it and be right here.

Note

The following is a list of various documents consulted during the writing of this article:

1. Bert Almon, *Gary Snyder*, Boise State University, Boise, 1979.
2. Alfred Aranowitz, 'The Yen for Zen,' *Escapade*, New York, October, 1960.
3. Alfred Aranowitz, 'Visit with a Fellaheen Man,' *Swank*, New York, September, 1961.
4. Lee Bartlett, editor, *The Beats: Essays in Criticism*, McFarland, Jefferson, 1981.
5. Samuel Charters, *Some Poems/Poets: Studies in American Underground Poetry Since 1945*, Oyez, Berkeley, 1971.
6. Bruce Cook, *The Beat Generation*, Scribner's, New York, 1971.
7. Michael Davidson, *The San Francisco Renaissance: Poetics and Community at Mid-Century*, Cambridge University Press, Cambridge, 1989.

8. William Everson, *Archetype West: The Pacific Coast as Literary Region*, Oyez, Berkeley, 1976.

9. Ekbert Faas, editor, *Towards a New American Poetics: Essays & Interviews*, Black Sparrow Press, Santa Barbara, 1978.

10. Thom Gunn, 'Walking with Wonder,' *The Listener*, London, May 2nd, 1968.

11. Jon Halper, editor, *Gary Snyder: Dimensions of a Life*, Sierra Club Books, San Francisco, 1991.

12. David Kherdian, *Gary Snyder: A Biographical Sketch & Descriptive Checklist*, Oyez, Berkeley, 1965.

13. David Kherdian, *Six San Francisco Poets*, Giglia Press, Fresno, 1969.

14. Joanne Kyger, *The Japan and India Journals 1960-1964*, Timbouctou Books, Bolinas, 1981.

15. Inger Thorup Laurldsen & Per Dalgard, editors, *The Beat Generation and the Russian New Wave*, Ardis Publishers, Ann Arbor, 1990.

16. Howard McCord, *Some Notes to Gary Snyder's Myths & Texts*, Sand Dollar, Berkeley, 1971.

17. Katherine McNeil, *Gary Snyder: A Bibliography*, Phoenix Bookshop, New York, 1983.

18. David Meltzer, *The San Francisco Poets*, Ballantine Books, New York, 1971.

19. John Montgomery, *Kerouac West Coast: A Bohemian Pilot: Detailed Navigational Instructions*, Fels & Firn Press, Palo Alto, 1976.

20. Gary Snyder, *Six Sections From Mountains & Rivers Without End*, Four Seasons Foundation, San Francisco, 1965.

21. Gary Snyder, *A Range of Poems*, Fulcrum Press, London, 1966.

22. Gary Snyder, *The Back Country*, Fulcrum Press, London, 1967.

23. Gary Snyder, *Earth House Hold*, New Directions, New York, 1969.

24. Gary Snyder, *Regarding Wave*, New Directions, New York, 1970.

25. Gary Snyder, *Turtle Island*, New Directions, New York, 1974.

26. Gary Snyder, *The Old Ways*, City Lights Books, San Francisco, 1977.

27. Interview with Gary Snyder in *The Beat Diary*, California, Pennsylvania, 1977.

28. Gary Snyder, *He Who Hunted Birds in His Father's Village*, Grey Fox

Press, Bolinas, 1979.

29. Gary Snyder, *The Real Work: Interviews & Talks*, 1964-1979, New Directions, New York, 1980.

30. Gary Snyder, *Axe Handles*, North Point Press, San Francisco, 1983.

31. Gary Snyder, *Left Out in the Rain: New Poems 1947-1985*, North Point Press, San Francisco, 1986.

32. Gary Snyder, *Passage Through India*, Grey Fox Press, San Francisco, 1992.

33. Alan Watts, *This Is It*, Collier Books, New York, 1967.

34. Kenneth White, *The Tribal Dharma: An Essay on the Work of Gary Snyder*, Unicorn Bookshop, Llanfynydd, 1975.

The above is not meant to be a complete list of either Snyder's own books or books by other writers which contain references to him. There have been various British and American editions of some of Snyder's collections of poems, and reprints which have combined earlier, smaller publications. The British edition of *A Range of Poems*, for example, includes *Riprap*, the *Cold Mountain* poems, *Myths & Texts*, *Miyazawa Kenji*, and part of *The Back Country* sequence. I have only listed those editions I had access to. Katherine McNeil's bibliography is useful for further information, though it is limited to the period from the early 1950s to the early 1980s.

LEW WELCH: GOLDEN GATE POET, 1981

'Dave Wain that lean rangy red headed Welchman.'

Jack Kerouac, *Big Sur*

R eaders of Jack Kerouac's books, and of Beat Generation literature
generally, will be familiar with a character named 'Dave Wain'
who is one of the people the narrator (Kerouac, of course) mixes with
in *Big Sur*. That book describes events in and around San Francisco
in 1960, but Kerouac and Lew Welch (which is who Dave Wain is)
had met before that. And their 1959 cross-country trip from the West
Coast to New York had been important to Welch's development as
a writer. But all this is to jump ahead of the story, and is really just
to draw attention to a poet whose work is sufficiently interesting to
stand on its own merits. In this article I'll try to give an outline of
Welch's life and work. Both are interesting, the life because it says a
great deal about the fifties and sixties, the work because the best of
it is still worth reading.

Welch was born in 1926 in Arizona. He grew up in an affluent
household, his mother's family being what he himself described as
'super rich.' There was a slightly unusual aspect, however, in that his
father was from a poorer background, and seems to have been
something of a drifter. From Welch's account it was almost a
Hollywood-style romance – poor boy, handsome and good at sports,
meets rich girl and sweeps her off her feet; they marry, the boy is
fixed up with a job by her family, but proves to be an unreliable type.

Welch's father was nicknamed 'Speed,' and you get a whole picture of the twenties (flapper girls, fast cars, hip flasks, raccoon coats, society parties, college football games – Scott Fitzgerald country, in fact) from that alone.

I won't go into a detailed account of Welch's life in the thirties and forties: suffice it to say that he lived in Southern California most of the time, certainly cossetted to a great degree by his mother's money, seeing his father only occasionally, but starting to excel at sports and to read a lot. In late 1944 he enroled at the University of California at Berkeley, but in January of the following year he was inducted into the Air Force. He served only a few months, being discharged as the war ended, and then went back to studying, though not at Berkeley. Between 1946 and 1948 he was at Stockton Junior College, and it was here that he seems to have discovered that he wanted to be a writer. A sympathetic tutor suggested that he try Reed College in Oregon. Reed was a place with a radical and creative tradition.

In the two years or so that Welch attended Reed he met and became friendly with Gary Snyder and Philip Whalen, two other aspiring young poets who were later to become key figures in Beat generation literature. Welch's letters from this period illuminate his state of mind which was that of a somewhat impressionable young man agog with excitement about the people he was meeting, the artistic work he was experiencing, and his own tentative efforts to get something worthwhile down on paper. Not only paper, either, because Welch had a keen interest in music. A letter to his mother dated July 1950 refers to some success he had around Reed at that time. He set a Shakespeare piece to a contemporary melody (according to Welch it was adopted from a 'West Texas blues source') and it became popular, got Welch some air time on the local radio, and according to him looked as if it could take off into the big-time. But there's probably something highly significant in the fact that a letter dated a few days later doesn't even mention the subject, but instead rambles on about Welch's plans to head for South America in order to escape the possibility of being drafted because of the Korean War situation. Just a few more days on and even that idea had gone by the board. Consistency was not a Welch characteristic, it seems. According to a letter in October he did make an attempt to get a ship to South America, but the plan fell through. Still, his whole time at Reed wasn't just spent in day-dreams and unfulfilled planning. It was during this period that William Carlos Williams made a visit to the college, and there is something very real and unaffected in Welch's response (as recorded in a letter to his mother) to the older poet's comments about the need for American poets to appreciate the possibilities of their own language rather than imitate English writers.

Welch spent some time in New York in 1950 and early 1951, and then went to Florida. From there he moved to Chicago and enroled at the university. More of his inconsistency made itself evident when he quit the Philosophy course he originally took, and switched to English. It was during this period that he had a nervous breakdown and had to go into psychoanalysis.

I think Welch was, at this point in his life, obviously unsure what he wanted to do. And it was an uncertainty further demonstrated by his taking a job in advertising in 1953. Not that there's a rule which says that would-be poets shouldn't work in advertising. Many have, and some still do, and I can think of several fine poets who have spent time earning a living in agencies. It's arguably better for a poet than spending his time in the academies, though I hate to generalise too much about these things. There are good and bad poets in every walk of life, and there's nothing to prove that a non-academic life-style will in itself assure a poet of artistic success. But Welch's letters do tend to show him as believing in an 'open' approach. The Beat feeling was there, though it constantly clashed with other things. For example, one finds Welch talking about money, career prospects, marriage, houses, work, and so on, in the manner of any junior executive. And there's a suspicious absence at times of references to poetry or the arts generally. Was it a case of the psychoanalyst 'normalising' Welch in the sense of persuading him to adjust to society by conforming?

Welch's letters to Gary Snyder in 1955 hint at his still being dissatisfied with his lot. He asks Snyder how he manages to survive, and refers to his own doubts about being tied down to a well-paid, but intellectually and emotionally stultifying job.

By the end of 1956 or the beginning of 1957 Welch had realised that something was about to break open on the literary scene. There's a significant January 1957 letter from Philip Whalen to Welch in which the former mentions various articles which were highlighting the new writers. Whalen refers to his earning a living by washing glasses in a laboratory for a few hours each day. And he says that he's heard Welch has 'commenced coming over all square.' All this started Welch writing poetry again, and pushed him into persuading the advertising agency to transfer him to their Oakland office, a move that signified the start of his life as a poet.

By April 1958 Welch had been fired by the advertising agency, and was talking about becoming a teacher. But he needed to earn a living and started driving a taxi, an occupation that is referred to in one of his poems, 'After Anacreon,' which ends:

> When I drive cab
> I watch for stragglers in the urban order of things.

> When I drive cab
> I end the only lit and waitful thing in miles of
> darkened houses.

Welch's marriage came to an end around this time, his reason being that his wife wanted what he called the 'American Homemaking Bit,' and to him that was all 'soap and machinery ritualised to a point beyond my understanding.' Various letters from this period refer to his general elation about the way things were going. He was writing fairly steadily, and the scene in San Francisco was then at its height, with poetry readings, magazines, and other activities flourishing.

When Jack Kerouac visited San Francisco in 1959 he and Welch struck up an immediate rapport. Welch had ended his work as a taxi-driver, and had been employed in a factory but was fired for bad timekeeping. His oddball behaviour may have had something to do with his losing the job, Welch's story being that he had an ear pierced and had a piece of string dangling from it. So when Kerouac, who wanted to get back to New York, suggested that Welch drive him there it seemed like a good idea. They, and Albert Saijo, left San Francisco in Welch's old jeep. Welch was an excellent driver, a fact attested to by Kerouac in *Big Sur* when he says:

> We call up Dave Wain who's back from Reno and he comes blattin down to the bar in his jeepster driving that marvellous way he does (once he was a cab-driver) talking all the time and never making a mistake.

Like Kerouac, Welch was a heavy drinker, and that gave them something in common to work on. But, as Albert Saijo recalled,

> ... both Jack and Lew were into popular songs from the 40s. They both had fine singing voices and repertoires. Jack knew many Sinatra tunes and could sing just like him. Lew was a great singer of scat. So there were hundreds of miles of talk and song.

Welch and Saijo didn't stay long in New York after they'd dropped off Kerouac, though the three of them did stay together for a visit to photographer Fred McDarrah's house where they had their pictures taken and concocted a rambling poem which later came out in the style-setting anthology, *The Beat Scene*. But by the end of 1959 Welch was at his mother's home in Reno, and inspired by his conversations with Kerouac, was working on an autobiographical novel. His intention was to build it into four 'books' which would chart the progress of the hero, Leo, from his days at college in the late forties through to the time of writing. Welch's idea was to use his own experiences as a kind of history of the period, and he had some interesting observations to make on the effect of an influx of mature students into the colleges in the late forties, the impact of the Korean War, and the development of the Beat mood of the fifties. He did manage to write a fair amount of the first 'book,' although the results were only published in the seventies. But he had grave doubts about the quality of the work, and

soon abandoned it. As he wrote to Jack Kerouac, 'have decided my
novel is badly written and (therefore) dull.' In the same letter he told
Kerouac he was working on short stories, and had managed to sell
one to *Evergreen Review*, one of the major platforms for the new writers
of the late fifties and early sixties.

If Welch's novel hadn't gone too well he was writing poetry which
showed he had developed a personal style. 'After Anacreon,' and an
earlier poem about Chicago, were included in the important anthology
The New American Poetry in 1960, but his first book, *Wobbly Rock*, which
appeared that year, perhaps gave a better indication of his concerns.
He had clearly absorbed a great deal from Snyder and Whalen, both
in terms of style and what might be called a philosophy of life, but
had shaped it to suit his own requirements. And his own comments
at the time make it clear that he thought of *Wobbly Rock* as being much
more important than his other poems. It is an attempt to both describe
something of the California landscape (and seascape) and also establish
a mood of being moulded by the elements and adapting to them. There
are a couple of significant lines, too, which point to his need to see
California as a place to find a home, and also perhaps to his need to
be stimulated into artistic activity. Welch had to have the Beat explosion
to push him into giving himself to poetry, and he had to have Snyder
and Whalen to direct him towards a useful path, but once on the path
he had to walk it in his own way:

> like everything else I have
> somebody showed it to me and I found it by myself

The Zen empathy with the natural elements indicates Snyder's
influence, but the construction is more out of Whalen. The short, almost
clipped statements, piled up like a tower of philosophical windows, are
very much in the manner in which Whalen was then writing.

Welch constantly expressed a desire to get out of the city – any city
– and into the country, partly because he personally needed peace and
quiet to write, partly because he thought cities destructive in their effect

on human beings. And yet he was such a restless type that he floated from one environment to the other, sometimes anxious for solitude, sometimes desperate for company and the hurly-burly of the literary scene. And he always drank heavily. As early as 1960 his letters speak of problems associated with alcoholism. And there also seems to be evidence to suggest that, despite the claims to want to disassociate himself from the rat-race, he badly needed to prove himself as a poet. In a way there's nothing wrong with this – the artistic urge often thrives on the ego – but it can be dangerous in an unsettled personality. The competitiveness of the literary scene is not guaranteed to give peace of mind to the fragile, and Welch doesn't seem to have had the willpower to detach himself sufficiently to ensure survival, despite making claims to being a major poet. His letters disclose a need to constantly point out where his poems were being published.

Kerouac had been West again in 1960, of course, and the events described in *Big Sur* had taken place. Welch and his girlfriend Lenore Kandel (she's in the book as Ramona Schwartz) were members of the group which accompanied Kerouac on the ill-fated trip when he slipped into an alcoholic depression and almost cracked up. Welch's own life wasn't exactly a bed of roses either, and his drinking often led him to the point where a breakdown seemed inevitable. He lived at the East-West house in San Francisco, giving occasional readings, and working on and off in commercial salmon fishing. But the fishing venture failed, and this coincided with the end of his affair with Lenore Kandel, a combination of events which did push Welch into a nervous breakdown. By July he was living in Lawrence Ferlinghetti's cabin in Big Sur (cryptic notes to his mother during this period refer to his beginning to grow calm again) and he then found an abandoned shack where he stayed for some months. The shack had originally been constructed by an old Wobbly and Welch's enthusiastic comments about it – he imagined the ghost of the old radical watching over him – stand out in his letters to friends. There is no doubt that, for a short time at least, Welch managed to find some peace of mind. On the other hand there is evidence in the letters of the desire to achieve not only artistic excellence, but also artistic recognition. As I said earlier, this is not necessarily bad, but when linked to Welch's other problems it clearly wasn't guaranteed to let him ignore the outer world, something he wanted to do.

The period was productive in many ways, however, and Welch wrote his 'Hermit Poems', perhaps some of the best he ever produced. Cleanly constructed, they reflect what Welch referred to as the 'total lack of fear' he felt in his surroundings. Writing, relaxing, doing occasional jobs, visiting neighbours, he was relatively happy, although he still drank heavily. Along with the 'Hermit Poems' he also worked on the poems which appear in *Ring of Bone* in the section headed 'The Way Back.' But Welch was eventually forced to take a full-time job in 1963, something he found useful from a financial point of view but disruptive to his writing. By early 1964 he was back in the San Francisco area, lively, but perhaps showing some disturbing signs. In a letter written in February he referred to money problems, and to the fact that he'd missed an appointment at the Unemployment Benefit office because he'd been too hungover to get there on time. But he was still writing, and participated in Bay Area poetry activities. In June 1964 he took part in a reading with Gary Snyder and Philip Whalen. Prior to the reading the trio appeared on a panel discussion programme on local radio during which the problems of surviving as a poet were discussed. Welch referred to his failure to earn anything of consequence from his writing, to the need to take a variety of jobs, and to his regret that he hadn't learned a skill when he was younger. His idea was that with a skill he would be able to live independently. He spoke about his writing techniques, laying stress on his interest in poetry as speech, and on his desire to write with the concept of public performance always in mind. The transcript of the discussion was later published in book form under the title *On Bread and Poetry*, and longer expositions of Welch's theories can also be found in the essays, 'Language is Speech' and 'How I Work as a Poet,' both of which were collected in a volume which included essays, stories, and plays.

Welch had met a woman named Magda Cregg in 1964 and lived with her until 1971, one of the steadiest relationships he ever had. His poetic reputation was reasonably established by this time, at least on the West Coast, and he was involved with various ventures, such as teaching at a poetry workshop, reading at colleges and universities, underground movies, short stints as a resident poet, and so on. To earn money to supplement his meagre earnings from poetry he worked as a longshoreman's clerk on the San Francisco docks. By 1969 he seemingly had prospects of being included with Snyder and Whalen in one of the Penguin Modern Poets series of books (it never actually appeared), and having his collected poems, *Ring of Bone*, published by Grove Press in New York. But again the problems intervened. Writing in September 1969 he said, 'this has been a hard summer for me. Bad depressions and big changes I don't seem to be able to handle very well. Mostly it's a matter of stopping the booze absolutely.' And in an October letter to Philip Whalen he commented,

> I guess I finally really hit bottom on the alky trip (a bummer from the front) – ended up in the hospital malnourished and flipped out, body screaming for peace and mind on bad death/suicide trips for the first time in my life.

But optimism was still possible, with 1970 promising a lot. Welch had a series of readings, and a five week stint as a resident poet at a college in Colorado, and Grove were supposed to bring out his book in the summer. But by the time he was in Colorado he was despondent about the book which Grove were delaying publishing. It's difficult to document what happened after that year because Welch's letters during that period were few and far between. By January 1971 he was writing to friends to tell them that he was breaking up with Magda Cregg, and saying, 'It's so hard for me now, but I'll make it somehow, tho I know I'll never be the same.' And by March he was writing to his mother to tell her that he was such an alcoholic mess that he didn't want to visit her for fear of what he might get up to. He drifted north, working on the docks in Portland, and planning to move to Nevada County to build a cabin on land owned by Allen Ginsberg. He was there by May, taking Antabuse to curb his drinking, planning the cabin, and contacting friends for loans. But at some point he slipped off the wagon, drank some cans of beer, and on the 23rd May he took a revolver and walked into the woods in a deep depression. (Antabuse is a depressant and mixing it with alcohol, also a depressant, is disastrous from that point of view). He left the following entry in a journal which Gary Snyder found in Welch's van:

> I never could make anything work out right and now I'm betraying my friends. I can't make anything out of it – never could. I had great visions but never could bring them together with reality. I used it all up. It's all gone. Don Allen is to be my literary executor – use MSS at Gary's and Grove Press. I have $2,000 in Nevada City Bank of America – use it to cover my affairs and debts. I don't owe Allen G. anything yet nor my mother. I went Southwest. Goodbye. Lew Welch.

Snyder immediately organised a search party, and for five days carried out an extensive hunt for Welch. But if he did commit suicide his body was never found. And if he simply disappeared to the Southwest, as he said, then he has managed to stay out of sight ever since. The most likely thing is that he did shoot himself and that his body was swallowed up by the forest or lost in the foothills of the Rockies.

Welch's story says a great deal about the life of the poet in America, and even perhaps in the twentieth century generally. Anxious to write well, conditioned by upbringing and education to seek success in commercial terms, and constantly having to compromise to stay alive, it's little wonder that he cracked up. The surprise is that he managed to produce a reasonably substantial body of work, the best of which still reads well. It is clear, often witty, warm, and successfully mixes some very real insights with a skilled and spirited form of delivery. It ought to be read as long as there are people around who care for good poetry.

Note

The following bibliography does not attempt to list all of Welch's books because the early ones were collected in *Ring of Bone*, and that item is much easier to obtain than the limited edition pamphlets from the sixties. Likewise, my listing of ancillary items is not meant to be complete. It merely ties in with my article, and hopefully guides the interested reader to a few places where material by and about Welch can be found.

1. Jack Kerouac, Albert Saijo, Lew Welch: *Trip Trap: Haiku along the road from San Francisco to New York 1959*. Grey Fox Press, Bolinas, 1973.
2. Jack Kerouac: *Big Sur*. Panther Books, London, 1980.
3. David Meltzer, ed: *The San Francisco Poets*. Ballantine Books, New York, 1971. Includes a long interview with Welch.
4. Aram Saroyan: *Genesis Angels: The Saga of Lew Welch & The Beat Generation*. Morrow, New York, 1979.
5. *On Bread & Poetry: A Panel Discussion with Gary Snyder, Lew Welch & Philip Whalen*. Grey Fox Press, Bolinas, 1977.
6. Lew Welch: *Ring of Bone: Collected Poems 1950-1971*. Grey Fox Press, Bolinas, 1973.
7. Lew Welch: *How I Work as a Poet & Other Essays/Plays/Stories*. Grey Fox Press, Bolinas, 1973.
8. Lew Welch: *I, Leo: An Unfinished Novel*. Grey Fox Press, Bolinas, 1977.
9. *I Remain: The Letters of Lew Welch & The Correspondence of his Friends, Volume 1, 1949 to 1960*; Volume 2, 1960 to 1971. Grey Fox Press, Bolinas, 1977.
10. Elias Wilentz, ed: *The Beat Scene*. Corinth Books, New York, 1960.

BEAT WOMEN, 1993

> As a female, she's not quite part of this convergence. A fact she ignores,
> sitting by in her excitement as the voices of the men, always the men,
> passionately rise and fall and their beer glasses collect and the smoke
> of their cigarettes rises towards the ceiling and the dead culture is surely
> being awakened.

That excerpt from *Minor Characters*, Joyce Johnson's poignant memoir
of her involvement with Jack Kerouac and other Beat writers,
rightly points to the way in which women were given a back seat, or
at least one in which they were expected to sit quietly while the men
talked and wrote. Very few women were actively associated with the
Beats from the point of view of their own writing, and it was only in
later years that Carolyn Cassady, Joyce Johnson, and Hettie Jones
produced books which told the story as they experienced it. Their
accounts are, in fact, among the most accurate documents of Beat life,
much more matter-of-fact and honest than male versions of the same
events. If you really want to know what Neal Cassady was like, read
Carolyn Cassady's *Off The Road*, and if you want to find out about the
day-to-day life of Beat New York in the late 1950s and early 1960s,
look at *Minor Characters* or Hettie Jones's evocative *How I Became Hettie
Jones*. All three books manage to combine vivid descriptions of Beat
life with truthful appraisals of its practices and pitfalls.

They are also remarkably free of bitterness, considering how the
women were often treated, and they acknowledge the advantages that
mixing with the male writers and poets could sometimes bring. There
was a sense of being caught up in something exciting and interesting.

But it would be wrong to overlook the disadvantages that accompanied relationships with male Beats, and a searing narrative of the chaotic side of some Beat activities can be found in Bonnie Bremser's *For Love of Ray*, which deals openly with what she was prepared to do to support them both when Ray Bremser fled to Mexico to escape prosecution and possible imprisonment. He was irresponsible and had problems with both drugs and alcohol, and Bonnie Bremser sometimes worked as a prostitute to raise money to meet his needs. It's surprising that her book had what a critic referred to as 'a curious optimism,' though the mixture of downbeat and upbeat impulses is not unusual in Beat literature. *For Love of Ray* (or *Troia: Mexican Memoirs* as it was called in the American edition) was originally published in 1969, and is an authentic Beat work which has never been given the recognition due to it. Bonnie Bremser published little of significance after *For Love of Ray* and seems to have dropped out of the literary scene in the 1970s.

For another version of the problem women often had with male Beats, readers might search out Mimi Albert's *The Second Story Man*, a fairly obscure novel published in 1975. It doesn't deal with anyone well known, and is written in a conventional style, but the action takes place around the East Village in the late 1950s, and seems to have an autobiographical touch to it. And, like Bonnie Bremser's book, it tells how the woman frequently demeans herself in order to support a heavy drinking and feckless male.

There are, of course, a number of reasons why women were required to accept their place in the Beat world, but I don't want to investigate that side of things. Matters of sex and gender, and of the historical reasons why women were accorded a certain status, can best be looked at by someone better qualified than I am to write on the subject. And it's a theoretical area I never feel comfortable with. Suffice to say that the Beats, for all their talk about new ways of consciousness, tended to reflect the old ways in their attitudes towards women. But as I said, this is something that someone else ought to explore, and it does have many aspects worth looking at in detail. It seems, for example, to be a fact that a number of Beat writers, particularly those from working-class backgrounds, simply couldn't cope with intelligent, well-educated women. That the women managed to cope, for a time, with the men perhaps says something about their qualities. But it also raises the question of why intelligent, well-educated women were often attracted to men who were almost guaranteed to give them a hard time. If anyone does want to consider what happened to women during the Beat years, then books like those by Carolyn Cassady, Joyce Johnson, Hettie Jones, and Bonnie Bremser, are obviously of key importance. There was, also, a sociological survey, published in 1961, which could be useful. *The Real Bohemia*, by Francis J. Rigney and L. Douglas Smith, was based on research in San Francisco in the late 1950s, and largely focuses on what unknown Beats got up to, though a few writers are also incorporated into the survey.

It seems to me of practical use, however, to write about a few of the women poets who were around at the time when the Beats hit the headlines. There were, of course, numerous women – wives, girlfriends, etc – who were portrayed in Beat novels and poems. But they weren't writers. Bohemia has always celebrated itself and what was probably the first novel to deal with the subject, Henry Murger's *Scènes de la Vie de Bohème*, immortalised an unknown Parisian working girl, Lucile Louvet, by calling her Mimi and having her die tragically in circumstances not far from the truth about Louvet's death. You might want to find a parallel in Allen Ginsberg's poem, 'Fragment: the Names II', which refers to Elise Cowen's death. And who were the ill-fated Sheila, Connie, Natalie, and Iris, that Ginsberg also refers to in the same poem? A little information can sometimes be turned up, but the point is that none of them were writers, or at least they weren't successful in print. A few of Elise Cowen's poems did appear in *City Lights Journal*, but they're frankly little more than notebook jottings and do not suggest that she could have gone on to better things. For those curious about her, Leo Skir's 'Elise Cowen: A Brief Memoir of the Fifties', published in *Evergreen Review* 48 in 1967, is worth reading. There may be a useful study to be written about Cowen, and other forgotten women of the Beat Generation, though finding information might not be easy.

The magazines and anthologies of the Beat heyday – roughly 1957 to 1962, give or take a year or two – are the best source for work by Beat women writers. Only a few of them published books, and Diane di Prima is probably the best known. She was born in New York in 1934, and in the early 1950s was in touch with Ezra Pound and Kenneth Patchen. She corresponded with Ginsberg and Ferlinghetti in 1956 and met Kerouac, Orlovsky, and Corso in 1957. Her first book of poems, *This Kind of Bird Flies Backwards*, was published in 1958. It showed her to be a bright young writer with a short-lined, anonymous style, and the poems were largely personal and could be flippant about love affairs and the like. It wasn't the kind of writing to be thought of as much more than bohemian ephemera, and it was only when her book of prose pieces, *Dinners and Nightmares*, appeared in 1960 that di Prima demonstrated that she had an individual voice.

This small volume (an enlarged edition was published in 1974) gave a brisk and often amusing picture of Beat life. She seemed to be aroused by it, but at the same time aware of some of its drawbacks. One of the 'Conversations', a series of short pieces built around dialogue, describes a poet who, as he calmly watches a man beat up his girlfriend, proclaims that he loves the world and weeps for lost children. Elsewhere, she cryptically describes the mood of the late 1950s, when suspicion against the unconventional still ran rife and it was, according to her, open season on 'men with lipstick/ women with crewcuts/ poets of all descriptions,' with 'junkies and jazz musicians' being even more hated. It was, I suppose, something of an exaggeration, and aimed at the kind of bohemian audience likely to read a book by an unknown writer from a small press. A colourful and erotic description of Diane di Prima's experiences in the 1950s can be found in her *Memoirs of a Beatnik*, published in 1969, in which some factual details about surviving in a bohemian community are mixed with graphic accounts of a variety of sexual escapades. The book was published by the Olympia Press during its short American existence, which explains the frequent dollops of sex in its pages.

Diane di Prima's work developed over the years and the 1963 *The New Handbook of Heaven* showed that she had become a poet of some importance. The social and political upheavals of the 1960s seemed to encourage her to make more expansive statements, and in 1968 she was in San Francisco, working with the Diggers, and her *Revolutionary Letters*, with their advocacy of be-ins, marches, demonstrations, and other forms of direct action, attracted attention in the underground press. They indicated di Prima's interest in environmental issues, as well as her political ideas, and she advocated abandoning most of the trappings of Western Civilisation, even of civilisation itself. Like many of the ideas thrown around in the 1960s by woolly-minded hippies, di Prima's lacked intellectual rigour, though her poems were readable and occasionally hit the right targets.

Before leaving di Prima, it's necessary to say something about her involvement with LeRoi Jones and the publication of *The Floating Bear*, a mimeographed newsletter. The personal side of the di Prima/Jones relationship is dealt with in Hettie Jones's *How I Became Hettie Jones* and Amiri Baraka's *The Autobiography of LeRoi Jones*, and I'm just concerned with the literary aspects of the partnership. *The Floating Bear* was started in 1961 and continued for thirty-seven issues until 1969, with the majority published between 1961 and 1965. Jones and di Prima drew on the Beats for material, but also used poems by Black Mountain poets, together with contributions from writers in San Francisco and Venice West. The contents were, in other words, representative of the new writing generally and not just the Beat movement. What is interesting is that, di Prima apart, very few women appeared in the magazine. There were occasional contributions from Denise Levertov, Carol Berge, and a few others (and none of them could be described as Beat) but the general impression is of a male-dominated world. It may be that this didn't arise from any prejudice against women writers and simply represented the fact that most of the manuscripts received were from men. It may be relevant, at this point, to mention that di Prima herself, when asked about those days and the likelihood of male prejudice excluding her from publication, replied: 'For the first 10 or

15 years I never really realised one way or the other or cared that much about what was going on in that way. It wasn't an issue for me.' But di Prima, as she acknowledged, may have been a special case, and she did admit that her work in the early sixties would probably have received closer attention had it been produced by a male writer.

If *The Floating Bear* didn't publish many women, some other magazines did pull in a few from the bohemian scene. Tuli Kupferberg's *Yeah*, another mimeographed publication, used poems by Brigid Murnaghan. She was also published in Seymour Krim's anthology, *The Beats*, and in *Swank*, a slick 'men's magazine' which ran four special sections of Beat writing, largely thanks to Krim's influence. Murnaghan was probably a character around the scene who wrote occasionally rather than as a dedicated poet, and her work inclined towards the cryptic and lightly amusing. Was she a Beat poet? Perhaps not, though the same could be said of a lot of the males who were published under the Beat banner. Barbara Moraff was another poet who appeared in little magazines around this time, and she was much more talented than Murnaghan. Her work was printed in *The Beat Scene* (where she used the name Barbara Ellen), *Beatitude Anthology* (as Barbara Moraff), *Yugen* (calling herself Barbara Ellen Moraff), *The Outsider, Nomad, Evergreen Review*, and *Beat Coast East*. It was a reasonable publishing record for the time, though she doesn't seem to have published a book until some years later. Her work is on a Beat wavelength, its quirky personal tone and almost deliberately erratic construction having much in common with most minor male Beat verse of the period. Moraff was one of the *Four Young Lady Poets*, published in 1962 by LeRoi Jones's Totem Press, where she was alongside Carol Berge, Diane Wakoski, and Rochelle Owens, all of them active in New York, performing at poetry readings and publishing in magazines. What seems to set Moraff a little apart from the others is, perhaps, her feeling of spontaneity, with the poems often reading as if they've been taken direct from notebooks rather than carefully shaped. She appears to have drifted off the scene later in the 1960s and, according to a note in Fred McDarrah's *Kerouac and Friends*, she was living in Vermont in the 1980s and working as a potter. She had stopped writing at one stage but started again in 1976 and published several small collections of her poetry.

If Barbara Moraff confused people by occasionally publishing as Barbara Ellen, the strange Kay Johnson must have really got them mixed up when she sometimes called herself Kaja. She even published in the same magazine under both names. She seems to have had some links to New Orleans and *The Outsider*, published in that city, used her work in several issues. A photograph in the third, which came out in 1963, shows her outside The Beat Hotel in Paris. She lived there for a time in the early 1960s and was featured in an article on that establishment in the December 1962 issue of *Town*, along with Burroughs, Brion Gysin, and Harold Norse. She seems to have been somewhat disillusioned by Paris and said: 'I came here to find artistic friendship and found only loneliness. It was as if I were out in the Sahara desert.' I don't know if this was meant to suggest that she was excluded from the magic (mostly male) circle at The Beat Hotel, though she does come across as something of a recluse. She is pictured in Harold Chapman's *The Beat Hotel*, his photographic record of the Beats in Paris.

Kay Johnson's work did appear in some good magazines, such as *The Outsider*, *Residu* (a short-lived publication that placed her alongside Ginsberg, Norse, and Philip Lamantia), *Olympia*, and *The Journal for the Protection of All Beings*. She also had a small collection of poems, *Human Songs*, published by City Lights in 1964. Some of her poems were intensely personal, and her prose tended to be reflective and unlikely to appeal to readers used to conventional novels and stories. She could often sound gloomy ('I am near the age that my mother was/when she killed herself.') but she did also write short poems which made oblique comments on human behaviour. Under the name of Kaja she published a witty poem called 'I Worship Paperclips!' in *Olympia* magazine, and as Kay Johnson she was in *Residu* with an excerpt from 'LSD-748', a long poem dealing with hallucinations and other drug experiences. It reminds me of Ginsberg in places but also has semi-surreal passages. Like a lot of similar material it ultimately conveys little to the reader. Johnson was much more interesting when she wrote short, relatively formal poems, and it may have been that she was trying too hard to fall into line with the conventions of The Beat Hotel. She was a painter, as well as a poet, but it's impossible to say how successful she was in that field, and she disappeared from the literary scene later in the 1960s. I wonder what became of her.

On the West coast of the United States, Lenore Kandel was linked to the Beats for some years. She was born in New York, lived in Los Angeles and San Francisco in the 1950s, and went back to the Bay Area in 1960 and was soon involved in a relationship with Lew Welch. This brought her into contact with Kerouac, who portrayed her as Ramona Schwartz in *Big Sur*. In 1966 a small collection of her poems, *The Love Book*, brought her some notoriety when it was prosecuted for obscenity. In its handful of pages it provided a frank appraisal of the physical side of love-making and had an obvious connection with Beat writing through its desire to speak openly and honestly about sex. Kandel had other poems in *Evergreen Review, Beatitude*, and other magazines, and a second book, *Word Alchemy*, was published by Grove Press in 1967. With lines like 'Too many of my friends are junkies' and 'I have seen the junkie angel winging his devious path over cities,' and several poems which were as explicit as those in *The Love Book*, it initially gave the impression that Kandel was intent on exploring specific areas of experience. But she could also write powerful protest poems, as in 'First They Slaughtered the Angels', and lyrical short pieces which had some charm and humour. There was one excellent poem, 'The Farmer, the Sailor', which provided a moving account of an old man regretting that he'd never seen the ocean. *Word Alchemy* did indicate that Kandel had the potential to become a varied and interesting poet, but she seems to have decided to drop out of sight for some reason and little or nothing has been heard of her since 1970 or so. It would be useful to know why she chose to abandon her work as a poet, or at least chose to stop publishing. Did she experience difficulties simply because she was a woman, or was it a case of being affected by the kind of problems that might intrude into

the lives of both male and female writers? After all, some poets just
stop writing or decide they want to do other things. You don't have
to stay a poet, or a Beat, all your life.

Joanne Kyger's *The Japan and India Journals, 1960-1964*, published by
Timbouctou Press in 1981, has relevance to any survey of women and
the Beats, though Kyger never claimed status as a member of the
movement. But she was in San Francisco in 1957 and later said, 'I
found poets...and poetry has been my involvement since then.' Her
relationship with Gary Snyder (they were married for several years)
took her to India and Japan, and her account makes interesting reading
alongside Snyder's 'Now, India' (see *Caterpillar* 19, 1972) and Ginsberg's
Indian Journals. Kyger had mixed with Jack Spicer and others in San
Francisco, had links to the New York school of poets, and obviously
knew the Beats, but she wasn't overwhelmed by any one particular
group. Michael Davidson, in his *The San Francisco Renaissance*, astutely
sums up her work when he says:

> Like both the Beats and the New York school poets, Kyger's work stresses
> immediacy and spontaneity. Her poems map mundane activities like eating,
> cooking, gardening, and socialising with a minimum of commentary. Her
> work is respectful – even celebratory of nature, but avoids the more
> bardic invocations of the natural world associated with her Beat
> compatriots. Like Philip Whalen (whose work has exerted an important
> influence) Kyger's poetry often seems taken directly from the notebook
> page, each line registering a quick glance of momentary observation.

Davidson's comments, incidentally, are from a valuable chapter in his
book in which he discusses the place of women poets in the San
Francisco community. He refers to 'the boys' club of San Francisco
bohemia,' which, he says, could be 'blind to its own exclusionary
possibilities,' even when it was advocating new social roles for individuals.
And he mentions that Kyger's poetry is difficult to obtain, whereas her
journal is still in print, probably because of the Snyder connection.

There are not all that many other women who can be included in
a survey of their involvement with the Beats. A few names do crop
up in magazines and anthologies, though usually with just one or two

poems, and it's difficult to establish whether or not they intended to make a career in poetry or writing generally. Park Honan used a poem by Sally Stern in his 1987 anthology, *The Beats* (it was originally published in *The Beat Scene*), but it's significant that he had little to say about her in his notes on the authors. If she published elsewhere, it doesn't seem to have been in Beat-related publications. There was also Margaret Randall, who Fred McDarrah described as 'a central figure on the New York Beat scene,' though her main claim to fame came when she moved to Mexico in 1961 and started a magazine called *El Corno Emplumado*, which printed Beats alongside many others. She became increasingly active politically, lived in Cuba and Nicaragua, and only returned to the United States in 1984. Little of Randall's work is available now, and one of the few sources from the 1960s for her poems is *The Outsider*, Jon Edgar Webb's superb magazine. Finally, there is Ruth Weiss, and I have to thank Warren French, author of the informative *The San Francisco Poetry Renaissance, 1955-1960*, for drawing my attention to her work. She was born in Berlin in 1928 and had experienced bohemian life in New York and New Orleans before arriving in San Francisco in 1952. During the Beat years she published in *Beatitude*, *Yugen*, and *The Galley Sail Review*, but it needs to be stressed that she had a wide and varied career in the arts both before and after her encounter with the Beats. Her work reflects an interest in jazz, ecology, and film, among other things, and she has been active as a performance artist. She is best described as someone who could be linked to the Beats because of her long-standing bohemian inclinations and her free-ranging attitude towards artistic creativity.

I'm aware that I've not mentioned Anne Waldman in this article. She is, of course, often identified with the Beats, but she once said that she felt herself to be part of the Lower East Side community of younger New York poets rather than one of the older generation of Beat poets. She grew up in Greenwich Village and saw the Beats on the streets, but it was only in 1966 that she became actively involved in poetry readings, editing anthologies, and contributing her own work to magazines. Her activities have been important – she helped set up

The Jack Kerouac School Of Disembodied Poetics – and her writing has obvious Beat connections, especially in its autobiographical tone and sense of movement, but she doesn't properly belong in a survey which aims to look at women who were directly involved as writers during the key years of the Beat movement. It had splintered and diversified when she arrived on the scene. It may be as well, at this point, for me to refer to Ann Charters, who has done so much to document the history of the Beats and provide collections of poems, prose and photographs, which enable younger readers to gain an idea of what the movement achieved. Obviously, she was not a creative writer involved in publishing with the Beats, but it would be wrong to overlook her for that reason.

I have not tried to be totally inclusive, and I've no doubt that readers will be able to suggest some other names. It occurs to me that Eileen Kaufman, widow of Bob Kaufman, could have been considered, though little of her work is available for study. A short excerpt from 'A Life in Progress', her memoir of the 1950s in San Francisco, was published in *One-Eighty-Five* (Mongrel Press, 1973), a curious anthology featuring a fair number of obscure San Francisco writers, both men and women, some of them active since the 1950s. It includes, for example, a poem by Laura Ulewicz, 'Written in Recollection of the Days Before a Movement Got Stopped by Being Named and Publicised Too Soon'. The piece by Kaufman doesn't enable us to ascertain her qualities as a writer, though it has obvious documentary interest, and it may be that she's fated to be remembered because of her husband's wider publishing record. In this connection it will be obvious that I haven't tried to use my survey as a stick with which to attack a system which clearly denied the women the opportunities granted to most men. I feel that intelligent readers ought to be able to draw their own conclusions about the place of women in the Beat movement, and whether or not they could and should have made a greater contribution. It seems to me quite evident that Diane di Prima deserved, and deserves, more attention than she's ever had, and that her City Lights book, *Pieces of a Song: Selected Poems*, has a place on any list of the better Beat

publications. Lenore Kandel and Barbara Moraff have a legitimate place
in Beat history, and Kay Johnson might need to be recognised for at
least some of her poems.

Did any of the others have the potential to become good poets? It
doesn't appear so if we use the evidence of the poems they did get
into print. But I have to point out that Diane di Prima's viewpoint
differs from mine, though she's clearly basing her judgement on extra-
literary matters. She said: 'I can't say a lot of really great women writers
were ignored in my time, but I can say a lot of potentially great women
writers wound up dead or crazy.' But the casualty rate among male
Beats was probably quite high (how many slipped into obscurity while
one Ginsberg or Corso survived?) and it could be that we have to
look at the nature of Beat life in general for the reasons for suicide
and madness. Perhaps it attracted people who were prone to those
things. Bohemias often do. And perhaps someone will one day have
the courage to look at the damage inflicted by drugs and other forms
of self-indulgence. Not all Beats were engaged in serious attempts to
expand their consciousness, and the fact that Burroughs could survive
addiction and use it as the basis for literature, or that Ginsberg wrote
poems under the influence of various hallucinogens, does not suggest
that every minor character on the scene had the same talent to channel
the experience into art. I don't doubt that many women did have a
relatively hard time among the Beats, and that some of them might
have become good poets, given the right circumstances to develop their
skills. On the other hand, no useful purpose is served by pretending
that every female would-be poet is likely to turn out to be great. Most
poets of either sex are never more than minor. What I do hope is that
my survey will encourage readers to turn to the old magazines,
anthologies, and slim volumes, so that they can consider the actual
work that was produced by the women connected with the Beat scene.

Note

Since this piece was written two anthologies of women writers linked to the Beats have appeared, and many of the poets and others I referred to are represented in either or both of them. Brenda Knight's *Women of the Beat Generation* was published by Conari Press, Berkeley, 1996, and *A Different Beat: Writings by Women of the Beat Generation*, edited by Richard Peabody, was published by Serpent's Tail, New York, 1997.

TALKING WITH GINSBERG, 1990

Interviewing Allen Ginsberg in the plush Olympia Hilton Hotel in London is quite an experience. I ask at reception and they direct me to the Boardroom and I find Ginsberg there, smart and benign-looking in a blue suit and seated in a large chair behind a table complete with Hilton pads and pens. For a moment I have the urge to enquire if he's Chairman of Beat Inc., but I let it pass. He's an affable type and I've no wish to appear sharp, and in any case a few minutes' conversation with him is enough to dispel any idea that the suit and tie indicate any surrender to conventional values.

He's in London to read at the Royal Festival Hall and to promote his new record, *The Lion for Real*, recently out from Island/Antilles. He talks about it with enthusiasm. It is, he says, 'my best musical collaboration to date.' Asked about his voice he describes himself as 'just a funky old blues singer,' but he didn't think it appropriate to sing this time and it's noticeable that he speaks the poems and lets the natural cadence in them come out, while the musicians provide backgrounds which have clearly been planned. It isn't merely another example of a poet reading over some loosely related musical doodlings, and the listener has the impression that a fair amount of thought went into the record date. Ginsberg confirms this. He'll do more records like it, he says, and he also mentions that William Burroughs has recorded an album with strings. 'Strings?' I ask, surprised, and he replies, 'Yes, and on it he sings a drunken version of the old German song, 'Falling In Love Again', the one that Marlene Dietrich sang in *The Blue Angel*.' He chuckles, and adds, 'You should hear it,' and I say I can't wait. Burroughs camping up a thirties torch song sounds like it might be really something. Ginsberg returns to the relationship between poetry and music, pointing out how Blake was known to have sung his poems. And he mentions his own friendships with musicians and singers over the years. Bob Dylan, of course, who 'was tuned in to American poetry through reading Kerouac's *Mexico City Blues*.' A few other names are recalled, including Ramblin' Jack Elliot. Laughter. 'I knew him in New York in 1950. He stole my girl!'

Ginsberg wants to talk about more things than his record and we're soon off on a tour which takes in various topics. But not before he adds a word or two about Benjamin Zephaniah, dub poet and his partner at the Festival Hall event. He points out that 'the oral tradition is the origin of all poetry,' and he says he's never been able to understand why there's so much prejudice in this country against poetry written for public performance. It's as if we deny our heritage. 'Read John Skelton,' he says enthusiastically, and chants out a few lines of sing-song verse by the fifteenth-century English poet. Listening to Ginsberg you can hear how what he calls 'Skeltonics' relates to some contemporary performance poetry.

We talk about his visits to this country over the years, and he reminisces about 1957. 'I came over from Paris, and there was the French pub in Soho and George Barker, and oh, what was his name ... a publisher and bookseller ... David Archer.' Ginsberg is a mine of information about British and American bohemias, past and present.

He read at the famous Albert Hall gathering in 1965, an event which did much to boost the idea of a British 'underground' and that brings us to another matter, Ginsberg's recent visit to Prague, a city he was thrown out of just prior to appearing in the Albert Hall. 'I went back this year to see if I could find the notebooks that were taken from me in 1965 by the security police. And to regain the crown given to me by the students when I was declared King of the May.' All this was commemorated in his poem, 'Kral Majales', which Ginsberg wrote on the jet bringing him from Prague to London. And he points out that he reads it on *The Lion For Real*. For his return trip he wrote a new poem, 'Return of the King of May', in which he says 'This silver anniversary, much hair has gone from my head' and 'I return through Heaven, flying to reclaim my paper crown'. Once the crown had been ceremoniously handed back to him by the Mayor of Prague ('who happens to be the Czech translator of Gary Snyder's poetry,' Ginsberg adds, to stress how the Beat poets were admired in Eastern Europe), he passed it on to the new King, a local student. 'It's 25 years since they had an election for a King of May,' he explains, 'and they told me I was the oldest, greatest and longest King of May in history.'

I ask about Ginsberg's links with Eastern Europe and the way in which his poetry, and that of the Beats generally, has influenced people. According to him it was accepted enthusiastically because it represented a 'declaration of private feeling as against public party line,' and so appealed to dissidents. And how about the current upheavals? 'It's a good time to be there. But I gave a speech warning people that they need a spiritual politics and that getting into a commodity culture akin to the West won't bring any real benefits.' He mentions the terrible pollution problems found in countries like Poland, East Germany, and Czechoslovakia, and this brings us to his passionate concern for environmental matters. He's not just a recent convert to this, either, and he quotes lines from his poems to prove it. He says that quite a few of the Beats were always sensitive to such issues and 'both Gary Snyder and Michael McClure read ecology poems at the Six Gallery reading in 1955.'

That reference to early Beat days gives me the opportunity to ask Ginsberg about his background. I've always been intrigued, I tell him, by his Jewish radical upbringing. His father was inclined towards the Left politically and his mother, as his great poem 'Kaddish' records, was a communist. And he reads the moving 'To Aunt Rose', with its litany of lost hopes, on *The Lion For Real*. All this may have had a greater influence than he sometimes seems to admit. After all, he's a poet ever willing to get involved in public matters, protests, etc. Agreed, he never puts forward a party line, but it's possible to see those old socialist/communist grass-roots dreams in his desire for spiritual as well as material change. I prod him a little and mention that somewhere in Kerouac or maybe Holmes there's a character based on Ginsberg who dreams of being a great Labour leader. He laughs and shouts,

> That was me! I had a 1915 I.W.W. vision of social revolution and leading the workers, you know. But it was Jack Kerouac who brought me down to earth. He pointed out that I'd never worked in a factory, or anywhere else, and didn't know any workers. So, I realised I was bullshitting myself.

OK, I say, so let's look at the literary influences. His father, Louis, was, in Ginsberg's own words, 'a well-known lyric poet,' and when he was 8 or 9 he knew about Milton and Wordsworth. And he's often mentioned Whitman, Blake, Smart and others as having an impact on his thinking about poetry. But growing up in the kind of household he was born into, he must have also read the twenties and thirties radical poets. And some from a little earlier? I tell him I've got old anthologies with titles like *May Days* and *Unrest 1930* in which his father appears, and which were presumably around the house. And what about poets like Arturo Giovannitti and Mike Gold, both of them often using long lines and declamatory statements not unlike 'HOWL'. He nods, and admits, 'Yes, I read all the old copies of *Masses*' (*The Masses*, and its successor *New Masses*, were left-wing American magazines), and he recalls that 'Giovannitti was in that Untermeyer anthology.' (*Modern American Poetry*, edited by Louis Untermeyer, was a 1920s and 1930s collection which did have work by Giovannitti as well as by Ginsberg's father.) 'But the poem from that period that had a big effect on me was Ben Maddow's "The City". That influenced me a lot when I was writing "HOWL".'

Referring to writers read in his youth starts Ginsberg talking about Edgar Allen Poe who he really discovered, really came alive to, when he was about twelve. Why? 'Because reading him made me realise that other people had weird thoughts. I thought it was just me until then.'

And his enthusiasm for Poe takes us back to Prague and a conversation he had with a student leader who helped bring about the revolution there, and who said, 'It all goes back to Poe', when referring to the world of the imagination which informs all strivings against repression. Ginsberg agrees with him.

> Before Baudelaire, before Rimbaud, before the surrealists, before anyone else, there was Poe. He was ahead of his time, and you always need an avant-garde, whether in politics or literature, otherwise nothing happens, nothing changes.

You can understand why we need an avant-garde, and why some people fear it, if you look at recent events in the United States, according to him. He pulls out a sheaf of papers and reads examples of growing censorship problems. There's a conspiracy of sorts, with neo-conservative and fundamentalist religious groups taking advantage of state and federal laws to narrow the range of work available on the radio and in the libraries. 'It's similar to McCarthyism,' Ginsberg insists, and you can also draw parallels with Nazi book-burning and Stalinist attacks on intellectuals as 'rootless cosmopolitans.' New laws will stop radio stations broadcasting 'HOWL', not to mention work by Kerouac, Genet, Henry Miller, and many others. Ginsberg sees it as part of a pattern which includes censorship of student publications, restrictions on press reporting of certain events, FBI surveillance of libraries, and a long list of similar activities. 'It's an attack on language,' he claims, and an attempt at thought control.

> Much of my poetry is specifically aimed to rouse the sense of liberty of thought and political/social expression of that thought in young adolescents. I believe I am conducting spiritual war for liberation of their souls from mass homogenisation of greedy materialistic commerce and emotional desensitisation. Pseudo-religious legal intolerance with my speech amounts to setting up a state religion much in the mode of intolerant Ayatollah or a Stalinoid bureaucratic party line.

The interesting thing is, Ginsberg points out, that the neo-conservatives and religious fanatics who are behind much of the drive for censorship are the types who, a few years ago, would have been in the forefront of anti-communist agitation. Now they use the same tactics as their one time opponents 'to enforce the authority of their own solidified thought police and ethical systems.' And is it strange that this should happen? 'No,' answers Ginsberg, 'Blake put his finger on it when he said, "They became what they beheld".'

I can't help sharing Ginsberg's worries about growing censorship, and I tend to agree with his theory that the decline of the Cold War may well cause the censors and thought police to focus more on internal matters now that the external enemy is in a state of collapse. But it's time to ask him about his own recent work. Has he any new books due out? 'I'm working on a collection of photographs and I'm two years behind with that, but *White Shroud* was the last book of poems and there's nothing else planned just now. But I haven't written a lot of poetry recently. I've been busy with other things. Photography, and a new opera, *Hydrogen Box*, that I wrote with Philip Glass. It was premiered at the Spoletto Festival in Italy.' It's amazing that he keeps so active? 'Well, I'm just having fun,' he says, 'And it's a good way of revitalising yourself.'

I have the feeling that I could talk to Ginsberg for another couple of hours, and that he'd keep a constant stream of fresh ideas and provocative comments flowing, but the afternoon is drawing on. I've a train to catch and the Hilton are dropping hints that they'd like us to vacate their Boardroom. He'd promised to read a 'chain poem' produced by a class he teaches in Brooklyn, but somehow we both forgot about that. Still, he did read a poem about CIA involvement in the drug trade, and he part sang a send-up of the old communist anthem, 'The Internationale', so I'd been entertained as well as instructed. He's generous with time, energy and information. I get up, shake hands with the man who gleefully refers to himself as 'a minor but notable rock star in Hungary' (where a couple of his poems have been set to music by a popular band and the kids in the street know

'The Shrouded Stranger') and who is also a member of the American Academy and Institute of Arts and Letters, not to mention Distinguished Professor of Brooklyn College of the City University of New York. 'I'm now a most respectable figure,' he says with a smile, even if his poems are banned on American radio. But he carries his new-found respectability like his age, and doesn't allow it to dampen his enthusiasm or his concern for things that really matter.

Later, I find myself thinking about Ginsberg and it strikes me that my talk with him has reinforced my view that his Jewish radical background had played a major part in his life and work. I can understand why he perhaps doesn't want to focus on it too much. He's possibly of the opinion that it could be a limiting factor. And maybe, in the forties and fifties (key decades for the Beats) it would have been easy to be typed as 'just another Jewish commie.' But the Jewish radical angle, and the old socialist and communist dream (which had a spiritual side before it became bureaucratised) are things worth paying tribute to, and it was my fault that I wasn't more forceful with Ginsberg in pointing out why I was probing in that direction. I've never been able to take some of his forays into Eastern religions and philosophies too seriously, and his liking for gurus and mysticism bores me, but the fact that he's survived in the way that he has, and is so knowledgeable about social and political matters, inclines me to think that his feet are quite firmly on the ground.

I also start thinking that Allen Ginsberg has more humour in his work than some people give him credit for, and that it's what Diana Trilling once referred to as 'funniness of a kind which has never had so sure and live a place as it did in the 30s, the embittered and fond funniness which has to do with one's own impossible origins, funniness plain and poetical, always aware of itself.' Which isn't to play down the very real seriousness of a lot of his work, nor its tragic side, as in *Kaddish*. But listening to *The Lion For Real* makes me think not only of Ginsberg's Jewish radical roots, but also of his ability to mock himself at times. He said at one point during our conversation that the Beats 'were expressing in public what we were really thinking seriously,' and that doesn't necessarily exclude a humorous appraisal of one's situation. You can see that humour in an early poem like 'America' ('America I'm putting my queer shoulder to the wheel') and in the very recent 'Return of the King of May', where he says he went back to Prague with 'high blood pressure, diabetes, gout, Bell's palsy, kidney stones', a catalogue of ailments which is treated lightly. And I begin to wish I had asked him if he was Chairman of Beat Inc., because I'm sure he would have seen the funny side of setting out so many subversive ideas in the Boardroom of the Olympia Hilton.

FAR OUT WITH LORD BUCKLEY, 1994

Look at all you Cats and Kitties out there!
Whippin' and a wailin' and jumpin' up and
down and suckin' up all that fine juice and
pattin' each other on the back and Rippin' each
other who the greatest Cat in the world is! Mr.
Melanencoff, Mr. Dalencoff and Mr. Zelencoff
and all them Coffs, and Mr. Eisenhower, Mr
Weesenwooser and all them Woosers, Mr
Woodhill and Mr Beachill and Mr Churchill and
all them Hills, Gonna get you straight! If they
can't get you straight, they know a Cat, that
knows a Cat, that'll straighten you!
But I'm gonna put a Cat on you, who was the
Sweetest, Grooviest, Strongest, Wailinest,
Swinginest, Jumpinest most far out Cat that
ever stomped on this Sweet Green Sphere, and
they called this here Cat, THE NAZ, that was the
Cat's name.

When Richard "Lord" Buckley was dying in a New York hospital in 1960 he was looked after by some nuns, and baffled them — no doubt gently, lovingly, and with no wish to hurt — by referring to himself as 'The Hip Messiah.' It wasn't a bad title, and I like to imagine that Buckley finally went out in the manner of the hero of Joyce Carey's *The Horse's Mouth*. You remember the scene? Gulley Jimson is talking to a nun and she tells him that, considering the situation he's in, he ought to laugh a little less and pray a little more. And Jimson looks at her and says, 'Same thing, mother.' It's a story Buckley often used in his performances, and he put it across with a great deal of enthusiasm, laughter to him having an almost religious purpose.

But who was Buckley? 'Lord of Flip Manor' – 'Royal Holiness of the Far Out' – 'Prophet of the Hip.' Nice names which don't really tell us a great deal about the man, though they seem to place him in the post-1945 period and alongside such characters as Harry 'The Hipster' Gibson, Slim Gaillard, Babs Gonzales, and others linked to the Frantic Forties and the crazy days of hip talk and zoot suits and bebop. But this is nowhere near the whole story and Buckley had a much more varied career than those details suggest. He was also something more than just a 'hip' character.

He was born in a small mining town in California in April, 1906, and was reputedly of part-Native American and part-Anglo stock. When he was a teenager. he worked as a lumberjack, and in the 1920s he set off to find a job in the Texas oil fields. Somewhere along the way he met an itinerant musician, formed an act with him, and so got into show business. According to Buckley his first date was at the Million Dollar Aztec Theatre in San Antonio, and the manager told him 'You are the lousiest act I ever played in my life.' But Buckley persevered, working as a comic and master of ceremonies for Depression-era dance marathons. He toured the old vaudeville circuit and was a disc jockey in Portland for a time, but it was when he arrived in Chicago in the 1930s that he began to make a name for himself. Working as a comedian in speakeasies he attracted the attention of Al Capone, who said that Buckley was the only man who could make him laugh. Capone financed a night-club that Buckley ran, and it was during his Chicago years that he got to know many jazzmen, finding their music, their way of life, and their manner of talking, much to his liking. According to people who knew him, Buckley earned and spent money easily, and his wives came and went in much the same way.

It's difficult to know exactly what kind of material Buckley employed in those early days, but by the 1940s he was using Black speech rhythms and slang when he toured with a unit that visited army camps and similar establishments. It was during this period that he met Ed Sullivan, who was so impressed by Buckley that he often used him on his TV show in the 1950s. When the Second World War came to an end Buckley worked around New York, appearing on Broadway and in night clubs. He also kept up his jazz links, and his publicity outline referred to him having been 'a featured entertainer with a great many name bands including Gene Krupa's and Woody Herman's.' And he continued to live it up. One writer describes him as playing 'host to an eclectic group of artists, jazz musicians, comics, dancers, socialites, bohemians and street urchins.'

Among those friendly with Buckley were the great jazz saxophonist Charlie Parker and his wife Chan. There are numerous stories about Buckley's oddball behaviour, some of them perhaps a little exaggerated but well in character. He was reputed to have walked up to a policeman outside Birdland and asked him for a light for the reefer he was about to smoke. On another occasion he gave an impromptu lecture on Chinese communism to the blue-collar clientele of a small bar he went into. And he rode through Chicago in a hearse, lying in the coffin and then suddenly sitting up to display a sign which said, 'This body comes alive at the Suzy Q,' the club where he was appearing. If these tales weren't true they should have been and, in any case, there probably were equally outrageous Buckley stories that were based on fact.

Buckley had finally met a woman he could live with permanently, or who could live with him, and decided to move to California in 1950, reasoning that there would be work in Hollywood and that he would also be within easy reach of the night clubs of Reno and Las Vegas. His Hollywood career never really got off the ground, and he appeared in only one film, a now forgotten Ginger Rogers vehicle called *We're Not Married*, which also had a brief appearance by Marilyn Monroe. But California proved to be the catalyst for the kind of performances that were to bring him to the attention of new audiences. Buckley had often entertained his friends with monologues which took historical events and translated them into stories told in the hip vernacular, and his wife suggested that he perform a similar routine on stage. He developed a style that mixed Black jive talk with an affected upper-class English accent, scat singing, and a collection of comments that outlined his approach to life. At the centre of his work was a vision of a 'big rock candy world,' where everyone would be happy. Love, hope laughter – an affirmative view of life in general – made up a major part of Buckley's philosophy. He wanted everyone to be 'cool,' and he didn't mean smart, fashionable, sophisticated. To him 'cool' meant 'to believe in the magic power of love,' and that's why he thought of Jesus and Gandhi (both of them featured in monologues) as 'cool cats.' He kept telling his audiences over and over again to stay cool. 'My Lords, my Ladies, Beloveds. Would it embarrass you very much if I were to tell you that I loved you?' he would ask, and as they giggled nervously he would say, triumphantly, 'It embarrasses you, doesn't it?'

A Buckley performance was a total experience, and during the course of it he would present his monologues ('The Naz', 'Jonah and the Whale', 'Nero', 'Scrooge', which were all hip talk versions of well known stories) and mix them with semi surreal sketches ('Murder', for example, which probes at the darker recesses of the mind), socio-political references ('Governor Gulpwell', a swipe at grasping and hypocritical politicians), bitter satire ('Georgia, Sweet and Kind', with a lynching providing the background for a performance of the banal lyrics of a popular song extolling the virtues of the state), and even history, if Buckley's hilarious views on the origins of the chastity belt can be called that. A rendering of Mark Antony's funeral oration starts off as: 'Hipsters, Flipsters, and finger-poppin' daddies, knock me your lobes.' And Buckley could make political points through humour, as in a piece called 'The Hip Gahn' or 'The All-Hip Mahatma' (like a jazz musician Buckley improvised and so the recorded versions of his monologues vary), which is about Gandhi and his fight against 'the Lion,' as the British are called:

> They called this Cat The All Hip Mahatma because his wig was so cool. Here's the way the scene went down. The Lion was Buggin' India. Every time India got a little extra Supply in the cupboard the Lion went ZOOM – snapped it up and swooped the scene and there stood the poor Indians scoffless. No Food. And the day that the All Hip Mahatma swung in on the scene, The Lion was into that supply

cupboard shoulder high, flippin' and flappin' his tail, trying to locate
that low bolt to pick up the whole supply. Well The all Hip Mahatma
did one of those long Indian Brood jumps WAPP, Stomped on that
Cat's tail so hard he swooped the Scene, and that's the last they saw
of him from that day to this and Naturally that Gassed India.

This kind of material appealed to people at odds with the conformity
of the 1950s. As someone once noted, 'it's difficult to convey just how
square the square world was in the 1950s and how far outside of it
(and out ahead of it) Lord Buckley was'. But jazz musicians, singers,
show-business types, writers, poets, artists and bohemians, liked him.
Playwright Clifford Odets praised his work and Henry Miller said it
was 'all very alive and jumping.' Buckley still had to look for work in
places like Las Vegas, where casinos and clubs provided a steady income,
but his new approach, with its hip humour and social satire, primarily
appealed to audiences in tune with its sentiments. He moved to Marin
County in 1960, attracted by the Bay Area's artistic community and
sympathetic subculture, and joined performers such as Lenny Bruce,
Mort Sahl, and Dick Gregory, at clubs like The Hungry I and The
Purple Onion. He was described as 'a jazz comic' and 'not a critic but
a preacher,' but the great thing about Buckley was that he couldn't
really be placed in any one classification. He was very much his own
man and created his own world.

In 1960 he made a cross-country trip by road, a trip that Buckley
called 'The Cosmic Tour.' The final destination was New York, but
along the way he carried out an engagement at the Gate of Horn in
Chicago and was interviewed by Studs Terkel on a local radio station.
One evening of the Gate of Horn gig was a special three-man show
called 'The Seacoast of Bohemia,' with Del Close and Severn Darden
joining Buckley on stage. Darden later recalled that Buckley hadn't been
in the best of health when he was in Chicago, but he seems to have
carried on with his engagement and then moved on to New York,
where he was due to appear at the Jazz Gallery. And it was there that
things began to go badly wrong. Like all those wanting to work in
New York clubs Buckley had to apply for a cabaret licence, something

which required police clearance. This often meant that a musician or other artist with a police record could be denied the right to work unless, of course, certain 'arrangements' were made with the officials issuing the licence. Billie Holiday, Lenny Bruce, Frank Sinatra, Charlie Parker, and numerous others, experienced police harassment in connection with cabaret licences. Buckley did obtain a licence, but a few days after opening at the Jazz Gallery it was suddenly withdrawn. The official reason was that Buckley had failed to declare an old arrest for drunkenness when applying for his licence, though it may have been that the authorities had different reasons for wanting to close his show. Buckley was probably looked on with suspicion by the square world, just as Lenny Bruce, the Beat poets, and anyone else linked to alternative culture were.

Buckley's wife tried to persuade him to return to California, but he stayed in New York, unhappy and with hardly any money. He contacted the writer Harold Humes (author of *Men Die* and *The Underground City*) and asked for a loan, saying that he had barely eaten for a week. And he complained to a friend that he had 'the bugbird' in him, a comment that chilled those who knew how, in Buckley's version of Edgar Allan Poe's 'The Raven', the bugbird is the symbol of impending death. He was taken to hospital and died on November 12th, 1960. One doctor said that death was due to a stroke, but the police, perhaps mindful of their part in harassing Buckley, issued a statement saying it was caused by an old kidney ailment. Seymour Krim gave a blunter, if less medically based, opinion when he said that Buckley's death was 'as much of a busted heart as anything else.' It does seem certain that he hadn't been in good health after leaving Chicago, and the withdrawal of his licence must have had a detrimental effect on his state of mind. His wife also pointed out that his pace of life hadn't helped. Buckley liked to have a ball, as they say, and was often surrounded by friends and admirers who encouraged him to perform both on and off stage. And, as she said: 'People used to wear him out, and he didn't realise that time had passed – he'd gotten older – it was too much for him.'

As I said earlier, it's difficult to categorise Buckley. He was an entertainer, but you couldn't call him a comedian because to do that would reduce his work to the level of telling jokes, and he deserves better. On the other hand it's probably a mistake to try to give him some kind of heroic status or to suggest that his work had greater qualities than can actually be found in it. He was original and he was funny, and at his best he had a sincerity and warmth that can still communicate several decades after his performances were captured on record. A good Buckley performance never dates, even if the hip language he used no longer has the same impact, because he always wanted to do more than simply play around with words. He wanted to say something, and that's why a piece like 'The Naz' (or his brief but joyous reference to *The Horse's Mouth*) can still retain the power to move. Of course, he didn't always appeal to everyone, and perhaps still doesn't, and Harold Humes summed him up well when he said:

> Revolutionaries didn't like him because he dug that it made no difference who be in the driver's seat since no matter who, he be bound to square up – since square be the shape of all driver's seats. Nice people didn't like him because he talked about freedom as if he meant it (and he did), and he was even hurt in the last weeks of his life by musicians who put him down for talking like a downhome Negro when he wasn't. He was hit hard by the cracker attack from both sides of the shadow line. But that's the way the corn shucks, I suppose. Nobody looks to motives anymore, just labels. And there are not many easy riders around to keep things level, either. But there you go. Everybody's got to have something to care about. And Buckley cared about Gandhi, who got more done in a few decades than perhaps any single man in recent history. He told me once that "it's the greedheads that will destroy this country, the greedheads." And he was right. Any other kind of head gets busted.

Another of Buckley's admirers said that he was 'talking the language of a generation yet to come,' but I seriously doubt that he ever spoke, or is likely to speak, for a generation. Personally, I prefer to think that he spoke, and speaks, to those with ears to hear, and that they're always a minority in any generation. And I wonder what he would make of today's scene? The violence, cynicism, greed, have all grown, and Buckley, were he around, might feel like a voice crying in the wilderness.

Still, some people would be able to take comfort from his appeal to stay cool. And perhaps Buckley's faith in the power of love would enable him to carry on with his humorous preaching. He once said:

> All over this world, in the alleys, in the valleys, on the plains, on the mesas, on the mountaintops, on the plateaus, through the sand, to the gulf, through the whole scene of this world – black, blue, green, yellow and pink – it's loaded with beautiful people who we never hear a thing about ... . But there they are. And those people are the protectors and possessors of the vault of love which is known as God.

It may seem a little sentimental in a world beset by problems of war, disease, hunger, and more, and yet it still has positive qualities that are refreshing. And Buckley would no doubt have gone on to add that a little laughter never did any harm, either. As he said of 'The Naz': 'When he laid it, HE LAID IT!'

Note

I first wrote about Buckley over thirty years ago ('The Hip Messiah', *The Guardian*, 12th August, 1963), but there was only a limited amount of information about him available in those days. Recent years have seen a resurgence of interest in his work, and I am grateful for two American contacts, David Barrett and Oliver Trager, for providing copies of various articles which have filled gaps in my knowledge of Buckley's life. Oliver Trager's 'Stompin 'The Sweet Swingin Sphere:' Celebrating Lord Buckley in Southern California', *Organica*, Summer 1992, and Douglas Cruickshank's 'All Hail Lord Buckley' (*San Francisco Examiner Image*, 6 September 1992) are particularly worth tracking down. Oliver Trager is currently working on an oral biography of Lord Buckley which will contain reminiscences by numerous people who knew him.

Seven Buckley monologues were transcribed and published, under the title *Hiparama of the Classics*, by City Lights in 1960. One of them, 'Nero', was also printed in the May 1961 issue of *Swank*, along with 'His Lordship's Last Days', by Harold Humes. *Swank* was an American girlie magazine which, thanks to Seymour Krim, printed four special sections of Beat-related writing in 1960/61, with Kerouac, LeRoi Jones, Lawrence Ferlinghetti, Allen Ginsberg, and others featured. There was a short tribute to Buckley by Francis Newton in *The New Statesman* (31 December, 1960). Buckley records have appeared and disappeared over the years, and amongst those once available in Britain have been: *Revelations of the Late Lord Buckley* (Nonesuch PPL208); *The Best of Lord Buckley* (Elektra 2410 002); *Lord Buckley Blowing His Mind* (Fontana TL5396); *Way Out Humour* (World Pacific WP - 1279); *Bad Rapping of the Marquis De Sade* (Demon VERB 6). In the United States I understand that *A Most Immaculately Hip Aristocrat* (Straight Records) and *Lord Buckley Live* (Shambola Lion Editions) have been available recently. Earlier Buckley LPs appeared in the USA on Vaya, Hip and RCA. Collectors are advised to check before attempting to find all the material referred to as some duplications may occur. The Elektra LP mentioned above seems to contain the monologues originally issued on Vaya, and the Fontana LP seems to have re-appeared as a Demon Verbal release. Some of Buckley's most popular routines – 'The Naz' (or 'The Nazz', as some versions have it) and 'Jonah and the Whale' – are on more than one issue, but as I pointed out, Buckley improvised a great deal, so they are not simply straight copies. I have three versions of 'The Naz', and they are all a delight to hear.

Dating Buckley's recorded material does not appear to be easy, though *Lord Buckley Blowing His Mind* stems from 1960, as does *Bad Rapping of the Marquis De Sade*. The World Pacific LP, *Way Out Humour*, is dated 1959. The most fascinating dates, however, relate to *The Best of Lord Buckley*, which shows a recording date of 1951, and *Revelations of the Late Lord Buckley*, recorded in 1952. These indicate how far ahead of his time he was in terms of the nature and presentation of his work.

JOHN MONTGOMERY, 1992

Most people will know of John Montgomery through his links to Jack Kerouac. He figures in *The Dharma Bums* and *Desolation Angels* as Henry Morley and Alex Fairbrother respectively, though it's probably the portrait in the former which has established him in Beat legend. I don't want to spend too much time looking at how Kerouac represented him. In *The Dharma Bums* he said:

> Henry Morley was a bespectacled fellow of great learning but an eccentric himself, more eccentric and *outré* than Japhy on campus, a librarian, with few friends, but a mountain climber.

It has been suggested that Morley is one of the most interesting personalities in Kerouac's work. Montgomery seems to have had a good-humoured attitude about how he was 'used' by Kerouac, though he did once say that 'what Jack did with my talk was to make me sound like Danny Kaye'. And he played down the colourful aspect of his character by saying, 'The people I've known are interesting. I'm not interesting.'

But who was John Montgomery? He was born in Spokane, Washington, in 1919, spent most of his early years in California, and graduated from Berkeley with a degree in economics in 1940. I suspect, though I can't prove it, that he may have had some leanings towards the Left at that time, though that wouldn't have been surprising. Any sensitive and aware young man living through the 1930s must have had some sympathies with the unemployed and dispossessed. Montgomery knew Kenneth Rexroth in 1940 and Rexroth, of course, did have involvements with communist and anarchist groups on the West Coast. This isn't proof that Montgomery had similar interests, but occasional asides and references in his published work, and in letters I had from him, did make me think that, if not necessarily an activist, he was familiar with the literature of protest. In one of his books he notes that he heard Malcolm Cowley say that 'there were only about eleven depression proletarian novels', and the suggestion is that this was an inaccurate estimate and that Montgomery knew better. But, as I have said, evidence like this is hardly conclusive and perhaps only indicates curiosity rather than commitment.

Montgomery attended law school for a time but eventually qualified as a librarian, something he worked as on and off. He also seems to have done a variety of other jobs, and the obituary in a local paper in California referred to him as a former postal worker. What does seem clear is that he didn't think of education as simply a means to a career. He was, in Jim Christy's words, 'a man of prodigious learning and multifarious activities', and his writing certainly backed up that description. I always had the feeling that Montgomery's poems packed in a great many oblique clues, not all of them likely to be immediately identified by even the most erudite reader. The saving grace was that he wore his learning lightly and with a smile, so the occasional bemusement that the reader felt was tempered by the knowledge that the writing was good-humoured and not just meant to demonstrate the poet's cleverness.

There isn't a great deal of information about what Montgomery did between 1940 and 1955, and he only came to the attention of a literary audience in 1955. As he described his introduction to Beat writers: 'One Friday evening as per custom I called on my friend Rexroth from whom I learned as much as from all my professors and found Snyder asking him where to give a poetry reading.' The event turned out to be the famous one at the Six Gallery at which Allen Ginsberg delivered his celebrated reading of 'HOWL' and Kerouac passed around a wine jug. Montgomery and Snyder had discovered a common interest in climbing and arranged to make a trip together, and Kerouac tagged along. The rest, as they say, is history, and it brought Montgomery into the limelight. It was after the publication of *The Dharma Bums* in 1958 that he began to be mentioned in print as an acquaintance of the Beats, if not necessarily one of the inner circle, and in 1959 he contributed an article, 'Report from the Beat Generation', to *The Library Journal*. Unlike many others then writing about them, Montgomery knew who the Beats really were, where they had come from, and what they represented in social and literary terms. He was not taken in by the negative aspects of the movement but he knew better than to dismiss all those connected with it as untalented or merely out to create a sensation.

He kept in touch with the Beats over the years and, in 1970, published the first of a series of small books which documented his awareness of and involvements with Kerouac and company. *Jack Kerouac: A Memoir in which is revealed Secret Lives and West Coast Whispers, Being the Confessions of Henry Morley, Alex Fairbrother & John Montgomery, Triune Madman of The Dharma Bums, Desolation Angels and Other Trips* is a long title covering a 16-page pamphlet published by Giligia Press which contains two short pieces about Montgomery's connection with Kerouac. He continued to re-work this material over the years, and another small book, *Kerouac West Coast: a Bohemian Pilot: Detailed Navigational Instructions* told much the same story, though with additional details and comments. In a way, these books or pamphlets typified Montgomery's general approach, because they outline the story and embellish it, sometimes with humour, sometimes with information, but always idiosyncratically. There's a passage in *Kerouac West Coast* which offers a summary of Beat characteristics:

> The physical, sports, movements action is I think a distinguishing characteristic of Beat prose and in a sense Beat is a misnomer. Particularly true of Ginsberg, also perhaps the most honest; in the case of Holmes, it seems to have a tearful note; with Jack, possibly related to the attitude that he is more virtuous than others in a honkytonk situation; with Neal, the note that I detect is that embarrassment is hugely comic; with Ginsberg, whose brother is an attorney, I note the continuity with his father; an extremely ethical man, of both decency and humility and a typically Jewish innate demand for justice for all.

It's quirky and provocative, but throws up a lot of ideas.

What Montgomery also did, besides putting his reminiscences of Kerouac and the Beats into a couple of small books, was assemble two collections of essays, tributes, and assorted pieces by a variety of writers. *The Kerouac We Knew* contained some excellent stuff, including Mike McGrady's *Jack Kerouac: Beat, even in Northport*, which captured the essence of Kerouac in his home setting, and Jim Christy's *Jack and Jazz: Woodsmoke and Trains*, an evocative memoir which is as much about Brew Moore and bass player Charlie Leeds as it is about Kerouac but still seems relevant. Montgomery had the knack of finding curious essays which caught the mood of Beat writing. If I can interject a personal reminiscence, it was always a source of pleasure to me that he chose a short piece of mine for inclusion in the second collection, *Kerouac at the 'Wild Boar' & Other Skirmishes*, and that he obviously appreciated the spirit in which I'd written it. He knew what the references to seeing Shelley plain and passing Brummell in a Brighton street were meant to indicate. Both collections were published by Montgomery's own Fels & Firn Press, and are essential additions to any collection of Beat-related writing. They carefully mix personal commentary, critical views, and useful information, along with a selection of idiosyncratic responses to Kerouac, and reflect Montgomery's tastes and interests as much as those of the writers concerned.

It would be unfair to overlook Montgomery's poetry which, if various assertions by him are to be believed, was largely a product of the post-1955 period. In fact, it would appear that most of his published poems appeared in print in the 70s and 80s. His one book, *Hip, Beat, Cool, and Antic*, brought together twenty-eight poems, though these were surely only a small selection of his total output. I can think of quite a few poems in magazines like *Alpha Beat Soup*, *Connections*, and my own *Palantir*, which weren't in the book. One of them, 'There were Hoofbeats at Sunset', printed in *Palantir* in 1979, is a particular favourite of mine. It neatly satirised the image of John Wayne that the movies had constructed, and by implication aspects of America, but it did it with a wry affection and some ambiguity. The poem starts with a brisk assertion of the origins of both Wayne and apple pie, an assertion that is pure Montgomery in its witty idiosyncrasy:

> John Wayne was as American as apple pie.
> They were both invented by the first Aryans
> To keep the boys from going South
> From Eden Canyon after they'd seen
> Minnehaha luxing her undies.
> Wayne and de Mille both stood
> Hats off loyal to the North.

From there the poem moves to reflections on American imperialism, Wayne's Hollywood career, and his private life. And it makes a succinct comment on the kind of principles enshrined in his film-making and, supposedly, his life:

> John Wayne taught young hopefuls like Ladd
> It's better to shoot straight than be mean;
> To keep your character simple
> So the critics can't analyse you.
> Hedda Hopper was afraid of him.
> He didn't have the heart to tell
> Louella Parsons she wasn't his type.

And, near the end, Montgomery describes, in a cryptic way, Wayne's death, which came:

> Not with a stroke, like a prize director
> Not with heart failure like an old leading lady
> But with cancer in interesting organs.
> John hit the gong in the American way.

The technique is unforced, and a dry voice comes through, a voice that mocks in a manner that is almost elegiac. The reader has the feeling that Montgomery, while satirising, is almost lamenting a lost dream of America, a dream that Wayne distorted by focusing too much on only certain aspects of it. You can understand why Montgomery was drawn to the Beats and they to him. The world wasn't what it should have been, their work said.

The use of names (people, places, events) to signpost a way through a poem was fairly typical, but didn't necessarily occur all the time. In his book there are several poems which are not unlike some of Kenneth Rexroth's work in their simplicity and directness:

> The honey in the hollow tree
> Fills the side valley
> With scent this year.
> How strong the worker bees
> Must be to bring all that
> Blossom from over the mountain.

There is the same feeling for the natural world, and the same easy rhythm. In another poem there's also the same kind of emotional power that Rexroth could pack into a few simple words:

> I was young once and I knew one
> In a quick-moving crowded time.
> And when they ask of her
> In my spacious later time,
> How can I tell them it is still
> With me, motionless; the shadow
> Still on her cheek, the dust
> On her sandal, my breastbone
> Freshly dented where it moved?

And, like Rexroth, there is an awe when faced with the immensity of the natural world, though it's never an awe which slides into sentimentality. Montgomery, like Rexroth, was far too sensible for that and knew that it was the human eye and mind which shaped the picture of the world:

> From a high-crowned headland I gaze,
> Contemplating the Pacific, misnamed
> Great watersheet of the world. Here

> In this solitude of unvisited second
> Growth redwood bestrewn with fog
> I handle thoughtfully the relics
> Of a vanished commerce; rusted cables,
> Antique machinery beside the stumps.

Montgomery wrote his share of Kerouac poems, those which recorded his admiration for the Beat novelist and his activities. The good thing was that he didn't get carried away with the overdone 'road' images, and instead preferred to concentrate on the real Kerouac:

> The map of Kerouac: its coordinates
> Goodbuddy workingmen's hotels
> Corners in old-fashioned bars
> Little secret sandy spots to sleep
> Between freights, Greyhounds and friendly trucks
> Shadows and schoolyards of a gone depression milltown.

And he acknowledged that Kerouac was 'learning all his life', something that Montgomery also did.

He was original, in his own small way, both in his poetry and prose. His short articles and book reviews were written in a crisp style, with opinions and relevant information shooting off at angles. He was at his best when writing about those he'd known, such as Kerouac, Rexroth, and Gary Snyder. Of Snyder, he said, 'his joy is sober it seems to me. It glows, then turns inward' and,

> Of my friends I assess Gary as the most consistent over the years. He does not see himself as exotic. He keeps on schedule and he never loses his cool. I can not visualise him retiring. Reading his poems conveys a philosophy of life.

Both comments are astute and illuminating. And Montgomery's letters were always interesting and amusing. I'm reluctant to use anything from the various letters and postcards I received over the years, but I hope it will not be taken amiss if I include a couple of things which particularly delighted me. In an exchange we had about the way people see other societies, he said

I gather that the same British idea of the USA as a place of large spaces, whoop de doo, vitality, social mobility, re-locating several times, together with a kind of exuberance expressed (in USA) by gangs, a healthy private gun industry, and aggressiveness makes the British a bit happy vicariously.

It's something that always comes to mind when I watch programmes on TV or read articles about America in the colour supplements. On another occasion, I referred to some links I had to the I.W.W., and he wrote back to say:

> I hadn't known that the IWW had branched out again. We seldom hear of it in the USA though their songbook was re-printed some years ago to good publicity. Curiously enough I have a copy of *Bars and Shadows*, Ralph Chaplin's poetry book (1922), with the owner's name: George Sterling (Bohemian Club) and some lines marked by him. Sterling was a leading bohemian (not of the club) in San Francisco who killed himself because the girl he loved married Upton Sinclair.

There was a whole world of American radicalism and bohemianism referred to in that one passage, and it wasn't unusual to find many like it in Montgomery's letters.

It's probably true that John Montgomery will never be remembered as a major writer, and that he may well be fated to go down in literary history as the basis for a character in a couple of Kerouac's books. But he did produce something of value of his own and deserves to be honoured for it. He was a delightful correspondent, a witty and intriguing poet, a wise editor, and an informed commentator on other people's work. He also had the generosity of wanting to promote that work, whenever he could. The world is a sadder place without him.

Note

Hip, Beat, Cool & Antic was published by Alpha Beat Press, Montreal, in 1988. The Giligia Press pamphlet was published in Fresno in 1970, and *Kerouac West Coast* was published by Fels & Firn Press, Palo Alto, 1976. *The Kerouac We Knew* came from Fels & Firn Press, Kentfield, 1982, and *Kerouac at the 'Wild Boar'* from Fels & Firn, San Anselmo, 1986.

'A Gary Snyder Reading' appeared in *Palantir* 23 (1983), 'Up the Matterhorn with Kerouac and Snyder' in *Alpha Beat Soup* 3 (1988), and 'My Friend Snyder' in *Alpha Beat Soup* 5 (1989).

MIGRANT, 1966

> If there be what I believe there is, in every nation a style which never
> becomes obsolete – a certain mode of phraseology so consonant and
> congenial to the analogy and principles of its respective language, as
> to remain settled and unaltered – this style is probably to be sought
> in the common intercourse of life, among those who speak only to
> be understood.

This quotation from Samuel Johnson's writings was printed as the editorial to the first issue of *Migrant*, a little magazine which made its initial appearance in July 1959, and came out regularly every other month until the eighth, and final, issue in September 1960. It may seem that its life-span was too short for it to have made any great impression, but nothing could be further from the truth. *Migrant* was one of the best magazines published here in recent years, and it helped focus attention both in the pages of *Migrant* itself, and through the series of booklets which were brought out in conjunction with it, on a neglected, but first-class, body of writers in this country, the best of whom were, and still are, about the only worthwhile British counterparts to the American poets of the 'Black Mountain' school. At the same time it used work by some of these American poets, as well as by writers of other nationalities.

The first number of *Migrant* contained just eighteen pages, but even so the quality aimed at, and the general tone of future issues, could be easily discerned. The American poet, Edward Dorn, was featured, and there was an interesting anonymous prose-piece – 'A Comment, Spring 1959' – which stated its author's views on the way things appeared to be going just then. It's worth quoting at least part of it – like the Samuel Johnson piece it gives a good picture of what concerned certain of the *Migrant* contributors.

> We are breeding sensibilities, discentred to such an extent and resignedly so, that they are all but incapable of any sense of values other than the merely pragmatic, the sloppily self-indulgent, living from moment to moment. I do not see how this would be possible for minds passionately active for a sense of past achievement, passionately concerned to translate that achievement, to extend it by self-discipline, into present meaning. Do I mean that an awareness of Ben Jonson would make of Kerouac a better writer? No, K. is a spiritual simpleton – nothing could do that. But an awareness of the kind of live intelligence Jonson represents could prevent an intelligentsia wasting its time on the Kerouacs, etc. But then, an awareness of Mark Twain would do that!

It will be seen from the above that *Migrant* certainly wasn't one of the many magazines on the Beat bandwagon which was getting so much attention about that time. In many ways it was carrying on in a tradition which magazines like the American *Black Mountain Review* and *Origin*, and the Canadian *Combustion*, had also been in, and it was no surprise to find some of the people who had been amongst the mainstays of these publications – Robert Creeley, Robert Duncan, and Cid Corman (the editor of *Origin* incidentally) – in the second issue of *Migrant*. The English contributors included Michael Shayer, a fine poet (his long work *Persephone* was published as a *Migrant* pamphlet, but unfortunately never received the attention it deserved) who was here featured with a lengthy essay on Osborne's *Look Back In Anger*.

The third and fourth issues maintained the high standard set by the previous numbers with work by Charles Tomlinson, Denise Levertov and several others. There was a group of good poems in the fourth issue by Hugh Creighton Hill, an English poet who had published in magazines like *Poetry (Chicago)* as far back as the early 1930s. One of his poems in *Migrant* (and later included in *Latterday Chrysalides*, a collection by Hill published in the booklet series) was the delightful 'Grishkin is Nice':

Those undeserving women
who provide poets with
the usual satisfaction

have a deal of fuss
made over them

and when you meet them
in the flesh

cripes!

In the same issue part of a letter to Gael Turnbull, the editor, was reproduced, and this, in its way, pinpoints some of the things about *Migrant* which could be criticised:

> The first issue of your new magazine reached me today. Like all these things now it left me feeling very depressed. Everyone seems to NAG so now, all so very sure they're right; and all the chatter about dissensions in the literary world, which is so unimportant, and so impotent finally, because it is not going to cause anything to happen. If only people would write what they have to, and leave the chatter to the odd-job men, the PhD-toters of this world. All right one has to think about from what one is writing; but surely one doesn't have to mount to one's own vantage point by this solid treading upon other worn-out faces. Surely Eliot doesn't have to be knocked down again, surely the 'Club' writers can be left now, not pulled up, dusted, and flung down again. Nobody can be amused by this anymore. Also, why is success in writing so necessarily filthy – I admit it can be – but look at all the real writers who've wanted it – Keats, Clare, Pope (the list is endless). Why is it so nasty to want to live off one's pen, if one can do it (which is unlikely, all right) without selling out. The whole issue here is so bloody minor; and the repeated nag about it eventually has to look like sour grapes – and it sets my teeth on edge.

It seems important to stress at this point that *Migrant* was obviously very much a 'workshop'; besides the poems printed there was a copious use of excerpts from contributors' letters and general comments. The prose-pieces were – with the exception of one or two short stories – usually of the type previously quoted from, or like Hugh Kenner's 'The

Drama Of Utterance' (a study of the work of William Carlos Williams)
in issue seven, and Alan Brownjohn's article on the poetry of Robert
Creeley and Philip Larkin. All contributions were, of course, of general
relevance to the atmosphere surrounding the *Migrant* group (I use the
word 'group' loosely here – the poets in the magazine, though obviously
having some things in common, were far too individual to ever run as
a pack), though they didn't necessarily reflect the opinions of the editor.
In a letter to me, in July 1965, Gael Turnbull said,

> These fragments did not always by any means represent any direct
> reflection of my own opinion, or that of Shayer – a few were put in
> merely by way of giving expression to valid feelings and reactions –
> what I wanted was some sort of context against which the poems could
> be read – something for the poems to relate to, etc. – a 'soil', if you
> like – and a sense, in it, of something of the flux of the everyday.

The eighth issue was an extra large one, and included work by most
of the English writers who had come to be associated with the magazine,
and who had books published in the *Migrant* series. Anselm Hollo,
Michael Shayer, Edwin Morgan, Ian Hamilton Finlay, and Roy Fisher
were all featured, and it was the latter who contributed a beautiful
poem, 'The Hospital in Winter,' which ended with these lines:

> Smoke filters across the town,
>   High panes are bleak;
> Pink of coral sinks to brown;
>   A dark bell brings the dark down.

The American poets in the final issue included Charles Olson, Larry
Eigner, and Barriss Mills.

Migrant operated under Gael Turnbull's editorship, and was published
– with Michael Shayer's assistance – from Worcester, England, and
Ventura, California. Although there appear to be no plans to revive it,
the booklet series has continued over the years – a collection by Turnbull
and a long poem by Matthew Mead were published in 1964 – and at
the time of writing it seems certain that it is to be extended. It's a

pity, really, that the magazine isn't to be reborn – there are one or two others which carry on in the same line, but none has managed to recreate the very personal tone of *Migrant*. It was, as I mentioned previously, a 'workshop,' and though, as in any workshop, things sometimes didn't go quite right, there was a good deal of honest work done, and a few first-class things, too. Many of the contributors are now quite well known, but all – known and unknown – helped to make *Migrant* what it was, and at a time when it looked as if some of the more extreme manifestations of the Beat mood might swamp good writing under, they held out for care and concern for their craft.

Looking back, it's possible to see just how important *Migrant* was. It's true it was short-lived, and that it had a restricted circulation, but its effect was far-reaching. Apart from spotlighting many of the writers mentioned in this article, it helped to bring English, American, and Canadian poets into closer contact with each other's work, and its influence is still felt amongst those who form the 'group' it encompassed and those who follow in their footsteps. It was not for nothing that Donald Allen chose to include *Migrant* in the select bibliographical section of his *The New American Poetry: 1945-1960* anthology, nor was it for nothing that the editors of *Mica*, a California magazine which commenced its life shortly after the demise of *Migrant*, said,

> In the belief that Gael Turnbull's *Migrant* stood among the best and most readable of the little-magazines, the editors of *Mica* want to continue in its footsteps. We hope that readers already familiar with *Migrant* will find in *Mica* the same human qualities which they recognised and praised in its predecessor.

It was quite a tribute and one well deserved.

Note

For information about Migrant Press see my article and check-list in *The Private Library*, Berkhamsted, 6:1, Spring 1973.

SATIS: THE HISTORY OF A LITTLE MAGAZINE, 1998

Satis exists to publish poems. We cannot specify in advance the poetry we want – and for which we cannot pay – but can only promise to recognise that poetry when we see it. The editor sits here sniffing among the manuscripts like A.E. Houseman's terrier.

That excerpt from the editorial in the first issue of *Satis* establishes a tone that may be familiar to anyone who has edited a little magazine. True, some editors do have a determined awareness of what they want, but others, perhaps the majority, prefer to keep an open mind, one which responds to the work arriving in the mail. Of course, getting the first issue off the ground usually involves soliciting poems, and the editor naturally writes to people he admires. A direction may then be suggested and would-be contributors might well recognise it as one which would suit their work.

It's interesting, with this in mind, to look at a particular publication, in this case a small magazine which appeared over five issues between Autumn, 1960, and Spring/Summer, 1962. This was a fertile period for little magazines, especially those with a link to the new poetry then appearing in the United States. *Migrant,* an influential publication with which Gael Turnbull and Roy Fisher were much involved, had appeared in 1959 and 1960, and others, such as *New Departures* and *Underdog,* both with a leaning towards the Beats, were also around. I mention these only in passing so as to set *Satis* in context, and there were many more, including *Ambit, Sidewalk,* and *Outburst.* There was, I think, a reaching out on the part of poets breaking free of the constraints of the 1950s to kindred spirits in the United States, where it seemed something of a renaissance was under way.

This is not to suggest that the editor and publisher of *Satis* were awed by American trends in the way that some of those who looked to the Beats were. But Matthew Mead, the editor, certainly seems to have kept in touch with developments on the other side of the Atlantic, to the extent that he recalled trying to distribute the American magazine, *Odyssey*, prior to deciding to start *Satis*. And the publisher, Malcolm Rutherford, went along with Mead's policy of encouraging contact with American poets.

Rutherford and Mead had met in Singapore in 1945 and shared an interest in the work of T.S. Eliot and Sidney Keyes, among others. Mead began writing poetry after the War and sought Rutherford's advice about the results. Their continuing friendship led to them deciding to launch a magazine in 1960, though Mead later recalled that there was not one specific reason for doing so:

> Why *Satis* was started is hard to recall; it was perhaps inevitable. The idea of starting a little magazine had lodged itself in my mind and Malcolm Rutherford was interested in the little magazine background. In such a situation a recitation of e.e. cummings' "let's start a little magazine" may be enough of a why.

The name *Satis* was chosen by Rutherford, and a note in the first issue explained that it came from a description alongside an inscribed Roman brick in the Silchester Collection in Reading Museum. 'Satis' means 'enough', and it could indicate that the brick was the last in a particular batch, or it could simply have been an idle remark by the workman.

Ten of the twenty-four pages of the first issue were used for Mead's own essay on Alun Lewis, primarily because he wanted to establish the idea of having some critical work in each issue. There were seven other contributors, and all but one had been asked to submit work. Mead, who thought of John Heath-Stubbs as 'the leading active English poet below the rank of God,' wrote to him to solicit poems, and he also contacted Frederick Eckman, an American whose poetry he knew from

Odyssey. He also wrote to Anne Cluysenaar, who had been featured in *Universities Poetry Two*, and Gael Turnbull and Michael Shayer, who he knew from *Migrant*. Mead's long work, *A Poem in Nine Parts*, had been published by Migrant Press in 1960. Another *Migrant* regular, the Finnish poet, Anselm Hollo, then living in London, was also contacted. The odd man out was Anthony Smythe, who had somehow heard about *Satis* and sent in a poem which Mead liked.

Was there a discernible line of thinking about poetry in the first *Satis*? It doesn't appear so in retrospect, which isn't to say that the contents lacked interest. Michael Shayer's extended work, 'Persephone', from which an excerpt was taken, is now mostly forgotten, but at the time its attempt to use the English provinces as a basis for a poetry of ideas, much along the lines of Williams Carlos Williams' *Paterson* was of great interest. And Turnbull's crisp 'Mareta,' with its dry social comment, still reads well today.

Once the first issue had circulated there was no need to invite submissions of poetry, though Mead always found that good prose was harder to come by. Gael Turnbull, then something of a key figure in the transatlantic exchange of ideas, provided a list of names and addresses to which copies of *Satis* were sent, and it inevitably included many Americans. Mead later said that the presence of a large number of Americans in subsequent issues 'was not deliberate. I took the best of the manuscripts I received regardless of where they came from,' but their influence was noticeable. The second issue had poems by Richard Weber and Barriss Mills, along with Turnbull's essay, 'A Gesture to be Clean,' which he described as 'some notes on the poetry of William Carlos Williams.' And the third issue was entirely devoted to American writers, because 'the idea of an American number was forced on us by the very weight of manuscripts which we received from the USA.' Not all of these were good, and Mead remembered one American poet whom he described as 'a scourge ... who would submit (from California) anything between 30 and 50 poems at a time and repeat the process on rejection. I still recall surviving that onslaught with satisfaction.'

Of the ten American writers (Turnbull was one of them, though he's not usually thought of as American), most have since slipped into obscurity, and even those whose names are still occasionally seen here and there – Robert Sward, Larry Eigner, David Raphael Wang – are hardly well-known. Nonetheless, their work in *Satis* was of interest at the time, and indicated that they were very much part of what was going on in America. None of them belonged to any of the then-definable camps, such as Beat, Black Mountain, New York, etc., though Eigner did have some currency with the avant-garde and his work was set alongside Creeley, Dorn, Joel Oppenheimer, and Charles Olson, in Donald Allen's anthology, *The New American Poetry 1945-1960*. But he was too idiosyncratic to be completely identified with a specific group. The tendency of the poets in the American *Satis* was towards open forms, but with precision of language and technique highlighted, and these factors may suggest how Mead's own leanings were shaping the magazine's tone. There were certainly no Beat histrionics, nor any obscurities, and clarity and conciseness were prized.

One matter of related interest, bearing in mind the earlier comments about links with America, was the advertisements for American magazines. *Midwest, Epos Quagga* (described as 'a quarterly of poetry and pataphysics published at the University of Texas'), *Descant*, and *Trace* were listed, as was *The Outsider*, which was handprinted in New Orleans by a couple of old-style bohemians, Jon Edgar Webb and Louise 'Gypsy Lou' Webb, whose tastes ran to a mixture of traditional jazz and modernist poetry. The handful of issues of their magazine, plus a couple of books published by their Loujon Press, are now collectors' items. From my own recollections of the magazines mentioned, they did have a loose identity, if only because they didn't throw in their lot with any one group or style. Beats, Black Mountaineers, and others did appear in their pages, but so did a variety of poets not identified with those labels. The fact that *Satis* had contact with such publications was not accidental, and points to shared values. The editorial in the American issue said, 'what we like in American poetry is a matter-of-fact romanticism,' and that statement does describe many of the poems.

The policy of using an essay in each issue had been suspended, but was revived in the fourth, and Donald Carroll contributed a piece entitled, 'Who was John Peale Bishop?' He was unapologetic about looking at a poet whose work was not well known:

> To most readers of Modern poetry John Peale Bishop is a name appearing on a library card somewhere between Auden and Bridges ... . To most of those few acquainted with his work he is a collector of used images, appearing everywhere behind Yeats and Eliot.

Carroll's short essay attempted to redress the balance so far as an appreciation of Bishop's work was concerned, and like the poetry in *Satis* was clear and concise.

Most of the poets featured in this issue – Cluysenaar, Turnbull, Weber, Shayer, Hollo – had been in *Satis* previously, but a couple of new names were added. Bernice Ames contributed four intense poems which were striking but ultimately forgettable – a not unusual characteristic of many little magazine poems, past and present – and Tom Malcolm, who could be said to have been writing a 'matter-of-fact romanticism,' came in with a couple of short poems in which direct use of language, and an uncluttered technique, combined to create a powerful and more lasting effect. The usual advertisements were also there, with this time a few British publications listed. Migrant Press had been a presence from the first issue, but *Prospect*, and Ian Hamilton Finlay's Wild Hawthorn Press, now made an appearance. There was, too, a plaintive notice which said: 'Poet, little-mag. editor, distressfully acquainted engineering, road haulage, export packing, etc., free early 1962, seeks post London/Home Counties or sinecure anywhere.'

All little-magazines eventually call it a day, some earlier than others, and *Satis* did so with the fifth issue, dated Spring/Summer, 1962. The editorial referred to 'adequate reasons of love, money and lassitude,' and Mead, when looking back, said, 'it would have had to cease in any case as far as I was concerned because it was getting in the way of my own writing. I think it was WCW who said of little mags that they are all part of one big magazine; and I felt perhaps that I had served my turn.' A continuity of sorts was proposed with an arrangement whereby Jeremy Prynne's *Prospect* took over responsibility for honouring Satis subscriptions which included the sixth issue.

The final issue expanded slightly beyond the 24 pages which had been the standard in the first four, and a few new contributors were added. Jeremy Prynne, Godfrey John, Ken Wlaschin, John Ambrose: with the exception of Prynne I know nothing about these people, and their work was admittedly readable but slight. Probably the most significant contributions were some poems by Charles Bukowski, together with an essay on his work by R.R. Cuscaden. These days, Bukowski is a cult figure, much admired by those who like their writers to be larger than life and twice as boozy, but little was known about him in this country in 1962. The poems in *Satis* were the first to appear in a British publication, and taken with the essay they pointed to a poet who had an individual voice and an approach which, though seemingly loose and even haphazard, was then serious and intelligent. Cuscaden's piece referred to 'a Jeffers-like pessimism' in Bukowski's work, and quoted him as saying, 'if I have a god it's Robinson Jeffers, although I realise that I don't write as he does.' The tough-guy stance was already evident in Bukowski's poems, but without the mannerisms that took over when he became conscious of writing for a specific audience. In the early 1960s he was, as Cuscaden rightly says, 'the poet of a ruined landscape,' with a despair that 'exists just because he continually hopes.' Opinions vary about Bukowski's work generally, but Mead was performing a correct editorial function when he featured it in *Satis* in those early days when it seemed fresh and interesting.

Commenting on his own feelings about the general situation when Satis was in existence, Matthew Mead said:

> It is difficult for me to recall how I felt about poetry in general in the UK at the time (1959-62) and again I ought to emphasise that poetry had always been very Anglo-American to me; that volume of Sandburg mentioned in the editorial of *Satis* 3 really was one of the early books of verse which I devoured and tried to imitate.

I've concentrated on the editorial side of *Satis* but the practical aspect of running a little magazine is always of importance. And the publisher, Malcolm Rutherford, deserves recognition for his part in keeping *Satis* afloat. The cost of producing it was evenly divided between Mead and Rutherford, with 300 copies of the first issue printed and 400 of each of the rest. The magazine was neatly printed in a small-size format and had red card covers. Some copies were sold through the 'half-a-dozen London bookshops which would, in those days, stock a little magazine and which I could negotiate before I tired of the London pavements.' (Mead's words). Each contributor was given six copies in lieu of cash payment, there was a small subscription list (mainly Americans), and review and exchange copies were mailed out to other publications. Complimentary copies were sent to poets like Basil Bunting and Robert Creeley. The Arts Council bought a copy of the first issue, but returned a free copy of the second which was sent to its office. Many years later the same organisation paid a price much in excess of the original for a complete set of the magazine.

Did *Satis* achieve anything, other than in terms of offering a number of individual poets an outlet for their work? Most little magazines rarely do more than that and, in retrospect, have little to recommend them beyond the possibility of finding a forgotten but interesting writer. But Mead's own tastes did give *Satis* a certain cohesion, even if many of the poems were not necessarily first-rate. It is still surprisingly readable, which is not always true of little magazines. To look at the five slim issues now is to recapture a period when there was a genuine striving for new approaches to the writing of poetry, and when it seemed essential to have some sort of contact with the United States. The history of the 1960s is too often written in terms of a so-called 'underground', but there were much more provocative things going on, especially in the early years of the decade. It should also be noted that *Satis*, like so many of the magazines which helped broaden the possibilities of British poetry, came from the provinces (it was published from Newcastle-upon-Tyne), something which is ignored in standard cultural histories of those years. Five issues of a little magazine may not seem like a major contribution to literary developments, but they had a valuable part to play and deserve to be rescued from oblivion.

I am grateful to Matthew Mead and Malcolm Rutherford who, some years ago, corresponded with me about *Satis*, and gave me permission to use their comments in this article.

CHARLES BUKOWSKI: EARLY DAYS IN ENGLAND, 1994

It was in the early 1960s that I first began to notice poems by Charles
Bukowski in such vital little magazines of the day as *Midwest, The
Outsider, Nomad, San Francisco Review, The Wormwood Review,* and *Satis,* the
latter published from Newcastle-upon-Tyne, and in its final issue
(Spring/Summer, 1962) containing a short essay by R.R. Cuscaden
which must have been one of the first, if not the first, serious reviews
of Bukowski's work to appear in an English publication. It is, I think,
significant that it was *Satis* – a non-establishment, provincial-based
magazine – which used this piece. Very few people had heard of
Bukowski in those days, and he certainly didn't interest academics or
the journalists working for the national press and glossy magazines. All
that came much later, and the initial favourable response to Bukowski's
poetry was to be found amongst a few poets and some readers of little
magazines. The editors of *Satis* were pioneers and got there long before
anyone else. For the record, most of Bukowski's work that was
published in Britain prior to his inclusion in the Penguin Modern Poets
series in 1969 was printed in provincial magazines. I recall one called
Iconolatre, based in West Hartlepool, which used several of his poems.
And, in 1966, I used a Bukowski poem in a little anthology, *Thirteen
American Poets,* published as a slim supplement to *Move,* the magazine
I was then editing from Preston.

It's interesting to speculate about why most British editors and readers
had no awareness of Bukowski or didn't like his poetry. I suspect that
his openness, both of style and subject matter, embarrassed them, or
would have done had they encountered his work. They perhaps found

it easier to relate to his prose, because there was a tradition of hard-bitten American writing that he seemed to fit into, and which the British have a vicarious taste for. But the poetry, even now, is often viewed with suspicion by those whose tastes have been formed by a formal education. For my own part, I think it was the openness that attracted me to Bukowski. That and his directness of expression and awareness of, to quote Cuscaden, 'How complete and deep has been his estrangement from the world in which he lived.' Cuscaden, speaking of the poet's position in society in the past two hundred years or so, went on to say:

> He has known how futile would be his claim to be legislator of anything at all in a world he never made and did not admire. Few of today's poets are as conscious of this, or write so well about it, as Charles Bukowski.

Or as Bukowski himself put it:

> and I walked into a dark hall
> where the landlady stood
> execrating and final,
> sending me to hell,
> waving her fat, sweaty arms
> and screaming
> screaming for rent
> because the world had failed us
> both.

The estrangement implicit in that is a recurring theme in virtually all of Bukowski's early poems, from the relatively minor pieces which chronicle the breakdown of an affair, or even just a conversation, to those which attempt a bitter look at the whole human condition:

> now the horns have stopped and
> the firecrackers and the thunder ...
> it's all over in five minutes ...
> all I hear is the rain
> on the palm leaves

and I think,
I will never understand men,
but I have lived
it through.

The difference between the two poems is, possibly, the resignation hinted at in the final three lines of the second one.

What was always additionally striking about Bukowski's poems was their sheer readability. The quality could be variable, it's true, because I don't think he could ever be called a selective or refined poet, but it was never a struggle to find a way through anything he wrote. This isn't to suggest that he was simplistic. But too many poems in the 1960s, and now, were and are difficult to finish. The words tangle with each other, the ideas take too long to appear (if an idea appears at all), and the lines wander and lack tension. Bukowski had his faults, but they were not usually of the kind referred to. And even when he was at his slightest and most sentimental (like other tough-guy writers, there was a soft streak deep inside him) his poems at least stated their intentions clearly:

I met a genius on the train
today
about 6 years old,
he sat beside me
and as the train
ran down along the coast
we came to the ocean
and then he looked at me
and said
it's not pretty.
It was the first time I'd
realised
that.

That's just one side of his directness, however, and there is a deeper, more serious strain to his work, as can be seen from this brief extract from the wonderfully titled 'Something for the touts, the nuns, the grocery clerks, and you ...'

We have everything and we have nothing
and some men do it in churches
and some men do it by tearing butterflies
in half
and some men do it in Palm Springs
laying it into butterblondes
with Cadillac souls

And so it goes on, tense and terse, and with a finely controlled despair which gives it a cutting edge:

and nothing and nothing. the days of
the bosses, yellow men
with bad breath and big feet, men
who look like frogs, hyenas, men who walk
as if melody had never been invented, men
who think it is intelligent to hire and fire and
profit, men with expensive wives they possess
like 60 acres of ground to be drilled
or shown-off or to be walled away from
the incompetent, men who'd kill you
because they're crazy and justify it because
it's the law, men who stand in front of
windows 30 feet wide and see nothing,
men with luxury yachts who can sail around
the world and yet never get out of their vest
pockets, men like snails, men like eels, men
like slugs, and not as good ... .

It should be clear that Bukowski, although often concerned with personal matters, could be a very sharp social critic, though he steered well clear of political commitment. Sometimes the criticism took the form of jeers at aesthetes, academics, and anyone else not matching up to Bukowski's notion of 'real' people. It was all entertaining, but eventually a little futile because, as Bukowski certainly knew, life just isn't that simple. The people we think of as involved with life-styles vastly different from our own might well turn out to be decent and intelligent, whereas the romanticised 'real' people may just be the ones who don't give a damn for poetry, civilised living, or anything else for that matter. And it doesn't help a writer's case if the targets are too easy, as Bukowski's sometimes were:

> The boy walks with his muddy feet across my soul
> talking about recitals, virtuosi, conductors,
> the lesser known novels of Dostoevsky;
> talking about how he corrected a waitress,
> a hasher who didn't know that French dressing
> was composed of so and so;
> he gabbles about the Arts until
> I hate the Arts,
> and there is nothing cleaner
> than getting back to a bar or
> back to the track and watching them run

Fine, we know the type, and who wouldn't dislike a creep who thinks it clever to brag about ridiculing a waitress. But the meanness goes deeper than that, and it's in evidence in the bars and at the racetracks just as much as it is on the fringes of the Arts.

In another poem, 'Voices', the anti-intellectualism spills over into a series of swipes at writers Bukowski either didn't like or was suspicious of. Again, it has entertainment value, but probably the only people who appreciated the poem were those like the boy in the piece quoted above, the types who can smirk and nudge one another, and say, 'That's so-and-so he's knocking,' and then wait to see if so-and-so will respond. Bukowski should have been bigger than that.

The deeper side of Bukowski's social sense – the side that looked beyond the literary cliques and phoneys and instead fastened onto a despairing vision of the whole society rather than just the idiocies of a few fools – was much more interesting:

> I see people in department stores and
> supermarkets
> walking down aisles
> buying things
> and I can see by the way their clothing
> fits them and by the way they walk

and by their faces and their eyes
that they care for nothing
and that nothing cares
for them

Unlike the too glib jibes at fellow-writers and literary groupies, that poem has a timeless quality. There is ultimately a deep sense of desolation at work in it, and it's a desolation which doesn't attempt an easy way out by preaching a political solution to a world writhing in the grip of it. The malaise is spiritual. And, as Hugh Fox, an early commentator on his poems, pointed out, he was at his best when he saw 'himself not as poor Bukowski (the individual pose), but Bukowski the poor man (the universal truth)':

the old gray-haired waitresses
in cafes at night
have given it up,
and as I walk down sidewalks of
light and look into windows
of nursing homes
I can see that it is no longer
with them.
I see people sitting on park benches
and I can see by the way they
sit and look
that it is gone.

Or, from another poem in which a real awareness of the way things are comes through:

it is the man you've never seen who
keeps you going
the one who might arrive
someday

I can see the man there, and feel for him, whereas the other Bukowski – the blood-spitting, boozing toughie – can sometimes be a bit tiring. I accept that it's the same person speaking, but as with a friend whose moods and behaviour vary, I tolerate Bukowski at times and like him at others.

A couple of final points before I end this brief reflection on why Bukowski appealed to me all those years ago. I referred to his inclinations towards a routine anti-intellectualism, but his obvious fondness for classical music was always in evidence. It isn't a complete list, but from the early poems I recall favourable references to Brahms, Borodin, Beethoven, Shostakovitch, Mozart, Donizetti, Dvorak, Franck, Bartok, and Greig. His use of music often seemed to be a means of coping with stress. And in his poem about Borodin he painted a neat picture of the composer as an eccentric who wrote music to relax and whose wife treated him with contempt. Perhaps Bukowski identified with this situation. But it does need to be noted that the anti-intellectualism was something of a pose, and the early poems actually contain a wide range of references to writers, painters and composers. Bukowski may have written, 'don't ever get the idea that I am a poet; you can see me/ at the racetrack any day half drunk,' but he knew he was.

The other point concerns his technique. On the face of it he used a very loose style, with entirely arbitrary line-breaks, not to mention haphazard use of punctuation. A close examination of the poems, though, leads to a realisation that the line structure relates completely to the mood and rhythm of the individual poems. Likewise the placing of punctuation. When it is sparingly used the poems tend to the lyrical and move smoothly. When it is more obvious the poems are terse, sometimes almost jagged, and spit out their statements. What this means is that the technique is there simply as an aid to understanding what the poems are saying.

I've not attempted more than a brief survey of Bukowski's early poems, and it's a survey made from a personal point of view. I've indicated that I had my doubts about some of his work and the attitudes it represented, and I suspect that basic insecurities in his character may have shaped the poses he adopted. But it was possible to see the poses as part of the whole man and so make allowances for them, and they were more than compensated for by his achievements and the singularity of his voice. I hold to the view that Bukowski probably wrote far too much later, and that the content of the poems suffered as a result of this, but the poetry produced in the late 1950s and early 1960s still seems to me to be worth reading. And it needs to be recorded how fresh and exciting it was when I first encountered it in those now forgotten little magazines.

Note

Bukowski's early poems can be found in *The Days Ran Away Like Wild Horses Over The Hills* (Black Sparrow Press, Los Angeles, 1969), and *Burning in Water Drowning in Flame* (Black Sparrow Press, Los Angeles, 1974). The selection in Penguin Modern Poets 13 (Penguin Books, Harmondsworth, 1969) is also of interest. Details of Bukowski's early appearances in print can be found in Hugh Fox's *Charles Bukowski: A Critical and Bibliographical Study* (Abyss Publications, Somerville, Massachusetts, 1969), which covers the period 1944 to 1968 and shows the importance of little magazines and small presses in Bukowski's development.

ALFRED KAZIN, 1996

There are a number of important surveys of the New York Intellectuals, the group of literary and social critics, many of them with their roots in Marxism, who came to the fore in the thirties and forties and dominated the cultural scene for several decades. And descriptions of what they represented can vary. For the purpose of this piece Irving Howe's explanation will suffice:

> My use of the phrase *New York Intellectuals* is simply a designation of convenience for what might awkwardly be spelled out as *the intellectuals of New York who began to appear in the Thirties, most of whom were Jewish.*

Howe himself was one of the leading second-generation New York Intellectuals, and so was Alfred Kazin, though their differences were sometimes as evident as their similarities. Howe was always close to politics, whereas Kazin, though growing up with images of socialism all around him, never allied himself with any one party or programme. In later years, when he looked back at himself as he was in the early thirties, he said: 'I wasn't much interested in anything except reading and reporting in my notebook the direct impact of everything I read.' He was, in fact, much more aware of social and political developments than that suggests, but the statement does indicate where his priorities lay.

But Kazin has always been an interesting and provocative writer, one whose work contains a strong element of social criticism. His dedication to books, and to the idea that writers ought to be aware of what is happening in society in general, has never been in any doubt. In his most recent book, *Writing Was Everything*, he discusses the lack of beliefs that extend beyond the personal, and comments:

Emerson, Whitman, Melville, Dickinson, and Faulkner, along with Dostoevsky, Kafka, and Camus, would have said that not having enough to think about beyond our health, our sex life, our status, we are not thinking at all.

Born in 1915 in Brooklyn, Kazin was one of the generation of writers and intellectuals who attended the City College of New York in the Thirties. There are stories about how the cafeteria at CCNY had separate alcoves where groups of young Trotskyists, communists, socialists, and others, would gather to debate their ideas, but Kazin doesn't seem to have settled in any one of them, at least not to the extent of being identified with specific views. He has been described by Alan Wald as 'an armchair left-wing socialist, attracted to Marxist intellectuals but not to Marxism as a doctrine.' Like many of his contemporaries he had grown up with radical beliefs almost as a family routine. His father had been a member of the Jewish-Socialist Bund in Russia, and in America joined the Socialist Party and admired Eugene Debs. And Kazin, as he grew up, attended political rallies and meetings and knew many activists. His first volume of autobiography, *A Walker in the City*, is coloured with references to the politics of the period. Looking back, he wonders:

> Where now is Mendy, with the venomous cowlick over his eyes, who went off from the slums of Thatford Avenue to disappear on the Ebro in defence of 'Spain,' and before he left dismissed me forever in rage and contempt – "intellectuals are not even worth shooting" – because I doubted the omniscience of Josef Vissarionovitch Stalin? And David, my excellent if pedantical friend David, with those thick lenses before his eyes severe as Marxist method, who dutifully suppressed his love of chemistry and poetry to go down into the wilds of darkest Georgia to advance the cause of the Negro oppressed?

Elsewhere in *A Walker in the City* he reminisces about his father's work as a house-painter, when there was work to be had, his mother working from home as a dressmaker, and his cousin and her friends, employed in the East Side sweatshops and all 'passionately loyal members of the International Ladies Garment Workers Union.' People with jobs were lucky and others became victims of the Depression and lost their homes. Kazin refers to

> The nude shamed look furniture on the street always had those terrible
> first winters of the Depression, when we stood around each newly
> evicted family to give them comfort and the young Communists raged
> up and down the street calling for volunteers to put the furniture back
> and crying aloud with their fists lifted to the sky.

It may be true that Kazin did not, in later life, show signs of strong
political leanings, but anyone reading his book will not be in any doubt
about how he was affected by the sufferings and injustices of the Thirties.
Many years after these events he was attacked by right-wing critics such
as Lionel Abel and Kenneth Lynn for an alleged anti-capitalist bias in
his work. Lynn, reviewing a re-issue of Kazin's *On Native Grounds*
(originally published in 1942 and a major survey of American literature
between 1890 and 1940) said that it was full of anti-business sentiments,
and Abel, a one-time Trotskyist who went conservative, claimed that
Kazin's *An American Procession* (1984) suggested a deepening of his doubts
about American society due to what he perceived as 'the astonishing
degradation of America in recent years.' The effects of the social
turbulence of the Thirties were to be felt for many years amongst the
generations of New York Intellectuals, whether they retained some sort
of liberal or left-wing ideas or swung to the right. Sidney Hook's
autobiography, *Out of Step*, which appeared in 1987, spent many pages
fighting the old battles of the thirties and forties and had some harsh
things to say about Kazin's activities and opinions.

A Walker in the City constantly highlights how culture, especially
literature, shaped Kazin's life more than politics did, though the two
were often hard to deal with separately. Radical politics often went
hand-in-hand with Modernist writing, so that, visiting a friend, it was
not unusual to see *Poetry* (the famous Chicago-based magazine which
printed leading contemporary poets) alongside *New Masses* (a
Communist Party cultural publication), while the same friend had a
'hallowed copy of *The Waste Land* that he carried around with him
wherever he went.' And in the second volume of his memoirs, *Starting
Out in the Thirties*, Kazin says:

Although I was a 'socialist', like everyone else I knew, I thought of socialism as orthodox Christians might think of the Second Coming – a wholly supernatural event which one might await with perfect faith, but which had no immediate relevance to my life.

A deep suspicion of ideology kept him away from tightly organised political groups, especially the Communists, who he had seen disrupt Socialist meetings, and whom, in the person of some student activists he knew, he distrusted, at least prior to the Popular Front days.

Kazin's entry into literary journalism came through a meeting with John Chamberlain, a man who made 'radicalism seem as American as baseball.' Chamberlain was then in a pro-communist phase, had a job as a reviewer for *The New York Times*, and had established a reputation with a book called *Farewell to Reform*, a radical critique of the Progressive movement in America which ended by suggesting that revolution not reform was the right way forward. Chamberlain's views later changed, so much so that he worked for right-wing magazines in the fifties and sixties. But in 1934 he was sufficiently sympathetic to Kazin's views and situation to help him pick up some work as a book reviewer for the *New Republic* and *Scribner's*. It was a breakthrough, and an early one, considering that Kazin was only nineteen, and it gave him a direction.

To my surprise – I had never thought of criticism as an occupation – I suddenly found a way of writing, a form, a path to the outside world. The *New Republic* was not merely a publication but a cause and the centre of many causes. I had a chance to meet writers in a society which in 1934 was still not far removed from the old Bohemia of Greenwich Village and Chelsea.

And Kazin's writing wasn't done in a social vacuum. He mixed with people concerned about current events – 'I had arrived at the *New Republic* to be told with grim satisfaction by Otis Ferguson, the assistant literary editor, that a general strike had just broken out in San Francisco' – and he was himself aware of what was happening at home and abroad, and how a new breed of writers was breaking into print. Kazin noted that the rebels from the twenties had mostly come from 'good' families – John Dos Passos, Hemingway, Edmund Wilson, Malcolm Cowley, were all in that category – but, as he said in *Starting Out in the Thirties*, the radicals now 'came from anywhere,' and he recalled some of them:

> Robert Cantwell had worked in a plywood factory in the far West, learning the craft of the novel from Henry James and imposing a highly literary symbolism on the factory system. James T. Farrell had worked as a clerk in an express company and in a cigar store. Edward Dahlberg's mother had run a barbershop in Kansas City and he had been a hobo before trying his luck at college. Albert Halper had worked in a mail-order house in Chicago. Daniel Fuchs came from one Brooklyn slum, Williamsburg, and Henry Roth from another, Brownsville; Richard Wright from a tenant farm in Mississippi; John Steinbeck had worked on farms and in a sugar refinery, and had laid bricks for the new Madison Square Garden; Erskine Caldwell, though his father was a Presbyterian minister, had worked as a mill labourer, farm hand and waiter; Nelson Algren had tended a filling station in Texas and Henry Miller had worked up and down New York before driving himself wild as a personnel boss at Western Union. With ideology or without ideology, they were typical of the new writers who came up in the Thirties, and they understandably flourished their experience, their hard knocks, their life on the road, their days on the picket line and in the hiring hall.

Starting Out in the Thirties is one of the most vivid memoirs of the period, at least from the point of view of a sensitive young man slowly establishing himself as a writer and responding to events and personalities. It is full of references to writers such as those mentioned above and others like Nathanael West and Clifford Odets. Kazin grew more sympathetic to the Communist Party for a time, when it seemed to be taking the lead in organising resistance to Fascism. He recalls meetings at which André Malraux and the British novelist and International Brigade volunteer Ralph Bates appealed for aid for the Spanish Republic. He was, he says,

> Tired of virtue, and now wanted to see some action. In the midst of the violent labour unrest in France, the great sit-down strikes in

American factories, the beginnings of the CIO, everything at home and abroad seemed to call for the same revolutionary energy.

But he was not wholly committed to communism as an ideology, nor as a way of life, as so many young writers and intellectuals seemed to be. The Moscow Trials, with their obvious show element, shocked him, and in any case his overriding concern was for cultural matters, something likely to set him apart from those who thought that politics ought to take priority. As he worked on the book that was to be published as *On Native Grounds* he wanted to reach back to 'our real literary brethren in the utopian and Socialist bohemians of 1912,' and he felt 'radicalism as a spiritual passion.' Writing literary criticism was a way of dealing with social matters, and he quotes Van Wyck Brooks on the relationship between literary and social criticism:

> Literary criticism is always impelled sooner or later to become social criticism ... because the future of our literature and art depends upon the wholesale reconstruction of a social life all the elements of which are as united in a sort of conspiracy against the growth and freedom of the spirit.

It was a summing up which, in many ways, described Kazin's own approach to writing.

New York during the war years, was 'a world city full of freedom, openness, hope.' Rejected for military service, Kazin continued to write, though broadening his work to take in reportage about the war effort at home and, later, abroad, and he also acted as a consultant to the Office of War Information. The massive governmental structure co-opted many intellectuals into working for the State in one role or another, albeit in the fight against fascism, and led to significant changes in the general status of radical intellectuals in the post-war years. But Kazin was still essentially free-lancing in the early forties. *On Native Grounds* had brought him some success in the intellectual community, though the five years it had taken to write it had been a time of part-time teaching, and occasional book-reviewing. What it significantly did was demonstrate how Kazin, a Jew from a poor background, had a close identification with American literature, something not necessarily true of slightly older New York Intellectuals, who often looked to Europe as much as America. American culture was Kazin's main focus, and Norman Podhoretz tellingly summarised the difference:

> When [Philip] Rahv, of the first generation, wrote about American literature – and he did so with originality and depth in several seminal essays – it was with the eye of the learned outsider. When the twenty-five-year-old Kazin, of the second generation, turned his amazingly precocious attention on the same subject in *On Native Grounds*, it was with the aggressive conviction that this literature was *his*.

Kazin's activities after the publication of *On Native Grounds* are recorded in *New York Jew*, his third autobiographical book. Amongst other things, he visited Hollywood, where he met one-time members of the Group Theatre, the famed radical New York theatrical unit, who had turned to working in films and were now sunning themselves by their swimming pools while still going through the motions of support for the Communist Party. Kazin's view of their compromises is harsh, the Hollywood affluence with its status symbols and cultural poverty clearly at odds with his own ideas of what is worthwhile in life. But he did also point out that many of the people concerned suffered for their early commitments when Hollywood began to purge its left-wingers in the late forties and early fifties.

He had a similarly doubtful view of a brief experience teaching at Black Mountain College in North Carolina. It had been founded in 1933 by John Andrew Rice, a dissident classics professor, as an alternative to the established higher education establishments. It's probably best known now for the period from the late 1940s to its closure in 1957, when Charles Olson dominated it and writers like Robert Creeley and Fielding Dawson were on campus, but in the late 1930s and the war years it had on its staff a number of 'gifted refugees,' amongst them the 'Bauhaus painter and master teacher Josef Albers, the Czech conductor Heinrich Jalowtez, the German psychiatrist Erwin

Strauss, the musicologist Edward Lowinsky.' Kazin's view of the student body was less enthusiastic, and he described some of them as 'waifs, psychic and intellectual orphans, children of agitated professional families in agitated New York, Cambridge and Chicago,' and he also noted that there was a constant stream of visitors:

> Artists from New York like Robert Motherwell, conscientious objectors on their way to and from the mental hospitals they served in as orderlies, vagrant idealists a decade before hippiedom who flopped on the college steps and wanted to live with us Thoreau's life of the spirit.

There is, perhaps, in Kazin's comments on the 'psychic and intellectual orphans' and the 'vagrant idealists' something of the puritanism of the autodidact, the man who had few advantages and had to obtain his education the hard way in public libraries and by systematic reading.

Kazin also visited England, arriving in Liverpool, where what he saw put him in mind of Melville's comment a century before: 'Poverty, poverty, poverty, in almost endless vistas: and want and woe staggered in arms along those miserable streets.' England, he thought, had never recovered from its industrial revolution:

> Along the docks everything was as dark and grimy as in the first days. Iron bridges overhead between the solid tiers of ware houses, high stone walls, cobbled passageways along which ran beautiful children red-cheeked in the cold. Would they become these men with working-class caps and scarves and yellow teeth who worked in that maze of shadows?

Talking about the impact of the war on English society, and the way in which the middle and upper classes had been forced to mix with their fellow-countrymen, Kazin says: 'Nowhere else in the Western world would the revelation of what one's own people looked like have come as such a shock. But some English still did not regard other English as people at all.' He adds: 'England was a social battleground. The English liked class differences. They thrived on the social drama.' He perceives that the working-class

could be more hide-bound and exclusive than royalty. Their customs
and traditions – even the rows of houses back to back – seemed dearer
to some than any possible ending of the class struggle. Their separate
speech, their pubs, their low feeding habits, their ancient bitter humour
were sacred to themselves.

Writing, always writing, working as an editor on various magazines,
teaching, Kazin observed the rise of anti-communism as an intellectual
trend in the late 1940s and early 1950s:

> The atmosphere was heavy with souped-up patriotism, and radiating
> from the many disillusioned and fretful ex-radicals like a new weapon,
> it was also intensely religious. All evil was now to be attached to
> communism, no doubt because some former communists felt their old
> attachment so intensely.

Loyalty hearings spread across America, in government offices,
schools, factories. People confessed to past affiliations and named names
or they lost their jobs. Sometimes they confessed and named names,
and still lost their jobs. Others took advantage of the situation:

> In New York many left-wing intellectuals, having just discovered that
> America stood for freedom and that Russian despotism was probably
> incurable, emerged from their proud longstanding 'alienation' to lead
> the new ideological crusade.

In *New York Jew*, Kazin bitterly records how some of the worst aspects
of literary life, the personal animosities, could be turned to advantage
by disguising them as righteous political struggles:

> Delmore Scwartz turned his many literary hatreds into political hatreds.
> Robert Lowell at Yaddo was to bring charges that the director, a devoted
> friend to many writers over the years, was a link to Soviet agents.

It was a bad time and Kazin recalls that 'the demand for orthodoxy'
suffocated him, though he accepted that, whatever its failures and
problems, America offered more than Russia, and that he had never

been one of those who went overboard for communism in the thirties. His social criticism, like his literary criticism, had always been directed from an independent radical position.

That position made it difficult for him to settle into what he refers to as 'the smug professional domesticity of the fifties' when he took on academic work and tried living in a small college town. He needed the more exciting intellectual challenge of New York, even though he was, over the years, to teach in a variety of universities across America. The fifties and sixties brought him relative prosperity and even a degree of fame. He was invited to meet President Kennedy, an encounter he described in a cool essay, 'The President and Other Intellectuals,' which didn't please either Kennedy or Kissinger. And one senses a slight unease with the success and its material rewards. 'We were all looking very well after ourselves,' he says, but the larger picture was unsettling. The sixties were years of 'sexual riot that praised itself as radical politics,' and people denied history: 'the past did not exist unless you had lived it yourself. There was no historical memory if you chose not to have one.' He had noted in an essay published in 1959 how contemporary novels so often focused on 'the self and its detractors,' and he quoted Tocqueville's observation that, 'in modern times the average man is absorbed in a very puny object, himself, to the point of satiety.' the result being in literature that 'we get novels in which society is merely a backdrop to the aloneness of the hero.' All these concerns, whether expressed in essays, short book reviews, or his three volumes of autobiography, point to Kazin as someone who, whatever his own social circumstances, is impelled to comment on the world he lives in and to make literary criticism into social criticism. It has always been a two-way process, of course, with the social criticism commenting on literary qualities. In a brief 1957 review of Nelson Algren's *A Walk on the Wild Side* he compared it unfavourably to an earlier Algren novel:

> It can be said, I think, that the characters in that harrowing and grimly honest book, *The Man with the Golden Arm*, were also freaks of a kind, and that this was the secret of Mr Algren's attraction to them. But although that book was equally sentimental and editorial in style, it was

about something real; the life and death of a man. And it was written out of such a genuine belief in determinism that any reader could feel life mercilessly crowding down on Frankie Machine. The book made sense, it hurt like a blow, because Mr Algren saw his lost and damned characters as victims of a system. He showed us how all parts of the system, from the politicians crowding the police at election time down to the smallest crooks, worked on and against each other to make up the iron meanness of Chicago. This new book shows, all too clearly, that Mr Algren's usual material no longer points an accusing finger at anything or anybody. It is just 'picturesque'.

It's a brilliant exposition of Kazin using his criticism to talk about books and society in equal measure, and with the comment flowing in both directions.

In his most recent book, the short but memorable *Writing Was Everything*, Alfred Kazin offers a brief summary of his life, builds it around the books he has read, the writers and intellectuals he has known, and the ideas he has applied his mind to, and ends it with a moving tribute to the power of the poetry of Czeslaw Milosz, which he contrasts to 'our 'alienated' poetry, full of introspective anxiety and artifice.' And he says of Milosz:

> Poetry to him is profoundly a recall, not a mere presentation of lived experience. It resembles what he calls 'the cries of Job,' not our endless defences and explorations of the ego.

Milosz, Kazin believes, is the kind of writer who knows

> in his heart that somehow, somewhere, despite the cruel wisdom of the age that nothing is less probable or perhaps less desirable, all lines do intersect. This kind of writer goes against the grain of those who now deride E.M. Forster's 'Only Connect!' as old-fashioned, too simple, too wistful.
>
> These ideologies ignore the imponderables of existence that are still with us after all the works of science, technology, analytical philosophy, psychology, deconstruction, or linguistics, after all the political, racial and sexual debate so hot in the academy. For the ideologues, there is no world except the one right in front of their eyes. And in this world nothing lasts; books are as perishable as magazines, advertisements,

movies, or television; and the academy is so preoccupied with status that it can proclaim literature to be only a branch of criticism, just another 'discourse.'

Those words, with their belief in the value of literature and their contempt for those who would abuse it, sum up Kazin's lifelong approach to writing. Neither a novelist, nor a poet, he has nonetheless created literature by writing about it in his criticism and his autobiographical works in a way that dignifies both the subject-matter and his treatment of it.

Finally, let me quote Kazin, again from *Writing Was Everything*, on what real criticism ought to do. It doesn't tell anyone how or what to read, he says, and in the following words one can hear the old autodidact at work:

> For many years now, academics high and low have pre-empted serious criticism, have been riding hard on students who are so unused to general reading that they have little taste of their own and are glad to be told how to read, especially what to discount. This will get them closer and closer to the work of art. What nonsense. What gets us closer to a work of art is not instruction but another work of art. Only a plurality of choices can open up the new *thinking* in a work of literature that excites and liberates us.

It is the purpose of good criticism to draw our attention to that 'plurality of choices,' not to choose for us, and Alfred Kazin's work can rightly be said to be good criticism. And good literature.

Note

Kazin's three volumes of autobiography are: *A Walker in the City* (Harcourt, Brace & World, New York, 1951); *Starting Out in the Thirties* (Secker & Warburg, London, 1966); *New York Jew* (Secker & Warburg, London, 1978). *Writing Was Everything* was published by Harvard University Press, 1995. Amongst his other books are: *The Inmost Leaf: Essays on American and European Writers* (Harcourt Brace Jovanovich,

New York, 1979); *Contemporaries: Essays on Modern Life and Literature* (Secker & Warburg, London, 1963); *An American Procession* (Secker & Warburg, London, 1985); *A Writer's America: Landscape in Literature* (Thames & Hudson, London, 1988). *On Native Grounds* was originally published by Reynal & Hitchcock, New York, 1942, though there have been later reprints.

Lionel Abel's famous attack, 'A Critic Without a Country: Alfred Kazin's Grand Procession,' can be found in his *Important Nonsense* (Prometheus Books, Buffalo, 1987), and Sidney Hook's comments on Kazin are in *Out of Step: An Unquiet Life in the 20th Century* (Harper & Row, New York, 1981). Of the various histories of the New York Intellectuals, Alexander Bloom's *Prodigal Sons* (Oxford University Press, New York, 1986) and Alan Wald's *The New York Intellectuals* (The University of North Carolina Press, Chapel Hill, 1987) are particularly informative about Kazin.

A Lifetime Burning in Every Moment: From the Journals of Alfred Kazin (Harper Collins, New York, 1996) appeared after this piece was written. Kazin died in 1998.

IRVING HOWE, 1995

When Irving Howe died in 1993 one of the tributes paid to him was that he was 'a man of books and of journals, and not of the media,' and reading that it struck me how true it was. You somehow couldn't imagine Howe happily participating in slick chat shows, nor could you see him churning out quick newspaper pieces which simply tried to attract attention by being controversial. Howe was from a different tradition, where intellectual depth was required and it was expected that a writer would have a commitment to something other than mere personal advancement. He was often linked to that 'herd of independent minds,' the New York Intellectuals, and yet he was very much his own man. When other New York writers and critics gave up on political involvement, or swung to the right, Howe continued to keep the faith by espousing socialist ideals.

But who was he and where did he come from? He wasn't perhaps well-known in this country, though some of his books were published here, and a man who could seriously state that his ambition was to be an intellectual is likely to be treated as if he's some sort of oddball and viewed with suspicion. The British are rarely comfortable with people whose chief currency is based on ideas, but Howe's high-mindedness never caused him to be pompous, though he always refused to compromise by lowering the level of his arguments.

He was born in the Bronx in 1920, the son of poor Jewish parents.

The area formed a thick tangle of streets crammed with Jewish immigrants from eastern Europe, almost all of them poor. We lived in narrow five-story tenements, wall flush against wall, and with slate-coloured stoops rising sharply in front. There never was enough space. The buildings, clenched into rows, looked down upon us like sentinels, and the apartments in the buildings were packed with relatives and children, many of them fugitives from unpaid rents. The tenements had first gone up during the early years of the century, and if not quite as grimy as those of the Lower East Side in Manhattan or the Brownsville section of Brooklyn, they were bad enough.

Howe's picture of those years, as he later painted it in *A Margin of Hope*, is vivid and compelling. His parents worked in the garment trade after his father's grocery store failed during the Depression, and Howe, as a thirteen-year-old, was pulled into the world of the left as the 1933 strike brought out garment workers all over New York. It was a significant experience for him, and he remembered how, once the strike was won, his family lived a little better and even managed to buy him a new shirt:

> The garment unions were an essential part of the immigrant life, helping to ease its hardships and giving our people a fragment of dignity. In later years, whenever I heard intellectuals of the Right or Left attack unionism, I would be seized by an uncontrollable rage that then gave way to frustration, how to explain to young people what the strike of 1933 had meant, how to find words to tell of the small comforts the union had brought, meat on the table and 'grown-up' shirts?

It was typical of Howe that he never forgot his background, nor what it meant to be poor and what trade unionists and others had done to improve matters. In this respect it's important to provide an account of his early years as a guide to what came later. He joined the Young People's Socialist League when he was fourteen and was soon involved with the argumentative life of the left.

> For several decades European Socialists had been struggling to work out a political response to liberal government enacting welfare reforms (social security, unemployment insurance, public works, pensions, and so forth) within capitalist society. For American Socialists this had

hardly been a problem, since the welfare state – what passes for one among us – came here later than in Europe. The far right of the European social democracy virtually blended into welfare liberalism, contenting itself with modest reforms. The far left, while not opposed to such reforms, saw them as mere palliatives and tried to maintain a revolutionary perspective. Between these polar tendencies wobbled the social democratic centre, dominant in most of the parties, which favoured reform programmes while maintaining – sometimes only on Sundays – a commitment to basic change. Similar divisions now flared up in the American movement, and all through the early 1930s they took a fierce, even ugly form. The problem was new to American Socialists, who had often contented themselves with sweeping denunciations of 'the system.' The very smallness of the movement in America made it almost certain that ideological disputes would be fought to the edge of death.

This factional fighting, so typical of the time and place but later even flavouring the cultural battles of the 1950s and beyond, continued when Howe went to the City College of New York and became involved with Trotskyism. It was a period of high hopes and intellectual ferment, as Howe explained in *A Margin of Hope*:

> The culture of New York was then still a culture of the word. For many young people the public library was still a place of refreshment and pleasure. Daily newspapers were numerous, but not yet challenged by other 'media.' Theatres presented plays with acknowledged scripts. Serious magazines really influenced educated opinion. Men with free time gathered in cafeterias and parks to discuss politics. Political campaigns meant speechmaking, not just handshaking. A high-school graduate would have read at least a novel by Dickens and a play by Shakespeare. There was a shared belief in the value – indeed, the honour – of gaining a high-school diploma, even among many who did not stay long enough to get it. This was not utopia, far from it. But the city did have a unity of culture, and that unity has since been broken.

Howe attended CCNY between 1936 and 1940, with 'a mediocre record, except for an unplanned course that lured me into unplanned enthusiasm.' The formal syllabus rarely provided the stimulus he needed, and some of the teaching was of poor quality, though Howe recognised that the nature of CCNY, with its heavy teaching loads and high turnover of students, didn't lend itself to first-rate tuition. The college had something of an open-door policy at a time when student numbers elsewhere were restricted and Jewish students, in particular, found it difficult to gain admittance to other establishments. But extra-curricular activities were important, and Howe said that the Trotskyist movement was 'my school in politics, my school in life,' and that it was his real introduction to the world of ideas and literature, especially literary modernism.

> The Trotskyists tilted towards highbrow culture. Trotsky set an example through his own skilful literary criticism and his friendship with André Breton and Diego Rivera. The first American follower of Trotsky had been the talented writer Max Eastman, and the main spokesmen in America were [Max] Shachtman and [James] Burnham, both intellectuals. Furthermore, our fondness for nuance and casuistry predisposed at least some of us to the problematic modes of modernist literature.

The drab cultural aims and interests of too many communists and socialists were not those of the Trotskyists.

After leaving CCNY, Howe spent a short time as editor of *Labour Action*, a Trotskyist magazine, and then went into the army. When he returned to New York in the mid-1940s he realised that things were changing. The war years had brought a boom in employment, and most left-wing parties and groups had increased their memberships, but the Cold War was soon to bring a clampdown on left-wingers, and the expansion in both the American and European economies persuaded many people that the need for radical action was past. Howe went back to working for the Trotskyists, but doubts were creeping in:

> Now we were all a little older and the question of earning a living, once so jauntily brushed aside, took on an urgency it could not have had in the Depression years. Meanwhile our political expectations were crumbling. The capitalist world, by no means in its 'final crisis,' was entering several decades of economic expansion, so that whatever remained of American radicalism was bound to suffer confusion.

There is a short story, 'The Party,' by the now almost forgotten Isaac Rosenfeld, which was published in 1947 and neatly satirised the

Trotskyists and their impossible dreams. As Howe said, 'Rosenfeld's story hurt to the point of rage, perhaps because we knew that in its fantastic way it was scraping against the truth.'

Howe had always read extensively, and developed his literary as well as his political interests, and he began to publish literary criticism in magazines. He worked with Dwight Macdonald on *Politics*, obtained work, almost by accident, as a book reviewer for *Time*, and began to contribute to *Partisan Review*, virtually the house magazine for the New York Intellectuals, and 'the vibrant centre of our intellectual life ... its prestige still high in the late forties.' He had almost abandoned his Trotskyist involvements and, like many of his friends, was

> beginning to see that for us the prime value was democracy, and that without it we could not even imagine a desirable socialism. The casual talk about 'revolution' one might still occasionally hear was a mere verbal hangover. We were becoming Social Democrats or, if you prefer, democratic Socialists.

This seems to me to highlight Howe's movement towards the world he was to become identified with, that of the New York Intellectuals, as well as towards the combination of political commitment (along the lines he outlined) and literary criticism that occupied him for the rest of his life. It was a time when

> What began to absorb the New York writers was a search for some principle by which to order the world after Hitler, culture after the Holocaust. The idea of centrality replaced the ideology of Marxism, though the idea can be seen as a stepchild of the ideology. To be central meant to engage with questions that gave our time its peculiarly terrible character.

Howe thought that the idea of the central was 'slippery,' which was what made it attractive in some ways, though this could lead to problems. People searched for something they could call 'central' and, as a result, novelty flourished, ideology declined, and personalities bloomed. Howe himself was slowly

stumbling upon an idea that could be traced back to Matthew Arnold
and would soon be picked up by Randall Jarrell: that in a secular age
literary criticism carries a heavy burden of intention, becoming a
surrogate mode of speech for people blocked in public life. Unable to
fulfil directly their vision of politics, morality and religion critics transfer
these to the seemingly narrower channels of literary criticism.

And he further noted that 'the most valuable critics have often doubled
as cultural spokesmen, moral prophets, political insurgents.'

Along with this realisation of the possibilities of literary criticism came
a reappraisal of the role of the great modernist writers. Pound, Eliot,
Yeats, and others were not lovers of democracy, and though Howe had,
at one time, considered that modernist art and modernist politics
(Trotskyism) went hand-in-hand, he was slowly changing his mind:

> It became fashionable in the early decades of this century for advanced
> writers – Joyce stands out as a wonderful exception! – to dismiss liberal
> democracy as a breeding ground of the mediocre masses and thereby
> an enemy of high culture. No, the union between cultural modernism
> and independent radicalism was neither a proper marriage nor a secure
> liaison, it was a meeting between parties hurrying in opposite directions,
> brief, hectic, messy.

The late 1940s debate about the activities of Ezra Pound ('a profascist
and anti-Semitic writer even if he had written the best poetry of 1948')
crystallised matters for Howe, and he asserted that, when aesthetic
standards and human values clash, as they did in Pound's case, then
the latter should be seen as primary. In *A Margin of Hope* he quoted a
marvellous passage from a piece by Clement Greenberg:

> I am sick of the art-adoration that prevails among cultured people,
> more in our time than in any other: that art-silliness which condones
> almost any moral or intellectual failing on the artist's part as long as
> he is or seems a successful artist. Psychopathy has become endemic
> among artists and writers, in whose company the moral idiot is tolerated
> as perhaps nowhere else in society.

It's fascinating to see Howe's working out of the position he was to adopt, give or take minor shifts of emphasis, for the rest of his life.

Of course, the practical dilemma of how to earn a living had to be dealt with, especially as subtle changes were taking place in intellectual life. Howe noted that 'a major shift in cultural demography began in the 1950s, the dispersion of literary people from urban centres and bohemian enclaves to university towns across the continent.' He wanted to stand against this dispersal of energies, as it seemed to him, but had to face up to the fact that the 'lines of separation that had defined intellectual life – lines between high and middlebrow, radical and acquiescent, serious and popular – were becoming blurred.' How best to find a way to survive, doing worthwhile work, in such a situation? Invitations to teach began to come in, and Howe accepted a post at Brandeis University,

> a remarkable place mixing college, political forum, and kibbutz, where the abundant energies of Jewish intellectuals – some of them free-lancers from New York and others refugees from Germany – found bread, speech, and audiences.

It was 1953 when Howe went to Brandeis, and after that his life was, from the point of view of a steady income, centred on academic work. He taught at Stanford University, and for many years at City University New York, but he always maintained a connection with the wider world through politics and his role as a social critic, his aim being to 'write literary criticism like that which Edmund Wilson or George Orwell wrote.' And he wanted 'to be an intellectual, one of those free-ranging speculative writers who grapple with the troubles of their time yet command some of the accumulated knowledge of the past.' He wasn't content to be an academic whose writing simply reflected what he taught. His next move demonstrated that quite clearly.

'When intellectuals can do nothing else they start a magazine,' Howe wrote in 1954 as he and several others founded *Dissent*, the publication he was to be identified with for the next forty years. And he later commented '*Dissent* arose out of the decomposition of American socialism or what tattered bits and pieces of it remained in the fifties,' a time when the Cold War, McCarthyism, and affluence, were combining to reduce interest in radical ideas to something pushed to the fringes of society. The magazine, financed by supporters and contributors, with the latter agreeing to write for nothing as well as giving donations to keep it going, pledged to combat conformism, to defend humanist and radical values, fight totalitarianism of any kind, and begin a dialogue with liberal opinion. And it also affirmed a belief in socialism. The launching of *Dissent* coincided with an important essay that Howe wrote for *Partisan Review*. It was designed as an attack on those one-time liberals who, Howe said, were now making their peace with the state, and he challenged this new orthodoxy. 'Intellectuals,' he wrote, 'far from thinking of themselves as a desperate opposition, have been enjoying a return to the bosom of the nation.' He agreed that there were tremendous pressures to conform, but insisted that there were greater virtues 'in preserving the attitude of critical scepticism and distance.' Howe was not the only New York writer to notice what was happening. Philip Rahv wrote that 'the intellectual bohemian or proletarian has turned into a marginal figure nowadays, reminding us in his rather quixotic aloneness of the ardours and truancies of the past.' In Howe's view,

> the institutional world of government, corporation, and mass culture needs intellectuals *because* they are intellectuals, but it does not want them as intellectuals. It needs them for their skills, knowledge, inclinations, even passions, without which they would be of no use. But it does not look too kindly upon, indeed does all it can to curb their traditional role as free-wheeling critics who direct their barbs not only upon enemies, but friends and allies, too.

And when intellectuals 'become absorbed into the accredited institutions of society they not only lose their traditional rebelliousness but to one extent or another they cease to function as intellectuals.' It is, of course, possible to see Howe himself, newly accepted into academic life, worrying away at how it would affect his role as social critic, but this doesn't lessen the value of his comments. And it's also possible to understand that starting *Dissent* was, perhaps, a means of maintaining some sort of independence, and an outlet through which he could channel his radical tendencies.

This is not the place to attempt a history of *Dissent* which, over the years, mixed matters of immediate concern with long-term political strategies and a range of cultural topics, but Howe was always heavily involved in both producing and writing for the magazine. He did much of the routine work of editing, raised funds, and somehow also managed to fulfil his academic tasks and additionally wrote a number of books on a variety of subjects, including histories of American communism and American socialism, critical studies of William Faulkner, Thomas Hardy, and Sherwood Anderson, a book on Trotsky, and several collections of essays. He edited a number of anthologies, some of them of Yiddish literature, and put together collections of the essential works on socialism and the writings of Trotsky. Two of his most important works were *Politics and the Novel* and *World of our Fathers*. In his survey of 'political novels,' Howe considered the general idea of how and why writers deal with politics in their work and looked at specific examples by Conrad, Stendhal, Turgenev, Koestler, Orwell, and others. It was written, he said, 'at a moment when I was gradually drifting away from orthodox Marxism ... orthodox Marxism in its serious versions, not the corrupt authoritarian slogans of the Communist movement.'

World of our Fathers is generally regarded as Howe's finest work, and is, probably, the one that will survive the passage of time. Researched over many years, it recreates the turbulent world of New York's Lower East Side when it was mostly a Jewish ghetto, with its Yiddish newspapers and poets, its pushcarts and dreamers, its sweat-shops and the unions that tried to change them, and its long history of work, family, culture, and dissent. As Howe said:

> We cannot be our fathers, we cannot live like our mothers, but we may look to their experience for images of rectitude and purities of devotion. It is the single commanding power of the Yiddish tradition that it seems immediately and insistently to thrust before us the most fundamental questions of human existence: how shall we live? What are the norms by which we can make judgements of the 'good life'? What modes of conduct may enable us to establish a genuine community?

And he added:

> We need not overvalue the immigrant Jewish experience in order to
> feel a lasting gratitude for having been part of it. A sense of natural
> piety towards one's origins can live side by side with a spirit of critical
> detachment. We take pleasure in having been related to those self-
> educated workers, those sustaining women, those almost-forgotten
> writers and speakers devoted to excitements of controversy and thought.

It was a personal note, and yet could apply to the feelings of many
people reflecting on their roots.

Howe achieved a small measure of fame with his book and admitted
to feeling uneasy about it and almost relieved when he once again
became 'simply a stoop-shouldered man with a bald spot' who could
sit unrecognised in a restaurant.

Towards the end of his life Howe produced a short piece for *Dissent*
in which he outlined his belief in the need to dream, to have a concept
of utopia always in mind, even if not in a scientific or systematic sense.
As early as 1954 Howe and Lewis Coser, with whom he co-operated
on various projects, had written an essay in which they looked at
different utopian theorists (Saint-Simon, Fourier, Cabet, etc.) and noted
their tendency to be dogmatic and even tyrannical, if it suited their
purpose. But, they pointed out, 'Utopia without egalitarianism, utopia
dominated by aristocracy of the mind, must quickly degenerate into a
vision of useful slavery.' As a rider to this, however, they said that 'a
life without some glimmer of a redeeming future [is] a life cut off from
the distinctively human.' Almost forty years later Howe reiterated his
conviction of the necessity of hope. What he called 'the great historical
disaster' of the decline and fall of the communist dream had led to
suspicion of radical politics generally, and the consequence was 'an
interval of weariness, disillusionment, pragmatism, and diminished
expectations.' The exhaustion could clearly be seen in the so-called
intellectual journals:

Some are sour (usually edited by ex-radicals) and others are timid (usually edited by quasiliberals). Some subsist by mocking the hopes of their youth. Others avoid any long-range expectations or desires. Still others narrow their focus of concern to the daily routines of politics, sometimes saying useful things, though not much more.

What Howe observed wasn't just typical of America, and although he didn't decry dealing with the immediate he stressed that long-range options were of equal importance. It was necessary to 'avoid the provincialism of the immediate,' and

> utopianism is a necessity of the moral imagination. It doesn't necessarily entail a particular politics; it doesn't ensure wisdom about current affairs. What it does provide is a guiding perspective, a belief or hope for the future, an understanding that nothing is more mistaken than the common notion that what exists today will continue to exist tomorrow. This kind of utopianism is really another way of appreciating the variety and surprise that history makes possible – possible, nothing more. It is a testimony to the resourcefulness that humanity now and then displays (together with other, far less attractive characteristics). It is a claim for the value of desire, the practicality of yearning – as against the deadliness of acquiescing in the 'given' simply because it is here.

This version of utopianism was not only Howe's personal belief, but also what he wanted *Dissent* to represent, and to those who had their doubts about this position, he said: 'to friend and foe, at a moment when the embers of utopianism seem very low, I'd say: You want to call us utopians? That's fine with me.'

Irving Howe was not without his critics, and anyone interested in knowing what they had to say can easily refer to the histories of the New York Intellectuals and the memoirs of individual writers and activists, such as Sidney Hook and Norman Podhoretz. But even those who didn't necessarily agree with him politically often admired his integrity. Alfred Kazin remarked that, as other one-time radicals exploited the 'cynical possibilities of ex-Marxist opportunism,' he 'looked to Irving Howe to uphold a fundamental standard of decency.' And Kazin pointed out that, at a time when too many were swayed by political correctness into lowering standards, the more he 'looked to Irving to remind a

negligent administration of a teacher's duty to stimulate the mind, not
to flatter the helpless. And it took an autodidact to do that.'

Howe's daughter remembered that he had 'conveyed to me a deep
love of literature,' and that his collection of books 'was fascinating,' but
she also made it clear that 'he was a man of many worlds, and I marvel
at how this was reflected in his day-to-day reading.' And others spoke
of the breadth of his knowledge. Leon Wieseltier, who was not at all
in agreement with Howe's socialism, knew Howe and liked him. Howe,
he said, 'understood the importance of the common touch, even if he
lacked it. He suspected things that dazzled. He liked ideas more than
theories, reasonableness more than correctness.' Wieseltier also stated
that Howe's 'greatest thrill was high art that felt democratic,' which is
why he wrote books about Anderson, Faulkner and Hardy, 'masters of
form who found in ordinary people difficulty and dignity enough,' and
why he loved Walt Whitman's poetry. And he added, perhaps slyly, that
he always thought of Howe as 'a welfare-state liberal with a fluency in
the Marxist tradition.' In the end, though, the labels don't matter. It's
the motives that count, and Irving Howe had the right ones.

Note

I've tried to use Howe's own words as much as possible, and have drawn
extensively from *A Margin of Hope: An Intellectual Autobiography* (Secker &
Warburg, London, 1983). Many of his important essays are in *Selected
Writings* 1950-1990 (Harcourt Brace Jovanovich, New York, 1990), and
a smaller, posthumously published collection, *A Critic's Notebook* (Harcourt
Brace & Co., New York, 1994) has some of his shorter literary pieces,
with clear, concise comments on Arnold Bennett, Kipling, Dickens,
Tolstoy, and others he admired. *Politics and the Novel*, originally published
in 1957, was re-issued by Columbia University Press, New York, in 1992.
World of our Fathers appeared in various editions and the one I used was
published by Harcourt Brace Jovanovich, New York, 1976. Finally, an
anthology, *Legacy of Dissent*, with a selection of material from *Dissent*
magazine, was published in 1994 by Simon & Schuster, New York.

GREENWICH VILLAGE, 1995

Greenwich Village: Culture and Counterculture edited by Rick Beard and
Leslie Cohen Berlowitz. Rutgers University Press, 1993.
Greenwich Village 1963: Avant-Garde Performance and the Effervescent Body
by Salley Barnes. Duke University Press, 1993.

Greenwich Village is synonymous with bohemianism. Caroline
Ware, in her authoritative survey, *Greenwich Village: 1920-1930*
(Houghton Miflin, Boston, 1935, reprinted 1994 by University of
California Press), said that although the Village was not the only place
in America where artists and social rebels congregated, it was the most
notorious. And its notoriety spread outside America, so that, like
Montparnasse in Paris, it was identified in the public mind with poets,
painters, free love, drunken excess, poverty, garrets, and even, now
and then, the production of a poem or painting. Things are different
now, and bohemia has lost some of its magic as its surface
manifestations have filtered into the wider society. Little bohemias can
be found everywhere, and it's difficult to tell who is a genuine bohemian.
What many people imagine to be the fashions of bohemianism are
often displayed by arts association bureaucrats, college lecturers, and
other professionals. The real bohemians probably look quite ordinary,
maybe a little shabby. Perhaps they always did? After all, someone
trying to live an economically simple life and focus on writing or
painting can't afford to waste money and time on dressing well or in
style. I'm reminded of something that the sociologist Ned Polsky said
in his splendid essay, 'The Village Beat Scene: Summer 1960' (included
in the book, *Hustlers, Beats and Others*, Aldine Publishing, Chicago, 1967):

'Moreover, the large majority of beats do not flaunt their physical presence before the public gaze. Most beats dress in an ordinary lower-class manner, distinctive only to middle-class eyes.' The point is, of course, that genuine bohemianism has little or nothing to do with the way one dresses. It is, as the old anarchist bohemian Hippolyte Havel once said, a state of mind.

Still, it's a fact that certain places have been identified with bohemianism, and Greenwich Village is amongst the most famous of them. But the Village was never just an area for those with artistic interests to live in, and it is largely a twentieth-century development that it has been identified as such. It's true, writers, artists, and their followers did meet there prior to 1900, but not in a systematic way. There were practical reasons for being in the Village, whereas after 1900 or so the reasons often had more to do with the way in which the Village was perceived by both would-be rebels and the general public. A new class of young dissenters and intellectuals had come into being, and to move to the Village was a social statement and identified the people concerned with certain artistic, political, and sexual views.

Movements always attract publicity, and publicity has usually been something of a problem for bohemians. As individuals they often desire to be left alone, but as writers and artists they want their work to be noticed and are not against attention from journalists. The latter are frequently attracted to the lifestyle of bohemia, and may well be budding novelists or poets, but they are never averse to a colourful story. Nor to the money they can earn by writing it. Bohemia then attracts the attention of the curious, and as Jan Seidler Ramirez remarks in an essay in *Greenwich Village: Culture and Counterculture*: 'Once its unique attributes are exposed for study and imitation by those alien to it, bohemia is devitalised.' Interestingly, it seems that even before the end of the nineteenth century some writers were lamenting the invasion of bohemia by the philistines. Ramirez refers to the story by James L. Ford, published in 1895, in which a lively Italian restaurant patronised by impoverished writers in search of cheap food is invaded by middle-class tourists, with the result the prices increase and the atmosphere coarsens. Ford did have the honesty to point out that the restaurant becomes popular because one of the writers couldn't resist publicising its attractions.

So, there is, and always has been, something of an ambivalence at the heart of bohemia, and it has been particularly noticeable in Greenwich Village, set in the heart of a city which thrives on novelty and sensation. But I don't want to focus on the contradictions of bohemia, nor on its characters and charlatans. If you want to read about them, and about many of the more talented who spent time in the Village, you can easily refer to some of the standard histories of American bohemianism, such as Albert Parry's *Garrets and Pretenders* (Covoci-Friede, Chicago, 1933, reprinted by Dover Publications, New York, 1960) and Emily Hahn's *Romantic Rebels* (Houghton Miflin, Boston, 1967). Both will make clear that as well as the high jinks, and the allegations of poseurs spending more time talking about art than creating it, there was a great deal of worthwhile work turned out. Joe Gould and Maxwell Bodenheim may have wandered drunkenly around the Village, but the area was also home to Malcolm Cowley, Edmund Wilson, Mike Gold, Max Eastman, Floyd Dell, and many others. Even Bodenheim, before he succumbed to drink, had been a productive poet and novelist and not without talent. When I mention many of these names I'm largely dealing with a specific period in the history of Greenwich Village when art and politics mixed easily, and the radical magazine, *The Masses*, lambasted hypocrisy, capitalism, warmongering, and injustice, and eventually got itself closed down by the government. What is fascinating about this early period is that a mass of teachers, social workers, and political activists provided the backcloth against which the writers functioned. Bohemia of the kind I'm talking about had an intellectual substance sadly lacking in some later versions.

Several earlier books about Greenwich Village have concentrated on the pictorial aspects of its streets. Fred McDarrah's *Greenwich Village* (Corinth Books, New York, 1963) combined his evocative photographs with a general guide to the area, and Edmund T. Delaney's *New York's Greenwich Village* (Barre Publishers, Barre, 1968) combined an illustrated historical account with contemporary pictures. But *Greenwich Village: Culture and Counterculture*, whilst having many pictures, presents a series of essays which look at aspects of both social and cultural history. As I mentioned earlier, it's a mistake to assume that the Village was home to bohemians only. Many others have also lived there, especially Italians, and they've often provided the services that the bohemians used. The Italians, for example, owned restaurants and coffee houses frequented by bohemians. Relations were not always affable – the relaxed moral stance of some bohemians, and the presence of gays and lesbians, didn't appeal to Italians with strong views about family life and religion – but the various groups got along on the whole. Some observers did note that the arrival of bohemians, and especially affluent would-be bohemians, often had a negative effect in that the rents increased. A social worker familiar with the living conditions of poor families in Greenwich Village commented:

> It was certainly amusing and astounding to us who had fought against cellar lodgings as unhealthful, damp and unfit for human habitation, as they were, to see them revived as 'one-room studios' and let often at six times the price of the former rentals.

The history of the 'real' Village, with its mixture of bohemians, working-class Italians, and others, is fascinating, but most people naturally turn to the activities of the writers, painters, activists of various kinds, and the hangers-on they attracted, when reading about it. And several essays cater for this interest. Leslie Fishbein's 'The Culture of Contradiction' looks at the radicals of the pre-1917 period, and Daniel Aaron's 'Disturbers of the Peace' deals with the 1920s, when e.e. cummings, John Dos Passos, and the communist writer, Mike Gold, were among the leading lights of Village life. Another piece, by Barry Miles, is about the Beats and Greenwich Village, though it's largely taken from his Ginsberg biography, and consequently misses an opportunity to inspect the Village Beat scene in full, rather than through the activities of a few well known writers, some of them with only passing links to the area. It could be that the lives of some minor

Beats would provide a better picture of how important the Village was to the movement. A book like *How I Became Hettie Jones* (Penguin Books, New York, 1991), for example, gives a vivid view of the day-to-day bohemian life in the late 1950s and early 1960s. But the Beats weren't the only writers around at that time, and Alfred Kazin's brisk essay about the poets, playwrights and novelists associated with the Village does mention Isaac Rosenfeld and Anatole Broyard, even if only in passing. Both had strong links to the Village, portrayed it in their writing, and deserve a place in bohemian history.

The abstract expressionist painters also had Village connections, and one of the best essays, Irving Sandler's 'Avant-Garde Artists of Greenwich Village', looks at what Jackson Pollock, Mark Rothko, William de Kooning, and their contemporaries, got up to. It wasn't all just drinking and arguing in the Cedar Street Tavern, and Sandler gives a sample of the kind of talks heard by the artists when The Club, as their meetings were called, got together. All this was prior to what Sandler calls 'the commodification of art,' and driving it was 'the need to talk about art to sympathetic colleagues.' But they didn't look inwards, and they invited musicians, philosophers, social critics and writers, to address them, heard poetry readings by Frank O'Hara and John Ashbery, and gave a party for Dylan Thomas when he visited America. Bohemian life then had a quality which, I'd suggest, went into decline when the pop ethos took over.

Greenwich Village: Culture and Counterculture ranges over a fairly wide area, both in terms of subject matter and time, but *Greenwich Village 1963* centres on the year referred to and has little, or nothing, to say about the wider sociological issues of Village life. It is about the bohemians, or at least about people linked to the arts, in one way or another. According to Sally Barnes, 1963 was 'a year that would change American life and culture forever,' and it was the year when the Sixties really began. It's interesting to note, in this connection, that the Beat movement had, in the words of Seymour Krim, 'splintered and broken up' by 1963, and it's certainly true that most of the major work in the Beat canon had been created by then. There was still plenty of literary activity, of course, with the Black Mountain poets, the New York poets, and many others, publishing books, anthologies and magazines, but there was also an increasing emphasis on the visual and performing arts. Off-Broadway theatre, Happenings, underground film, dance and free jazz, all began to boom. This isn't to say that such things had not been around before, because they clearly had, but 1963 was the year when the activity seemed to reach a peak of innovation and experiment. There was a kind of spontaneous explosion of artistic endeavour in which there was a 'reinvention of community.' Sally Barnes's opening chapters are effective summaries of the build-up to 1963, and although necessarily sketchy they do provide a great deal of information. She rightly refers to Diane di Prima's influential magazine *The Floating Bear*, which was a meeting place in print for a wide variety of poets, musicians and others, though she overlooks another equally important publication, *Kulchur*, which attempted to present poetry alongside articles about music, dance, theatre and art, as well as politics and civil rights. It would seem to me that anyone wanting to sample the intellectual atmosphere of the early 1960s ought to consult both *The Floating Bear* and *Kulchur*. They were in existence prior to 1963 and continued for some years after, and between them provide a useful survey of what was seen as important and necessary. *The Floating Bear* was valuable because it mixed minor writers and scattered pieces with work from well-known poets, and so now offers a good guide to what was done generally rather than just by a few successful writers. *Kulchur* was a much tidier magazine, though the same people (Frank O'Hara, Ginsberg, LeRoi Jones, Charles Olson) often appeared in both, and used more criticism and essays, but it still captured the spirit of the time.

I don't want to give the impression that Sally Barnes's book is primarily about writers. Its subtitle, *Avant-Garde Performance and the Effervescent Body*, highlights its concern with theatre, especially that of The Living Theatre under the direction of Julian Beck and Judith Malina, with Happenings, dance and film. She catalogues a world which included Andy Warhol, John Cage, Claes Oldenberg, the then little known Sam Shepard and Harvey Keitel, and many others, and she points to the way in which they attempted to 'heal the various splits that Establishment culture had created – between mind and body, between artists and audience, between 'high art' and 'low art,' between art and science, and between art and life.' She also indicates that contradiction existed:

> There was an overriding moral imperative towards quality, but at the same time eccentricity and differences were celebrated. A yen for spiritual oneness was viewed ambivalently. It seems the vibrancy of this early sixties art was, in fact, partly the product of an array of paradoxes.

The same could probably be said of most of the art produced in Greenwich Village, or any other bohemian community.

Together, these two books, one taking a broad historical and sociological view, the other examining in detail a more concentrated scene, add up to a spirited and often provocative survey of Greenwich Village and bohemianism. As I said earlier, it's difficult to define bohemia, and it's sometimes taken to represent display rather than activity, parade as opposed to production. But the sheer volume of achievement in literature, painting, music, and the rest that is referred to is surely enough to show that Greenwich Village, both as a physical location and a state of mind, has always provided a home for the energetic as well as the eccentric. And, in any case, the two could easily combine. There must be numerous poets, painters, and others who, even if they spent little time in the Village, were sustained by the idea of it and by the example of those writers and artists who were there. It can be argued that for every successful artist a dozen or more failures also walked the streets. Perhaps so, but as the Italians used to say: 'Give flowers to the rebels failed.'

HENRY ROTH, 1996

When Henry Roth died in 1995 his name had recently been in the news due to the publication of the first two volumes of a six-volume novel sequence. What had caused much of the interest was the fact that these books marked Roth's reappearance as a novelist after a sixty years break. His first book, *Call It Sleep*, had been published in 1934, but Roth then slipped into virtual silence as a writer, with the exception of a few short stories and other prose pieces which appeared in magazines. *Call It Sleep* was rediscovered in 1964 and gained both critical and popular acclaim, but few people thought that Roth was likely to produce any more major works of fiction. That he should start to publish novels again when he was almost ninety seemed incredible.

Roth's death may have affected the plans to publish the six novels on an annual basis, starting in 1994. It would seem that the third is ready for publication, but that the rest may need some skilful editing before they can be put into print. Roth and his editors were working on them when he died, and his absence will obviously delay the process of editing.

Who was Henry Roth and why was there such a long gap between books? He was born in 1906 in what is now a part of the Ukraine, and was the son of Jewish parents who brought him to America when he was two years old. The family lived in Brooklyn, the Lower East Side of New York (once described by Roth as 'a virtual Jewish mini-state'), and finally an area of Harlem which was then largely populated by Irish and Italian immigrants. The final move was a significant one for Roth, bringing a sense of isolation and alienation which he had never felt on the Lower East Side. In later life he said: 'Had I stayed there on the Lower East Side I'm sure I would have been a lot happier and I might have been a rabbi – who knows? Or a good zoologist, had a happy Jewish family. ... The point was I'd have been rather happy, no matter what, instead of this tormented life that I've lived.'

It is the early New York years, roughly 1910 to 1914, when the family went to Harlem, which are dealt with in *Call It Sleep* and which tell the story of David Schearl, who is sensitive, smart, and easily disturbed. He is close to his mother, but afraid of his father, a moody, sometimes violent man. Thomas J. Ferraro, in a book about the immigrant experience as it is expressed in American novels, neatly summarises the basic situation in *Call It Sleep*:

> A lone male child, terrified of sex yet driven to an increasingly hallucinatory probing of his parents' troubled sexuality: the father economically and culturally disenfranchised, prone to impotence and a compensatory paternal rage, feeling increasingly isolated from wife and child: the mother betrayed in her marriage, turning vengefully to the affection of the son, exposing him to the ultimate divergence of his awakening desire and her growing need.

And in a significant passage in the book Roth describes David's distance from his father:

> As far back as he could remember, this was the first time that he had ever gone anywhere alone with his father, and already he felt desolated, stirred with dismal forebodings, longing desperately for his mother. His father was so silent and so remote that he felt as though he were alone even at his side. What if his father should abandon him, leave him in some lonely street. The thought sent shudders of horror through his body. No! No! He couldn't do that!

It's not my intention to deal with *Call It Sleep* in detail. The book is impressionistic and my main aim is to give an impression of it. What it deals with, in addition to David's feelings about his parents, is his response to the world he experiences outside the home. There is a passage where Roth describes the move to the Lower East Side and what David finds there:

In February David's father found the job he wanted – he was to be a milkman. And in order that he might be nearer the stables, they moved a few days later to 9th Street and Avenue D on the Lower East Side. For David it was a new and violent world, as different from Brownsville as quiet from turmoil. Here in 9th Street it wasn't the sun that swamped one as one left the doormat, it was sound – an avalanche of sound. There were countless children, there were countless baby carriages, there were countless mothers. And to the screams, rebukes and bickerings of these, a seemingly endless file of hucksters joined their brawling cries. On Avenue D horse-cars clattered and banged. Avenue D was thronged with beer wagons, garbage carts and coal trucks. There were many automobiles, some blunt and rangy, some with high straw poops, honking. Beyond Avenue D, at the end of a stunted, ruined block that began with shacks and smithies and seltzer bottling works and ended in a junk heap, was the East River on which many boat horns sounded. On 10th Street, the 8th Street Crosstown car ground its way towards the switch.

There is, of course, a highly autobiographical element in Roth's fiction, but it should not be assumed that he was writing autobiography in *Call It Sleep*. Roth was selective. In real life he had a sister, but in the book, to quote Roth, she

> almost doesn't come into the picture for a number of reasons. Primarily because I was that much of an egotist as a child or young man. I so continually monopolised my mother's affection that I regarded myself as the one and only child around – with the exception of my father.

And in the same interview he added:

> At the time I wrote *Call It Sleep* I thought I was honestly portraying my childhood. ... I think this is one of the things which gives the novel its strength. Now I think I wasn't really portraying myself at all: the child is much too innocent, almost completely victimised, passive. It was simply an idealisation based on the notion that I was a much finer sensibility than what was around me – so fine I was being persecuted and victimised.

Call It Sleep, as I've already noted, covers only a few of Roth's childhood years. His biographical details show that after completing high school he entered the City College of New York, one of the few

places where a Jewish student with little or no money could study for
a degree. His intention was to study biology and then possibly work
in that line or as a zoologist, but two significant things happened while
he was at CCNY. He wrote a piece for an English class which his
tutor thought so good that he recommended it for publication in the
college magazine. Roth, it ought to be said, was an avid reader as a
child, with the public library serving almost as a refuge from the
pressures of home and the streets, and he had a natural understanding
of how a piece of writing can be structured and what it is required to
do. It's interesting to read the story, 'Impressions of a Plumber,' which
was based on Roth's experiences working as a plumber's mate during
the summer of 1924 and was an attempt to capture the rhythms of
the working day and the speech patterns of the various characters. Roth
phoneticised what the people said so as to show the vibrancy and
variety of language in New York and to stress how the immigrants
used English in their own way. He used this technique again in *Call
It Sleep*, though in the novel the family appear to speak 'pure' English
when they are conversing in Yiddish. This was a stylistic gambit,
designed by Roth to heighten the clash in David's mind between the
language he heard at home and that heard on the streets. 'Impressions
of a Plumber' is valuable, too, in terms of what it says about Roth's
attitude towards work, bosses, and the capitalist system. It does not
have any direct political comment, other than a brief reference to how
workers view the boss, but its proletarian subject-matter would not
have been unwelcome in left-wing circles.

The second major event in Roth's life around this time was his meeting
Eda Lou Walton, a lecturer at New York University who had some
standing as a minor poet and hostess of a literary salon which included
Hart Crane, Leonie Adams, and Louise Bogan. Roth's *A Diving Rock on
the Hudson*, the second volume of *Mercy of a Rude Stream* (his six-volume
work), covers Roth's initial encounters with Walton and has a scene
where he attends a poetry reading given by Leonie Adams. The third
part, when it appears, will presumably tell the story of how Roth had
an affair with Walton, a woman twelve years his senior, and moved into
her apartment in Greenwich Village, which had the effect of almost

cutting him off from his family whilst at the same time introducing him
to the world of the avant-garde in politics and art. It was during the
years that he lived with Walton that he wrote *Call It Sleep*, which was
heavily influenced by his reading of James Joyce's *Ulysses*. When asked
what he thought he had gained from Joyce, he replied:

> What I gained was this awed realisation that you didn't have to go
> anywhere at all except around the corner to flesh out a literary work
> of art – given some kind of vision, of course. In stream of consciousness
> I recognised that my own continual dialogue with myself could be made
> into literature. It was a tremendous impetus toward writing.

Roth had joined the Communist Party in 1933, an act which he later
described as 'a sentimental thing,' and when *Call It Sleep* was published
in 1934 it was attacked by some left-wing critics who saw its
impressionistic view of urban life as lacking in political commitment
and failing to correspond to the social realism expected of proletarian
literature. Early in 1935 the Communist Party cultural magazine, *New
Masses*, printed a review which ended by saying: 'It is a pity that so
many young writers drawn from the proletariat can make no better use
of their working-class experience than as material for introspective and
febrile novels.' But although some literary historians have suggested
that left-wing reaction to Roth's book was totally hostile, the records
indicate otherwise. Several readers wrote to protest about the review,
and the noted critic Edwin Seaver came to the novel's defence, saying:
'What better use could Roth have made of his working-class experience
as a child than to have shown honestly and exactly what that experience
consisted of?' And another Communist Party publication, *The Daily
Worker*, printed a favourable review of *Call It Sleep* by Alfred Hayes,
then a young left-wing poet and later a talented novelist. It would seem,
too, that the novel did not sell badly by the standards of the time,
1934 being one of the worst of the Depression years in the United
States. But the economic situation did work against Roth and his
publisher went bankrupt, with the result that *Call It Sleep* was soon
forgotten by all but a few of its admirers.

The ideological atmosphere of the 1930s did have its effect on Roth, as he admitted many years later:

> About mid-1935, after the trauma of *Call It Sleep* had worn off, I began to get the itch to write again. Now here is where the Party must have had its influence – because I now felt that I wanted to break away from an extension of the immigrant East Side Jewish childhood and do something from the American Middle West. Now suppose I hadn't known anything about the Party – I probably would have done the adolescent years, perhaps taking it as far as meeting Eda Lou or growing consciousness of artistic abilities. Instead, I broke away and was going to do the proletariat, right out of the American scene.

He planned a novel which would have a central character based on someone he'd met who seemed to represent the sort of proletarian hero liked by the Party, and he did complete over one hundred pages of this book and was given an advance against it by the noted publishers Scribner's. But it was never finished and, in Roth's own words, 'after that came the block.'

Some accounts tend to suggest that Roth stopped writing altogether once *Call It Sleep* was completed, but as mentioned above he did begin to work on his 'proletarian novel,' and some of what he wrote was published in a magazine in 1936. He also published stories in *The New Yorker* in 1939 and 1940, and one or two other short pieces also appeared, including a curious 1937 piece for *New Masses*. Called 'Where My Sympathy Lies,' it was an expression of support for Stalin and said of the Moscow trials:

> There are several things about this trial about which I am confused. Nevertheless, enough and more than enough has been revealed to convince me of the guilt of the accused; and by guilt, I mean that all their efforts were calculated to nullify or destroy the very growth of the safeguards that would ensure the freedom and fraternity of millions of men.

Roth went on to attack Trotsky and Trotskyism and referred to it as 'a sure way to paralyse all our efforts for a united front against fascism.' Of course, Roth wasn't alone in his views and in a 1985 interview he admitted how wrong he'd been:

That's the very example of, the perfect example of conversion, the
definition of the very thing I would condemn utterly, today, after I
had once completely committed myself to blind allegiance. It's
something you have to live down, and it's something that (needless to
repeat) continually haunts you.

If and when the appropriate volume of *Mercy of a Rude Stream* is published
it will be interesting to see how Roth deals with this phase of his life.
He did once refer in an interview to burning the original manuscript
of his proletarian novel, together with some valuable journals, during
the McCarthy period because he thought they contained self-
incriminating political material. As far as I know, he was never subjected
to FBI harassment in the 1940s and 1950s, nor was he ever called
before any sort of committee investigating political activities and
allegiances. But the nervousness about it was clearly there.

Roth made a break with the Communist Party in the late 1930s,
around the same time that he left Eda Lou Walton, and it is from this
period that his almost total disappearance from the literary scene can
be marked. He had met Muriel Parker in 1938 at Yaddo, the retreat
for artists, writers, and musicians, and married her in 1939. She gave
up a promising musical career and became a schoolteacher, and Roth
took to a succession of jobs, including being a machinist, teacher, forest
firefighter, plumber's assistant, and insane asylum attendant. In 1953
he bought some ducks and geese and started a business in Maine,
selling feathers and preparing carcasses for the table. He remained there
until the 1964 publication of *Call It Sleep* brought some unwelcome
publicity but also the money to travel and eventually settle in New
Mexico. He began writing again in earnest in the 1960s – a story which
was excerpted from a novel he worked on was published in *The New
Yorker* – but it was only in 1980 that he began to put together the
first volume of *Mercy of a Rude Stream*.

Obviously, the 'facts' of Roth's life do inform his fiction, but it may
be that *Mercy of a Rude Stream* is more factual than *Call It Sleep*. The
earlier work does have accurate descriptions of New York ghetto life
in the early part of the century, but its stylistic devices act against it

being a realistic novel. Like Joyce's *Ulysses* it stands as a single, highly idiosyncratic and almost unrepeatable achievement, something Roth perhaps knew in his heart and which might explain why he felt frustrated about proceeding any further. *Mercy of a Rude Stream* does have some self-consciously experimental aspects – there is a running commentary by an ageing author who ruminates throughout the books about his past and present problems and sometimes engages in a dialogue with his computer – but they are the least interesting parts, and the value of the writing lies in its vivid descriptions of the past and the way in which it evokes what it was like to be alive and engaged in certain activities (childhood, schooling, work, intellectual adventures, sexual strivings, etc.) at specific times. The writing is often almost pleasingly 'old-fashioned' in the sense of the language being direct and without any pretension, and I was occasionally reminded of the kind of novels produced by James T. Farrell (does anyone read him these days?), which were fascinating social documents and aim to record things exactly as they were. As I was reading the two published volumes of *Mercy of a Rude Stream* I was also looking at *Metropolitan Lives*, a book about the painters of the so-called Ashcan School (John Sloan, George Bellows, Everett Shinn, etc.) and realising how accurate were Roth's descriptions of New York. And the vividness of the pictures he paints of the ghetto slums was confirmed for me when I referred to the writings and photographs of the great reformer, Jacob Riis. It's unfair to compare *Mercy of a Rude Stream* to *Call It Sleep*, even if they are linked by more than their subject-matter and author, and it deserves instead to be put alongside other major works of the Jewish experience in America, such as Abraham Cahan's *The Rise of David Levinsky* and Michael Gold's *Jew Without Money*. And that is to rate it highly. Henry Roth may have written only one book, *Call It Sleep*, which deserves to be called a major work, but there is much in his other writings worthy of admiration.

Note

Call It Sleep was originally published in 1934. It was published in this country in 1963 by Michael Joseph in a hardback edition which has a useful introduction by Walter Allen. Various editions have appeared here and in America since then, and it is currently in print as a Penguin paperback. *A Star Shines Over Mt. Morris Park* and *A Diving Rock on the Hudson*, the first two volumes of *Mercy of a Rude Stream*, were published in 1994 and 1995 respectively by Weidenfeld & Nicolson.

Shifting Landscape is a collection of short stories and other prose and is linked with a commentary and excerpts from interviews. It is an extremely valuable book from the point of view of providing a backcloth for the novels. It was published in 1995 by Weidenfeld & Nicolson.

Thomas J. Ferraro's *Ethnic Passages: Literary Immigrants in Twentieth-Century America* was published in 1993 by the University of Chicago Press. It has some interesting comments on Roth's *Call It Sleep*. A discussion of the controversy in left-wing circles when the book was first published can be found in James F. Murphy's *The Proletarian Moment: The Controversy over Leftism in Literature*, published in 1991 by the University of Illinois Press.

Abraham Cahan's *The Rise of David Levinsky* has been in print in a Penguin edition in recent times, and Michael Gold's *Jews Without Money* in an edition from Carroll & Graf, New York, published in 1984. James T. Farrell is known today mostly for his *Studs Lonigan* trilogy which is occasionally reprinted. His other novels and short stories, which are of admittedly variable quality but can be good, are now all out of print.

Metropolitan Lives: The Ashcan Artists and their New York by Rebecca Zurier, Robert W. Snyder, and Virginia M. Mecklenburg, was published by Norton in 1995.

Since this piece was written two more volumes of *Mercy of a Rude Stream* have been published by Weidenfeld & Nicolson: *From Bondage* (1996) and *Requiem for Harlem* (1998). It would appear that the latter is the final volume.

ISAAC ROSENFELD, 1997

> I am used to thinking of the writer, then, as a man who stands at a
> certain extreme, at a certain remove from society. He stands over against
> the commercial culture, the business enterprise, that whole fantastic
> make-believe world which some people would like us to believe is the
> real world. Of course it can't be that for the writer.

The above is from a talk that Isaac Rosenfeld gave to the staff of
the magazine, *Chicago Review*, in 1956, the year when he also died
at the age of thirty-eight. It neatly sums up his basic attitude, which
was one that had kept him from riding on the postwar bandwagon
that allowed many writers to participate in what Rosenfeld thought of
as a 'fantastic make-believe world' of publicity and profit. He had been
uncompromising in his refusal to join in, so much so that he was seen
as a man who 'followed a discipline of conduct that looked like
unswerving downward mobility.' Rosenfeld had been a brilliant scholar
and writer who impressed almost everyone who knew him, and yet he
never fulfilled the promise that others saw in him, perhaps because to
do so would have been tantamount to being involved in the 'fantastic
make-believe world' he disliked so much. Of course, it's necessary also
to consider whether or not forms of personal waywardness affected
his judgements. Someone who knew him well called him 'the last
Bohemian,' but Alfred Kazin thought that his bohemianism probably
held back the development of his literary talents. When he first started
publishing Rosenfeld was often mentioned alongside Saul Bellow, but
as Kazin observed: 'Unlike Bellow, who could use every morsel of his
experiences, Isaac lived his fantasies and in company.' There is a

suggestion here that the bohemianism, and the refusal to make an effort to change his views, may have been a cover for a failed writer. There is a degree of truth in that idea in so far as Rosenfeld failed to produce the work that was expected of him. But what he did produce was of much more interest than the tidy but dull writings of authors who played the literary game and consciously sought success. Herman Melville accurately described such people:

> He who has never failed somewhere, that man cannot be great. Failure is the true test of greatness. ... And if it be said, that continual success is proof that a man wisely knows his powers, – it is only to be added, that in that case, he knows them to be small. Let us believe it, then, once for all, that there is no hope for us in these smooth pleasing writers that know their powers.

Whatever else can be said of Isaac Rosenfeld, he can never be dismissed as simply a 'smooth pleasing writer.'

He was born in 1918 in Chicago and grew up 'in the contentious atmosphere of free-thinking Russian Jews who were saturated in rebellion and socialism.' Rosenfeld and Saul Bellow were friends in the early 1930s, and both were attracted to Trotskyism while still in high school. In 1933 they enrolled at the University of Chicago, where Rosenfeld studied philosophy. There are, in memoirs of the period, engaging portraits of Rosenfeld as a teenage intellectual, and Bellow has recalled him delivering erudite papers to college debating societies at an age when most boys would have been reading comics. Rosenfeld passed through various Trotskyist groups, and continued his interest in politics when he moved to New York in 1941, his intention being to study for his PhD in philosophy. But his literary interests, which had always paralleled his philosophical and political enthusiasms, began to take precedence, and he abandoned academic work and started to publish reviews and short stories in such magazines as the *New Republic* and *Partisan Review*. It is true, as Alfred Kazin said, that Rosenfeld did not milk his experiences for use in his fiction, but he did sometimes write stories which drew on his background to a degree. 'The Hand

That Fed Me,' for example, which appeared in *Partisan Review* in 1944, concerns a young Jewish writer who, whilst enrolling for the WPA Writers' Project, meets a Gentile girl who later abandons him. The story is written in the form of a series of letters from the writer. Interestingly, the piece, though having a form of socio-economic framework because of its setting, is not at all political. The writer is more concerned with his personal relationship with the girl, and the story is essentially an exercise in a psychological study of its central character. Rosenfeld had read deeply in Russian literature – he and Bellow were sometimes referred to as 'underground men' – and he was also an admirer of Kafka, and his writing reflected the interest he had in those areas of literature.

A display of Rosenfeld's darkly satiric intentions can be found in another early story, 'The Party,' which revolves around a political party that falls apart when its members become bored with its failure to actually do anything. Rosenfeld's experiences amongst the Trotskyists had clearly shaped this piece, and it was probably based on the Workers' Party and its leading theoretical light, Max Shachtman. As Alan Wald put it:

> Rosenfeld describes the peculiar mentality of a devout but self-abnegating member loyal to the forms of the movement – the rituals of party interventions and social affairs, the veneration of 'old guard' leaders and the dynamics of faction struggle – even as its political content is lost. .... Rosenfeld's ideologues are brutally satirised because they remain impervious to experience.

That this story transcends the limitations of a specific period is easily seen when one refers to contemporary Trotskyist sects, with their magazines which continue to promote irrelevant ideas and often seem to rely on 'the dynamics of faction struggle' for their continued existence. And it's not unusual to come across Shachtman's name in them, even now!

Still, if Rosenfeld by the mid-1940s had withdrawn from direct involvement with radical politics, he certainly never lost his interest in political ideas, nor did he deny that his early experiences had helped shape his overall approach to writing. Just before he died he wrote an essay, 'Life in Chicago', in which he cast a cold eye on the city and, in particular, its university which, he thought, had lost something when money and social success became its guiding principles, and the students switched their interests from politics to sport and popular music. In Rosenfeld's view, 'politics furnishes the best of all bases for secular culture,' and he remembered the 1930s when 'politics was form and substance, accident and modification, the metaphor of all things.' Theodore Solotaroff, who admired Rosenfeld's work as a reviewer and essayist, said of him:

> Like many of the young writers who came out of the Depression, he had learned, as he says, "through political activity, to admire the vigour which a social orientation will impart to thought," and from the start his criticism was given vitality and point by his consciousness of what a given book was saying – implicitly and unconsciously as well as explicitly – about the times, about us.

The thrust of Rosenfeld's comments in 'Life in Chicago' was that the quality of intellectual life had declined, and he was particularly cutting about the way in which even supposedly bright students had taken to cultivating the 'cool' lifestyle of the hipster and the habits of what was soon to be labelled 'Beat.' He noted that it was still possible to find 'students without nonsense whose culture heroes might be some great poet, novelist, painter, philosopher, or composer, rather than the jazz musician,' but too many others were simply involved in a 'masquerade' that Rosenfeld obviously had little time for.

His approach to writing naturally placed him alongside many of the critics described as New York Intellectuals in the 1940s, and he was regularly published in *Partisan Review*, *Commentary*, and the *New Republic*. What he did as a reviewer was widespread in terms of the kind of books he wrote about, and a glance at his bibliography sees him dealing with poetry, novels, and other odds and ends, usually within a framework of one thousand words or so, and I would guess taking pot luck as to which books were given him to review. He was, in other words, reviewing as a job, and his style was described as designed for unscholarly but intelligent readers. But he was never just a hack, churning out weekly pieces for a price. A review by Rosenfeld, even of a minor work, always had a serious side, and he was, as Theodore Solotaroff said, concerned to develop 'a specific awareness of what was happening to the human image and to the values of the heart and mind that preserve it, during what he called an age of enormity.' He didn't have a 'methodology,' and instead relied on his natural instincts about the purpose of literature to take him to the core of the book he was reviewing. He wanted, he claimed, to restore 'confidence in our abilities, within our right, to take a simply human measure of literature,' and Theodore Solotaroff said that, in doing so, he 'helped keep alive the fundamental reasons for bothering about literature at all.'

Writing regular short reviews can be a death-trap for a young writer, as Seymour Krim so brilliantly described in 'What's *This* Cat's Story,' where he told how his addiction to the quick fix of the review, and its immediate response from the intellectual community, destroyed his talents as a short-story writer and would-be novelist. Rosenfeld did work on a novel, though, and it was published to some acclaim in 1946. Partly autobiographical, *Passage From Home* tells the story of a young Jewish boy who, bored with the restrictions of family life and the presence of a seemingly dull father and mother, develops a liking for an aunt who lives in what appears to be a colourful and exciting bohemian manner, and therefore offers an alternative for him to follow. The book, though having an obvious Jewish dimension, was not just about a Jewish rite of passage, and its central theme of alienation could easily be understood by anyone sensing a clash of values in a relationship with their parents and indeed in their response to the world they lived in. The hero of Rosenfeld's novel eventually realises that, in Alan Wald's words,

> the bohemian alternative to the alienation of conventional life is illusory, and he becomes resigned to his outsider status. Thus experience teaches that alienation is the permanent condition of humanity.

Passage From Home was highly praised when it appeared, and the
book became something of a key work of the New York Intellectuals,
portraying as it did the struggle between fathers and sons that so many
of them experienced as they broke away from traditional ways of life
and gravitated to the bohemian world of New York. But although
Rosenfeld developed a theory of alienation it could not be said that
he used it to follow a fashionable line. Alienation could, in some
circumstances, lead to an 'underground' existence, but in a 1952 review
of Sartre's collection of stories, *Intimacy*, he asserted that much of its
supposed identification with an 'underground' philosophy was sheer
posturing, and that, as Theodore Solotaroff summarised it, 'writers have
no more right to their disaffection than anyone else, particularly in view
of the self-preening uses to which it is put.' To develop a philosophy
of 'contactlessness, the emptiness and superfluity of existence, the sexual
miseries and perversions, violence and self-destruction' from the lives
and experiences of a small group of café habitués was surely misleading.
And in a significant passage, Rosenfeld highlighted the difference
between how he saw the writer standing at a distance from 'a fantastic
make-believe world' and those people who imagine themselves in some
sort of 'underground' situation:

> To some extent flattery deceives us on this topic: we like to imagine
> ourselves underground, living at a perpetual extreme, and we seize on
> every aspect of our age, its disorder and violence, amorality and unbelief,
> which confirms this estimate. We achieve by this means a passive
> heroism, to which romantic periods are prone, especially when the
> active modes promise little success. But there is still another way in
> which we deceive ourselves – this is a fundamental error and its cause
> lies in our predominant style of perception into human matters. We
> are used to seeing a subject through its individual accidents; we call
> on biography to give the direction and pursue the unique and the
> aberrant to such an extent that almost all understanding has become
> a form of psychopathological analysis. This has put a high value on
> confessions, disclosures of the private life and its feelings, usually
> revulsions, which earlier ages have found neither interesting nor
> tolerable. The tone of very much modern writing is, accordingly, one
> of malaise. But we are so accustomed to it, we are seldom aware of
> it as such; and when we do take this malaise into direct account, we
> readily mistake it for what it is not – a report from the underground.

Rosenfeld went on to point out how Sartre's fiction was constructed to

> allow his characters to proclaim and act out their disgust with life. The
> symptoms are the standard neurotic ones – contactlessness, the
> emptiness and superfluity of existence, the sexual miseries and
> perversions, violence and self-destruction. ... Neurosis becomes the
> equivalent of life. The ordinary syndromes, which we would otherwise
> discount to sickness, become on this inflated interpretation synonymous
> with subjectivity, crisis, anxiety, and other existential categories, and we
> read as ontology what we should recognise as disease.

Reviews such as this demonstrated how Rosenfeld could deal with ideas
within the framework of a few hundred words. As Theodore Solotaroff
pointed out:

> He had been trained in philosophical analysis by such men as Eliseo
> Vivas and Rudolf Carnap, and when he came to write practical criticism,
> he was able to fortify it by a precise use of general ideas, without which
> book-reviewing soon becomes a relaxed form of prejudice or advertising.

The cool, considered prose with which Rosenfeld constructed his
reviews and essays was in contrast to a personal life that became
increasingly disordered in the post-war years. He had hit a block, as
far as creative work was concerned, and though a few short stories
and some excerpts from an unpublished novel did appear in magazines,
he was looked on as a writer whose career was on a downward spiral.
He thought that his writing block had some relation to sexual inhibition
and he was attracted to the orgone box theories of Wilhelm Reich, in
whose theory of the orgasm he saw

> the possibility of carrying his search for freedom into the three sectors
> of his character: his natural drives and the struggle against his inhibitions;
> his intellect and its commitments to first principles of thought and
> conduct deriving from and in harmony with nature; his spirit and its
> thirst for the full being and transcendency of ecstasy.

Rosenfeld could associate his personal needs with his political ideas
because Reich theorised 'that a self-regulated man and community would
develop from complete sexual freedom and satisfaction,' and that

seemed to Rosenfeld 'the most powerful means of transforming culture so as to remove its terror and the potential for further terror.' Similar ideas were thrown around by the Beats and others in the 1960s, and William Phillips, one-time editor of *Partisan Review*, thought that Rosenfeld had 'the kind of perverse and radical sensibility that would have flourished in the sixties.'

Leaving New York, Rosenfeld took teaching posts in Minnesota and then at the University of Chicago, though he seems to have existed on the fringes of academic life rather than at its centre. Memoirs portray him as living in bohemian disarray. Saul Bellow thought that he 'preferred to have things about him in a mess. I have an idea that he found good, middle-class order devitalising,' and Mark Shechner added, 'there was a principle of perverse monasticism in this life, a disorder, as Bellow observed, that had become a discipline.' But he was never a self-conscious bohemian, dressing and behaving in a way meant to attract attention. As Bellow said, 'he did not pursue eccentricity for its own sake, for its colour. He followed an inner necessity which led him into difficulty and solitude.' He died, alone, in a furnished room in Chicago in 1956.

Rosenfeld's output was small if one compares it to other, more successful writers. One novel, a collection of stories, and a collection of essays and reviews. And the latter two were published posthumously. There were also scattered pieces in magazines which were never collected. He planned other novels, including one which was set in Greenwich Village. A posthumously published story, 'Wolfie,' also has that setting, and is a dark exploration of an oddball character's obsessive need to see a woman he admires seduced by someone else. Had Rosenfeld ever completed his novel he might well have come up with something which went beyond the usual picaresque account of bohemian capers. It may have been, of course, that his penchant for ideas and his philosophical training got in the way of his fictional skills, though not of his other prose work. His stories, though interesting, are not always well-developed as fiction, and his taste for allegory may not have been beneficial, though it was said that he was, in later years, 'trying to break away from the large, symbolic design of Kafka and write about his own experiences

in the world in more immediately concrete ways.' It's perhaps fair to
say that, of the work that did see print, it is his novel, the best of his
essays and reviews, and a few of his short stories, which should be
remembered. Having said that, I'm of the opinion that anything written
by Isaac Rosenfeld was, and still is, of interest, and that it is of more
value than the bland, careful writing, or the slick, attention-seeking work,
that so many other writers produced. There was a seriousness to all he
wrote, and it was a seriousness that indicated he was a man who cared
about life and about writing.

Note

Passage From Home, originally published in 1946, was re-issued in 1988 by
Markus Wiener Publishing, New York. Rosenfeld's stories were collected
in *Alpha and Omega* (MacGibbon & Kee, London, 1966) and the essays
and reviews in *An Age of Enormity* (World Publishing Co., Cleveland, 1962).
Much of the material from these two books, together with some extracts
from Rosenfeld's journals, is in *Preserving the Hunger: An Isaac Rosenfeld
Reader*, edited by Mark Shechner, and published by Wayne State University
Press, Detroit, 1988. This also has an informative introduction by Shechner
which, together with the introduction by Theodore Solotaroff to *An Age
of Enormity*, provides a good picture of Rosenfeld. Both books also contain
a short memoir by Saul Bellow, which is also included in his *It All Adds
Up* (Viking Press, New York, 1944).

A fictional portrait of Rosenfeld by Bellow can be found in 'Zetland:
By a Character Witness,' in the collection, *Him with his Foot in his Mouth
and Other Stories* (Penguin Books, Harmondsworth, 1985). Wallace
Markfield's novel, *To An Early Grave* (Jonathan Cape, London, 1965),
is about four Jewish intellectuals on their way to attend the funeral of
someone who closely resembles Rosenfeld, and their conversation
evokes memories of the man and his activities.

Rosenfeld's 'On the Role of the Writer and the Little Magazine,' can
be found in *The Chicago Review Anthology*, edited by David Ray, published
by the University of Chicago Press, 1959.

There are references to Rosenfeld in various histories of the New York Intellectuals. See, for example, Terry Cooney's *The Rise of the New York Intellectuals* (University of Wisconsin Press, Madison, 1986), Alexander Bloom's *Prodigal Sons* (Oxford University Press, 1986), and Alan Wald's *The New York Intellectuals* (University of North Carolina Press, Chapel Hill, 1987).

Individual memoirs by members of the New York Intellectuals group refer to Rosenfeld. William Phillips's *A Partisan View* (Stein & Day, New York, 1983) and Alfred Kazin's *New York Jew* (Secker & Warburg, London, 1978) are two of the more interesting, with Phillips being less enthusiastic than Kazin. The latter's portrait of Rosenfeld has been described as 'an accurate and penetrating miniature, the best short portrait of him available.' It is movingly honest about what Kazin saw as Rosenfeld's 'inability to compromise with the things of this world' and his resultant failure to fulfil his earlier promise.

SEYMOUR KRIM, 1971

To an English reader, at least, the name of Seymour Krim will most probably evoke memories of the heady days of the Beat movement. Krim edited *The Beats* (Gold Medal Books, Greenwich, 1960), one of the best anthologies to come out of that chaotic period, appeared in *The Beat Scene*, and was featured in such publications as *Evergreen Review* and *The Village Voice*. He also worked on two girlie-magazines, *Swank* and *Nugget*, during which time both managed to publish a remarkable number of writers normally found in little magazines and related publications. *Swank* (see *Ambit* 21 for a brief survey of Krim's connection with this publication) ran four issues which included a special section – The Swinging Modern Scene – devoted to 'literary' work. Among the writers spotlighted were Frank O'Hara, Ferlinghetti, Kerouac, Ginsberg, LeRoi Jones, Joel Oppenheimer, Hubert Selby, to mention only a few of the better-known names. *Nugget* was less specific but one could usually find stories and articles by Terry Southern, John Rechy, John Clellon Holmes, Leslie Garrett, Chandler Brossard, Kenneth Rexroth and others like them tucked between the breasts and buttocks.

Krim's activities haven't been limited to his associations with the Beats (or, to be more accurate, the post 1955 literary scene), however. True, he didn't get properly into his stride until the late fifties and his previous work – mainly criticism and a few scattered short stories (two of them in *New Directions* anthologies) – hadn't shown him to be anything more than an intelligent and moderately gifted young writer. The rise of the Beats coincided with some personal problems and seems to have provided the release Krim needed. The interesting thing is that he didn't then devote his time to fiction (and, as I'll mention later,

Krim had a special 'need' to prove himself in this field) but to the form – I suppose the term 'essay' best describes it – too often relegated to the rear ranks of literature. It's my opinion that Krim has gone a fair way towards making this as valid as (if not more than) the so-called creative forms.

Krim, in his own productions, has set a pace which anyone following will find hard to equal. 'What's *This* Cat's Story?' is possibly the key piece to date in the Krim canon. A long and fascinating account of his involvement with the New York literary scene, it not only evokes the qualities of a particularly brilliant group (basically centred on Greenwich Village and including such people as Chandler Brossard, Milton Klonsky, Clement Greenburg, Anatole Broyard, Weldon Kees, Manny Farber and Isaac Rosenfeld, most of whom were/are talented writers) but also an individual's – Krim's – place in that group at that time. It is, as well, an honest-to-God account of how Krim, wanting to write fiction, took to criticism because (a) it was an easier way of getting into print, and (b) it gave him the status he needed amongst the intellectually skilled types he mixed with. And, as Krim says,

> Having tasted the blood of print I couldn't stop; criticism was very much in the air, was hip, impressive, the sign of rank, fiction was for brainless impressionists (thus ran my snobbery) and even though I felt split about reviewing from the start and kept telling myself it was only a temporary filler the drug of seeing my glistening thoughts in print hooked me and I didn't have the courage to stop.

When Krim wrote that piece in 1960 as the introduction, so to speak, to his first collection, *Views Of A Nearsighted Cannoneer*, he had already moved away from the literary area he had previously inhabited and into what he called 'the definitely more initiative-taking articles which I did for *The Village Voice* (1957-1959) and *Exodus* (1959-1960).' In these he partly maintained his critical role (though the accent was on social rather than literary matters) – especially in *The Village Voice* – but also headed towards the autobiographical pieces which are, I feel, his best writing to date. In 'Ask For A White Cadillac' and 'The Insanity Bit' – as in 'What's *This* Cat's Story?' – he began to document his own experiences as a person caught up in the typical intellectual concerns and stresses of the post-war period. 'Cadillac' is an open and detailed 'confession' of Krim's search for affinity with the Negroes of New York. It would be wrong of me to attempt to comment on his picture of Harlem – it seems to be accurate (and James Baldwin has praised Krim's objectivity on the subject) but I'm naturally basing my judgement on information picked up from other writers. But what is more important is that he has caught the attempts of an individual to identify with a group he thinks of as having some basic qualities lacking in himself and his own kind. (I suppose the nearest equivalent in this country is the situation where someone from the middle-class attempts to relate to the 'workers'.) What is especially impressive about Krim (in a way he reminds me of Orwell in that he cuts through to the essence of things instead of wasting time in a lot of fake sociological jargon and analysing) is that he can list those minor details that denote a man who has experienced something as opposed to one who has observed it. Here he is on Harlem bar-room manners and morals:

> Never turn your back on a bar when standing there, it makes you conspicuous and is in bad taste; ask for no favours, butt into no fights or arguments; always buy a bouncer or bartender a drink when you can afford it; remember that music, sports and money are driving, magnetic topics in Harlem and will always get you an interesting conversation if you're hung-up or ill at ease.

'The Insanity Bit' has links with both 'Cadillac' and 'Cat's Story' by chronicling the breakdown brought on by the pressures – some of them mentioned in those two pieces – Krim felt. It is straight – most of the time a factual and bleak account of what happened – but does manage to suggest that Krim's experience might not be all that unusual. I'm not detracting from its quality in saying this – merely pointing out that he typified the problems of a talented individual running up against the brick wall of contemporary society.

I've concentrated on three essays from Krim's *Cannoneer* but it shouldn't be presumed that the balance of the material is not of interest. The long extract from an unfinished work, 'Two Teachers – Nuts, Two

Human Beings!', apart from again evoking a particular period (the forties and early fifties), also provides a fine portrait of Milton Klonsky. And even if an English reader is not interested in Klonsky the piece is still valuable because it describes a familiar (though not formal) teacher-pupil relationship as many writers will know it from their own lives. This, to me, is a major Krim attribute, his ability to involve the reader on two levels – (a) by interesting him in the subject he's writing about and (b) by subtly suggesting that the reader will understand Krim because he too will have experienced a similar situation.

Several short articles, some reviews, and one or two bits of fiction round off the collection. All are of relevance to the main pieces (in 'Cat's Story' Krim has added notes to show where the short things relate to the chart he draws) but at the same time they do have qualities of their own. Krim is a good critic when writing about someone he feels involved with and anyone curious about American literature will find the items on Dreiser, Hemingway, Wolfe and Whitman well worth reading.

With Krim's second (and to date only other) book, *Shake It For The World, Smartass* (1970), we move into the period after the important essays in *Cannoneer* had been written and Krim had, in fact, thrown himself more into a less refined literary life (it was in the early sixties that he worked on *Swank* and *Nugget*, the latter providing the longer and more complicated stint). He abandoned his attempts to write fiction and turned his back on the 'standard' criticism he had been doing. Instead, he hammered away at essays which invariably revolved around contemporary topics and personalities. It was, in a way, a kind of literary journalism, and invariably there was a note of autobiography (of someone living his literature) about it, and a personal response of the kind usually frowned on in 'straight' literary circles. I'm not sure that – with one or two exceptions – there are any in-depth autobiographical pieces in *Smartass* of the calibre of those in *Cannoneer*. And there is some evidence of padding out with fragments which, though interesting to someone like me, are not valuable in themselves. It would seem that a liking for Krim also indicates a taste for the writers he admires, such as W.H. Manville, Leslie Garrett, Nat Hentoff, John Clellon

Holmes and Fielding Dawson, all of whom I've enjoyed reading over the years. To be fair, I take it that Krim has wanted to compile a record of his involvement with the literary scene in the sixties and thus these fragments – a handful of letters are also included – are of importance to the book as a whole.

Most of the pieces in *Smartass* use another writer as a springboard for Krim. If it isn't a writer it's someone like Lenny Bruce or Abbie Hoffman. And although the book doesn't have any obvious political overtones it does point towards a committed position on Krim's part, i.e. committed to the intellectual life of his time. Mailer, Eldridge Cleaver, Baldwin, James Jones – he writes about them all. And about the forerunners of the current mood – Nelson Algren, Paul Goodman. There's a reprint of his justly famous essay on Kerouac, and an interview with Alan Kapelner (little known in this country, though his first novel, *Lonely Boy Blues*, has been drifting around in paperback for some years) which has pertinent things to say about political 'commitment' and the role of the writer in society.

'The American Novel Made Me' is one of the best essays in *Smartass* and leads into what has become a major concern of Krim's in recent years – the relationship between literature and journalism, and the spawning of a non-fictional prose form. Krim documents how he grew up thinking that the novel was *the* main medium to aspire to, the one that would not only bring the rewards – financial and otherwise – but would also allow the writer to speak to a large audience about matters of importance. The novelists of pre-World War Two were his staple diet, particularly the social realists of the thirties when fiction did have power and impact. The piece has added value, too, in that it describes an era when magazines such as *New Masses* and *Anvil* regularly printed stories and other work by the hopeful young radicals. 'Meridel Le Sueur where are you now?' Krim asks rhetorically and yes, what did happen to Le Sueur and Grace Lumpkin and Ben Field and Tillie Lerner and all the others? I don't suppose many young poets and novelists have heard of them, let alone read their work, but scattered amongst the hack political passages and the well-meant but sentimental expressions of faith there are some patches of good writing.

Sales of proletarian novels were small – writers such as Steinbeck, O'Hara, Erskine Caldwell, Jerome Weidman (all of them realists though hardly radicals) were far more popular – but, all in all, prose was a potent force for many individuals in America and Krim is after something that will re-create the potency. The formal novel is played out, hence it's time to move on to a new form and this is being devised by what Krim terms the 'new communicators.' He mentions Tom Wolfe, Frederick Exley, Fielding Dawson – of *An Emotional Memoir of Franz Kline* and *The Black Mountain Book* – Irving Rosenthal, Mailer, Dan Wakefield, David McReynolds and others as being of his breed. They often write free-wheeling books that have the tensions and sometimes the structure of a novel but are basically autobiographical and detail the writer's involvements with current concerns. Personally, I'm not totally convinced that a sufficiently large body of work has been created to back up the claims for this form, although I must admit to having a great deal of sympathy for it and to liking most of what I've read by the writers mentioned.

If 'American Novel' defines Krim's stance as regards the novel-length works he says we need, much of the rest of *Smartass* backs up his arguments for, or outlines his belief in, the 'new journalism.' Many of his pieces are often more akin to 'journalism' than to what little magazine writers (especially in this country) think of as 'literature.' But Krim says that the 'new journalism' is where the action is and he may be right. In 'The Newspaper As Literature/Literature As Leadership' he analyses closely his reasons for admiring the people he claims are doing the important work in this line. The problem here is that although an English reader can gets the books Krim mentions, and even most of the quarterly and monthly magazines, it's difficult to see the daily or weekly papers regularly. So it's virtually impossible to comment on whether or not Krim has put his faith in the right cause. (It's only fair to point out that some newspaper articles do, of course, find their way into books – Jimmy Breslin's work has been published in this country.) I would have thought that the restrictions of journalism could prove dangerous for a 'creative' writer. Agreed, good journalism is often under-rated, being genuinely better than some so-called 'creative work,' but it isn't a form likely to give anyone time to collect his thoughts properly. Personally, I wish I could work a little more in this line without getting hooked on it as a means of earning a living; an attitude Krim would condemn – he would probably suggest jumping in at the deep end and either sinking or swimming. Moreover, the restrictions on expression (and I don't just mean the right to say 'fuck') are more likely to come from a newspaper editor than from a little magazine editor or publisher. Krim's desire for a more committed literature is understandable but one has to be careful that the need to activate, to reach a mass audience, doesn't swamp the aim to tell the truth, unpalatable as it may sometimes be.

On the whole *Smartass* is a less definite collection than *Cannoneer* but it is still a very good book, highly readable and stimulating. As a record of the sixties (certain areas of the period, at least) it is invaluable; as a record of Krim's activities it is fascinating. Here is a man who really does put all of himself into his writing, whether it's a book review, a letter, or an essay. Gilbert Sorrentino once said of Krim's writing, 'Thick, heavy, embarrassing reliance on hip slang words, but he tells the 'truth'. Which is commendable, though does not make an art.' It is a criticism with a fair amount of accuracy in it – Krim can sometimes come on with a coyness which completely spoils the serious intention of his work – but I think a handful of his essays stand outside the faults mentioned. And these essays have made 'an art.' It may be that the years will not be kind to much of Krim's writing – some of the more ephemeral pieces in *Smartass* are already starting to show their age badly – but I do firmly believe that things like 'What's *This* Cat's Story?', 'The Insanity Bit,' 'Ask For A White Cadillac,' 'The American Novel Made Me,' and one or two others will last, not only because they are well-written, but because they provide an honest and detailed picture of a period. Not every writer can manage even that.

One final point: on the face of it Krim seems totally bound up with the 'American experience' and English readers might well ask what the value of his writings is to them. Well, I would guess that much of what is termed the 'American experience' is rapidly becoming an international experience (and, don't forget, Krim's response is always a personal one). In any case the importance of events in America should be obvious to even the most casual newspaper reader. Also, one should be prepared to seek out good writing no matter where it comes from. I wouldn't want to propose following Krim's stylistic lessons – they do seem particularly American in many ways – but the general principles he discusses (his development of the essay form, his interest in the 'new journalism,' his concern for a non-fictional creativeness) could provide some healthy lessons for us.

Note

The books mentioned are *Views Of A Nearsighted Cannoneer* (Dutton, New York, 1968) and *Shake It For The World, Smartass* (Dial Press, New York, 1970). The Dutton edition of *Cannoneer* is a considerably enlarged edition of the original, published by Excelsior Press, New York, in 1961, though all the material in it dates from before 1960. *Cannoneer* has been published in this country by Alan Ross (1969) but this edition excludes the additional items in the Dutton version. In other words it is, apart from a lengthened version of 'Two Teachers – Nuts, Two Human Beings!' the Excelsior Press issue. The important pieces are in the Ross edition; the Dutton is useful from the point of view of the minor items which inter-connect with 'What's *This* Cat's Story?'

Shake It For The World, Smartass was published in Britain by Alison & Busby in 1971, though with 'Smartass' dropped from the title. A third Krim book, *You & Me*, was published by Holt, Rinehart & Winston, New York, in 1974, and like the others collected pieces from various newspapers and magazines. Krim committed suicide in 1989.

Index

'4 A.M.' (Fearing) 62-3
Abel, Lionel 178,188
Adrift Among Geniuses (Smoller) 40, 45
'After Anacreon' (Welch) 103, 110
Albert, Mimi 117
Albert Hall (1965) 30
Algren, Nelson 185-6
'All Hail Lord Buckley' (Cruickshank) 144
'The All-Hip Mahatma' (Buckley) 140-1
Allen, Donald 114, 159
'America' (Ginsberg) 84, 136
American Earth (Caldwell) 49, 50
'The American Novel Made Me' (Krim) 231
An American Procession (Kazin) 178
'American Rhapsody (5)' (Fearing) 63
Ames, Bernice 164
Angel Arms (Fearing) 58
Archetype West: The Pacific Coast (Everson) 99
Armory Show (1913) 32
'Asbestos' (Rolfe) 66
'Ask for a White Cadillac' (Krim) 228-9
An Autobiographical Novel (Rexroth) 32
The Autobiography of LeRoi Jones (Baraka) 120
'Autumn in New York' (Burns) 18-19
'Avant-Garde Artists of Greenwich Village' (Sandler) 205
The Back Country (Snyder) 90, 104
Baraka, Amiri 120
Barnes, Sally 205-7
Barrett, David 144
The Bastard (Caldwell) 49
Beat Coast East 121
Beat Hotel, Paris 122

The Beat Scene 109, 121, 125
Beatitude (magazine) 123, 125
Beatitude Anthology 121
The Beats (anthology) 121, 125, 227
Before the Brave (Patchen) 73
Being Geniuses Together (McAlmon) 42, 45
Bellow, Saul 218, 224, 225
Berge, Carol 120, 121
Berkeley UCLA 92, 106
'The Berry Feast' (Snyder) 91, 94
The Big Clock (Fearing) 56, 61
Big Sur (Kerouac) 105, 109, 111
Black Mountain College 17, 182-3
Black Mountain Review (magazine) 156
Black Spring (Miller, H.) 94
Blake, William 130
'Blue Boy' (Caldwell) 54
blues (magazine) 49
bop *see* jazz culture
Bowles, Paul 72
Braine, John 27
Brand, Millen 75
Bremser, Bonnie and Ray 117
Brewer, Dick 92
Brooks, Van Wyke 181
Broughton, James 93
Bruce, Lenny 86, 141, 142
Buckley, Richard 'Lord' 86:
    early life and career 137-40; magic
    power of love 140, 144;
    monologues 140-1; final ('Cosmic')
    tour 141-2; recordings 145; works:
    'The Naz' 137, 140, 143, 144;
    'Nero' 140, 143, 144; bibliography
    of 144-5
'Buddhist Anarchism' (Snyder) 97

Bukowski, Charles 13, 165:
    publications, England 168;
    directness 169-71; anti-
    intellectualism 171-4; technique
    174; works: 'Something for the
    touts, the nuns, the grocery clerks,
    and you...' 170-1; 'Voices' 172;
    bibliography of 175
Bunting, Basil 26
Burns, Jim:
    biographical details 11-19; The
    American Influence 23-8; works:
    'Autumn in New York' 18-19;
    'Change' 18; Confessions of an Old
    Believer 17; 'The Hip Messiah' 144;
    'Village Life' 17;
Burroughs, William 82, 127, 129-30
Caldwell, Erskine 12, 13:
    early career 47-50; story writing;
    50-2; politics 52-3; autobiography
    and travel writing 53-4; works:
    American Earth 49, 50-1; Call It
    Experience 54; Deep South 53; Georgia
    Boy 53; God's Little Acre 47, 51-2;
    'Midsummer Passion' 50; Poor Fool
    49; 'Saturday Afternoon' 52;
    'Savannah River Payday' 51; Tobacco
    Road 47, 51, 52; 'Wild Flowers' 55;
    biographies of 55
'Bury Them in God' (Patchen) 73-4
California 89, 110, 159 see also
    Hollywood, Pacific Coast, San
    Francisco
Call It Experience (Caldwell) 54
Cantwell, Robert 180
Capone, Al 138
Carroll, Donald 164
'Cartagena' (Snyder) 90
Cary, Joyce 137
Cassady, Carolyn 116
Chamber Jazz Sextet 77
Chamberlain, John 179
'Change' (Burns) 18

Chapman, Harold 122
Charters, Ann 126
Chicago Review (magazine) 217
Chicago 107, 218, 220 see also Rosenfeld
Children of Fantasy (Humphrey) 33-9
    see also Greenwich Village
City College, New York 177, 191-2, 210
'The City' (Maddow) 71, 132
City Lights (publishers) 77, 122
Clark, Walter Van Tilberg 54
'Class of 1934' (Patchen) 79
Close, Del 141
Cold Mountain Poems (Snyder) 102
Collected Poems (Patchen) 81
Collected Poems (Rolfe) 65, 71
Combustion (magazine) 156
'A Comment, Spring 1959' 155-6
Communist Political Association 84
Complete Poems (Fearing) 62, 64
Confessions of an Old Believer (Burns) 17
Conroy, Jack 78
Contact (magazine) 41
Contempo (magazine) 67
Corman, Cid 156
Coser, Lewis 198
Cowen, Elise 118
Cowley, Malcolm 147
Creeley, Robert 85, 156
'A Critic Without A Country' (Abel) 188
Cruickshank, Douglas 144
'Cultural Notes' (Fearing) 58
'The Culture of Contradiction'
    (Fishbein) 204
cummings, e.e. 74
Cuscaden, R.R. 165, 169
Dahlberg, Edward 72
Darden, Severn 141
The Dark Thorn (Gardiner) 75
Davidson, Michael 124
Death of a Salesman (Miller, A.) 56
'Decision' (Fearing) 59
Debs, E.V. 33
Deep South (Caldwell) 53

Dell, Floyd 34-5, 37
'Denouement' (Fearing) 59
Desolation Angels (Kerouac) 146
The Dharma Bums (Kerouac) 87, 94
di Prima, Diane 86, 119-121, 126-7
A Different Beat: Writings by women of
    the Beat Generation 128
Dinners and Nightmares (di Prima) 119
'Dirge' (Fearing) 56
Dissent (magazine) 195-6
Distinguished Air (Grim Fairy Tales)
    (McAlmon) 44
'Disturbers of the Peace' (Aaron) 204
Dodge, Mabel 36
Don't Look Now (Patchen play) 77
Dorn, Edward 155-6
'The Drama of Utterance' (Kenner) 158
Du Maurier, George 31
Duchamp, Marcel 32
Duncan, Robert 93, 156
Dylan, Bob 130
Earth House (Welch) 97-8
Eastman, Max 33-4, 37, 192
Eigner, Larry 163
El Corno Emplumado (magazine) 125
Ellen, Barbara see Moraff, Barbara
Ellerman, Winifred 41
Elliot, Ramblin' Jack 130
Engels, Friedrich 98
England see London; Migrant; Satis
Ethnic Passages (Ferraro) 216
'Evening on the Riviera' (McAlmon) 43
Evergreen Review (magazine) 110, 118,
    121, 123
Everson, William 93, 99
'Family Album' (Fearing) 61
Farewell to Reform (Chamberlain) 179
'The Farmer, the Sailor' (Kandel) 123
Farrell, James T. 215, 216
FBI see McCarthyism
Fearing, Kenneth 75:
    early life and career 56-8; social
    radicalism 58-62; on poetry 60;

works: '4 A.M.' 62-3; Angel Arms
    58; The Big Clock 56, 61; 'Cultural
    Notes' 58; 'Decision'
    61;'Denouement' 59; 'Dirge' 56;
    'Family Album' 61; 'Hold the Wire'
    62; 'Q & A' 59; 'St Agnes Eve'
    57-8; 'Villanelle of Marvellous
    Winds' 57
Fel and Firn Press 149
Ferguson, Otis 47, 179
Ferlinghetti, Lawrence 76, 78, 85, 93,
    111, 119
Ferraro, Thomas J. 209, 216
'First Love' (Rolfe) 67-8
'First They Slaughtered the Angels'
    (Kandel) 123
Fisher, Roy 158
The Floating Bear (magazine) 120-1, 206
For Love of Ray (Bremser) 117
Ford, James L. 202-3
Four Young Lady Poets 121
'The Fourth Decade' (Rosten) 71
'Fragment: the Names II' (Ginsberg) 118
Fred Engels in Woolworth's (Burns) 18
French, Warren 125
Front (magazine) 49
The Galley Sail Review (magazine) 125
Gardiner, Wrey 75
Gascoyne, David 75-6
Gastonia, strike (1929) 52
Gate of Horn (club) 141
The Gathering Storm (Page) 52
Georgia Boy (Caldwell) 53
'Georgia, Sweet and Kind' (Buckley) 140
'A Gesture to be Clean' (Turnbull) 162
Gillespie, Dizzy 25
Ginsberg, Allen 27, 71, 81, 113, 127:
    poetic and Jewish radical roots 84-
    5, 131-3, 135-6, 148; Six Gallery
    reading 93-4; Europe (1950-60)
    130-1; on censorship and
    materialism 133-4; works: 'America'
    84, 136; 'To Aunt Rose' 131;

'Fragment: the Names II' 118;
'HOWL' 71, 82, 132, 133; *Hydrogen Box* (opera) 134; Indian *Journals* 124; 'Kaddish' 84, 131, 135; 'Kral Majales' 130-1; *The Lion For Real* (record) 129, 131, 135; 'Return of the King of May' 131, 136; *White Shroud* 134
Giovannitti, Arturo 85, 132
Glass, Philip 134
The Glass Room 68
God's Little Acre (Caldwell) 47, 51, 52-3
Gold, Michael 59, 85, 132, 216
Goldman, Emma 33
Goodman, Paul 72, 75
'Governor Gulpwell' (Buckley) 140
Greenberg, Clement 194
Greenwich Village:
history and bohemianism 30-3, 201-3; books on 203-7 *see also Children of Fantasy;* New York
Greenwich Village (McDarrah) 203
Greenwich Village 1920-1930 (Ware) 201
Greenwich Village 1963 (Barnes) 205-7
Greenwich Village: Culture and Counterculture 201, 202, 204, 205
'Grishkin is Nice' (Hill) 156-7
Grove Press 113, 114, 123
Halper, Albert 59
Han Shan 101, 102
'The Hand That Fed Me' (Rosenfeld) 219
Hapgood, Hutchins 33, 35-6, 37, 38
A Hasty Bunch (McAlmon) 43
Havel, Hippolyte 202
Hayes, Alfred 212
Heath-Stubbs, John 161
Hemingway, Ernest 43
'Hermit Poems' (Welch) 112
'The Highly Prized Pyjamas' (McAlmon) 43
Hill, Hugh Creighton 156
Hip, Beat, Cool, and Antic (Montgomery) 149

'The Hip Gahn' (Buckley) 140
'Hold the Wire' (Fearing) 62
Holiday, Billie 142
Hollywood 61, 139, 182 *see also* California
Holmes, John Clellon 81, 83-4, 85
'Homage to Kenneth Patchen' (Corrington) 78
Honan, Park 125
Hook, Sidney 178, 188
The Horse's Mouth (Cary) 137-8
'The Hospital in Winter' (Fisher) 158
House-UnAmerican Activities Committee *see* McCarthyism
How I Became Hettie Jones 116, 120, 205
'How I Work as a Poet' (Welch) 112
Howe, Irving 16-17, 176 199:
early life 189-92; Trotskyist movement 192-3, 197; literary criticism 193-5; *Dissent* (magazine) 195-7, 198; utopianism 198-9; works: *A Margin of Hope* 190-1; *Politics and the Novel* 197; *World of our Fathers* 197-8; bibliography of 200
'HOWL' (Ginsberg) 71, 82, 93, 132, 133
Human Songs (Johnson, K.) 122
Humes, Harold 142, 143, 144
Humphrey, Robert E. 33-9
Hydrogen Box (Ginsberg) 134
'I Worship Paperclips' (Kaja) 122
The Iceman Cometh (O'Neill) 35
Iconolatre (magazine) 168
'An Illiterate but Interesting Woman' (McAlmon) 41-2
'In-Between Ladies' (McAlmon) 43
'The Incredible Survival of Coyote' (Snyder) 99
The Indefinite Huntress (McAlmon) 43
Indian Journals (Ginsberg) 124
'The Insanity Bit' (Krim) 229, 233
Intimacy (Sartre) 222-3
'It's All Very Complicated' (McAlmon) 43
I.W.W (Industrial Workers of the

World) 33, 95, 98, 153
Jack and Jazz: Woodsmoke and Trains (Christy) 149
Jack Kerouac: A Memoir (Montgomery) 148
Jack Kerouac: Beat, even in Northport (McGrady) 149
Jackpot (Caldwell collection) 54
The Japan and India Journals 1960-1964 (Kyger) 96, 124
jazz culture 25, 82, 85-6, 129-30
   see also Buckley
Jazz Gallery 141-2
Jews Without Money (Gold) 216
Joans, Ted 86
'Joe Hill Listens to the Praying' (Patchen) 73, 79
Johnson, Joyce 116
Johnson, Kay 122-3
'Jonah and the Whale' (Buckley) 140
Jones, Hettie 116, 120
Jones, LeRoi 86, 120
The Journal of Albion Moonlight (Patchen) 74, 75, 79-80
'Kaddish' (Ginsberg) 84, 131, 135
Kandel, Lenore 111, 123-4
Kapelner, Alan 231
Kaufman, Bob 85
Kaufman, Eileen 126
Kazin, Alfred 17, 18:
   early career and politics 176-81, 184-5; on Black Mountain College 182-3; on England 183-4; literary criticism 185-7, 199-200, 217; works: *An American Procession* 178; *New York Jew* 182, 184; *On Native Grounds* 178, 181-2; 'The President and Other Intellectuals' 185; *Starting Out in the Thirties* 178-9; *A Walker in the City* 177, 178; *Writing Was Everything* 176-7, 186, 187; bibliography of 187-8
Kees, Weldon 66

Kenner, Hugh 157-8
Kerouac, Jack 14, 85, 93, 96, 116, 132
   works: *Big Sur* 105, 109, 111; *Desolation_Angels* 146; *The Dharma Bums* 87, 94, 146; *Mexicon City Blues* 130; *On the Road* 82
Kerouac at the 'Wild Boar' & Other Skirmishes 149
The Kerouac We Knew 149
Kerouac West Coast (Montgomery) 94, 184
Kirkland, Jack 52
Klevar, Harvey L. 55
Klonsky, Milton 230
Knoll, Robert E. 45
Koda, Carole 97
'Kral Majales' (Ginsberg) 130-1
Krim, Seymour 142, 221:
   career details 227-8; and 'new journalism' 232-3; works: 'The American Novel Made Me' 231; 'Ask for a White Cadillac' 228- 9, 233; 'The Insanity Bit' 229, 233; 'The Newspaper As Literature/Literature As Leadership' 232; *Shake It For The World,_Smartass* 230-1, 232, 234; 'Two Teachers – Nuts, Two Human Beings!' 229-30, 34; *Views of a Nearsighted Cannoneer* 228, 234; 'What's *This* Cat's Story?' 221, 228, 233
Kulchur (magazine) 206
Kupferberg, Tuli 121
Kyger, Joanne 95, 96, 124
Labour Action (magazine) 192
Ladies Home Companion (magazine) 80
Lamantia, Philip 93
'Language is Speech' (Welch) 112
The Last Romantic (O'Neill) 34
Latterday Chrysalides (Hill) 156
Leeds, Charlie 149
Levertov, Denise 120, 156
Lewis, Sinclair 44
The Liberator (magazine) 34

A Life in Progress (Kaufman, E.) 126
'Life in Chicago' (Rosenfeld) 220
The Lincoln Battalion (Rolfe) 65
The Lion For Real (Ginsberg record) 129
'Little Ballad for Americans – 1954'
     (Rolfe) 69
The Little Review (magazine) 32
Living Theatre, The 206
London 129-130, 166
Louvet, Lucile 118
The Love Book (Kandel) 123
Love in Greenwich Village (Dell) 35
Lowenfels, Walter 94
'LSD – 748' (Johnson) 122-3
Lumpkin, Grace 52
Lynn, Kenneth 178
Maddow, Ben 71, 132
magazines, little 48-9 *see also*
Migrant; *Satis*; individual titles
Malcolm, Tom 164
Maltz, Albert 68
The Man with the Golden Arm (Algren)
     185-6
A Margin of Hope (Howe) 190-1
Markfield, Wallace 225
The Masses (magazine) 33-4, 132, 203 *see*
     also New Masses
'Masses of Men' (Caldwell) 54
McAlmon, Robert 40:
     early career 40-2; stories: (of
     expatriate life 43) (of the low life
     44); works: *Distinguished Air (Grim*
     Fairy Tales) 44; *An Illiterate but*
     Interesting Woman 37-8; 'Machine
     Age Romance' 44; 'Miss Knight'
     44, 46; *North America, Continent of*
     Conjecture 46; *Not Alone Lost* 42;
     Post-Adolescence 44-5, 46;
     bibliography of 45-6
McAlmon and the Lost Generation (Knoll)
     45
McCarthy, Albert 75
McCarthyism 61-2, 68-70, 89, 91, 184,

214
McClure, Michael 93
McDarrah, Fred 109, 121, 125, 203
McGrady, Mike 149
McGrath, Thomas 70-1
Mead, Matthew 161-2, 164, 165, 166
Melville, Herman 183, 218
Memoirs of a Beatnik (di Prima) 119
Memoirs of a Shy Pornographer
     (Patchen) 80
Mexicon City Blues (Kerouac) 130
Mica (magazine) 159
'Midsummer Passion' (Caldwell) 50
Migrant (magazine): quality and tone
     155-6; contributors 156, 158, 162;
     criticism of 157; influence of 158-9
Miller, Arthur 56
Miller, Dan B. 55
Miller, Henry 94, 141
Million Dollar Aztec Theatre 138
Milosz, Czeslaw 186-7
Mingus, Charles 77
Minor Characters (Johnson) 116
Miyazawa Kenji (Snyder) 104
Modern American Poetry 132
Montgomery, John:
     early career 146-7; Beats
     (acquaintance with 147-8) (edits
     essays and tributes 149); Rexroth
     and Kerouac influences 151-2; on
     British idea of USA 153; works:
     Hip, Beat, Cool, and Antic 149;
     Kerouac West Coast 148; 'Report
     from the Beat Generation' 148;
     'There were Hoofbeats at Sunset'
     149-50; bibliography of 153-4
Moon Calf (Dell) 35
Moore, Brew 149
Moraff, Barbara 121-2
Move (magazine) 15, 168
'Murder' (Buckley) 140
Murger, Henry 118
Murnaghan, Brigid 121

Muscle Beach (film) 68
Myths & Texts (Snyder) 95, 104
'The Naz' (Buckley) 137, 140, 143, 144
The Nation (magazine) 62, 70
'Nero' (Buckley) 140, 143, 144
Nelson, Cary 65, 69
New American Caravan (magazine) 49
The New American Poetry 110, 159, 163
New Directions 74, 81
The New Handbook of Heaven (di Prima)
    210
New Masses (magazine) 52, 58, 67, 73
    178, 212, 213, 231 *see also The*
    Masses
New Republic (magazine) 179
New York:
    books about 116; Bronx,
    immigrant life 189-90; City College
    177, 191-2; Harlem 229 *see also*
    Greenwich Village New York
    Intellectuals 220, 222, 226 *see also*
    Howe; Kazin
The New York Intellectuals (Wald) 188
New York's Greenwich Village (Delaney)
    203
The Newspaper As Literature/ Literature
    As Leadership (Krim) 124
Nomad (magazine) 121
North America, Continent of Conjecture
    (McAlmon) 46
'North Beach' (Snyder) 95
North Beach Beat movement 76-7, 91
Not Alone Lost (McAlmon) 42
'Now India' (Snyder) 124
'Nude Descending a Staircase'
    (Duchamp) 32
Nugget (magazine) 227
Odets, Clifford 68, 69
Odyssey (magazine) 161
'Off the Road' (Cassady) 116
Olympia Press 119
On Bread and Poetry 112

On Native Grounds (Kazin) 178, 181-2
On the Road (Kerouac) 82
'On the Role of the Writer and the
    Little Magazine' (Rosenfeld) 225
One-Eighty-Five 126
O'Neill, Eugene 35
Origin (magazine) 156
Origin of the Family (Engels) 98
Out of Step (Hook) 178, 188
'Out of the Soil and Rock' (Snyder) 90
Outlaw of the Lowest Planet (Patchen) 75-6
The Outsider (magazine) 78, 121, 122,
    125
Owens, Rochelle 121
Pacific Coast states 99: *see also*
    California; Hollywood; San
    Francisco
Pagany (magazine) 67
Page, Myra 52
Palantir (magazine) 15, 149
Paris 12, 48, 118, 122
Parker, Charlie 85, 139, 142
Parker, Dorothy 43
Parker, Muriel 214
Partisan Review (magazine) 67, 193, 196
'The Party' (Rosenfeld) 192-3
Passage From Home (Rosenfeld) 221-2,
    225
'Passage to More Than India' (Snyder)
    98
Patchen, Kenneth 119:
    early life and career, pre-Beats 72-
    6; illness 74, 77; on North Beach
    Beats 76-7; and jazz 77; criticisms
    of 78-9; works: *Before the Brave* 73;
    'Bury Them in God' 73-4; *Collected*
    Poems 81; *Don't Look Now* (play)
    77; 'Joe Hill Listens to the Praying'
    73, 79; *The Journal of Albion*
    Moonlight 74, 75, 79-80; *Memoirs of a*
    Shy Pornographer 80; *Outlaw of the*
    Lowest Planet 75-6; *Poems of Humor*
    and Protest 77; *See You In the*

Morning 80; *Sleepers Awake* 80; *They Keep Riding Down All The Time* 80
Paterson (Williams) 26
Peabody, Richard 14
Perkins, Maxwell 49, 51
Persephone (Shayer) 156
Phillips, William 224
Pieces of a Song (di Prima) 126
Podhoretz, Norman 182
Poe, Edgar Allen 132-3, 142
A Poem in Nine Parts (Mead) 162
'A Poem to Delight My Friends Who Laugh at Science-Fiction' (Rolfe) 69
'Poems of Humor and Protest' (Patchen) 77
Poetry (magazine) 32, 156
Poetry Quarterly (magazine) 75
Politics and the Novel (Howe) 197
Polsky, Ned 201
Poor Fool (Caldwell) 49
Post-Adolescence (McAlmon) 44-5, 46
Pound, Ezra 194
Prague 130-1, 133
'The President and Other Intellectuals' (Kazin) 185
The Proletarian Moment (Murphy) 216
Propper, Dan 86
Prospect (magazine) 165
Provincetown Players 35
Prynne, Jeremy 165
'Q & A' (Fearing) 59
Quagga (magazine) 163
Rahv, Philip 196
Rakosi, Carl 60
Randall, Margaret 125
The Real Bohemia 118
The Real Work (Snyder) 99
Reed, John 36-7, 38
Reed College 89-90, 94, 99, 106
Regarding Wave (Snyder) 96
Reich, Wilhelm 223
'Report from the Beat Generation' (Montgomery) 148

Residu (magazine) 122
'Return of the King of May' (Ginsberg) 131, 136
Revolutionary Letters (di Prima) 120
Rexroth, Kenneth: *An Autobiographical Novel* 32; on Kenneth Fearing 60-1; influence 19, 92, 93, 147, 151; on Kenneth Patchen 76, 77, 78
Ring of Bone (Welch) 112, 113
Riprap (Snyder) 90, 93, 94, 104
The Rise of David Levinsky (Cahan) 216
Rolfe, Edwin:
early life and politics 65-8;
Hollywood and McCarthyism 68-70; works: 'Asbestos' 66; 'First Love' 67-8; *The Lincoln Battalion* 65; 'Little Ballad For Americans – 1954' 69; 'A Poem to Delight My Friends Who Laugh at Science-Fiction' 69; bibliography of 71
Rosenfeld, Isaac 192-3, 217:
early life 218; politics 219-220; reviews 220-1; later life 223-4; works: *The Hand That Fed Me* 219; 'Life in Chicago' 220; 'The Party' 219; *Passage From Home* 221-2, 225; 'On the Role of the Writer and the Little Magazine' 225; 'Wolfie' 224; bibliography of 225-6
Rosenthal, M.L. 62
Rosten, Norman 71
Roth, Henry:
biographical details 208-212; and Eda Lou Walton 211-212, 214 ; politics 212-14; and Muriel Parker 214; works: *Call it Sleep* 208-10, 211, 212, 214, 216; *A Diving Rock on the Hudson* 211; 'Impressions of a Plumber' 211; *Mercy of a Rude Stream* 214-215; 216; 'Where My Sympathy Lies' 213
Russia 67, 100
Rutherford, Malcolm 161, 166

Ryley, Robert M. 62, 64
Saijo, Albert 109
Salud! Poems, stories and sketches of Spain by American Writers 65
San Francisco: books on 115, 118, 126; North Beach 76-7, 95
San Francisco Poetry Renaissance, 1955-1960 (French) 125
The San Francisco Renaissance (Davidson) 124
Sartre, Jean-Paul 222-3
Satis (magazine) 15, 160-5
'Saturday Afternoon' (Caldwell) 52
'Savannah River Pay Day' (Caldwell) 51
Scènes de la Vie de Bohème (Murger) 118
Scott Fitzgerald, F. 43
Scribner's 49, 51
'Scrooge' (Buckley) 140
Seaver, Edwin 212
The Second Story Man (Albert) 117
See You In the Morning (Patchen) 80
Shachtman, Max 219
Shake It For The World, Smartass (Krim) 230-1, 232, 234
Shayer, Michael 156, 158 162
Shechner, Mark 224, 225
Sinclair, Upton 153
Six Gallery (1955) 131, 147
Skelton, John 130
Skir, Leo 118
Sleepers Awake (Patchen) 80
Smith, L. Douglas 118
Smith, Larry R. 78, 80
Smoller, Sandford J. 40, 45
Snyder, Gary 85, 86, 110: fictionalised in *The Dharma Bums* 87; early memories and experiences 87-9; Reed College 89-90, 99; marriages 90, 95, 96; San Francisco 91-3, 95; Berkeley 92; Japan 94, 95-6; Sierra County 96; East/West 'tribes' philosophy 97-101; and Lew Welch 107-8, 110, 114; works:

The Back Country 90, 104; 'The Berry Feast' 91, 94; 'Buddhist Anarchism' 97; 'Cartagena' 90; *Cold Mountain Poems* 102, 104; *Earth House* 97-8; 'The Incredible Survival of Coyote' 99; 'A Journey to Rishikesh and Hardwar' 96; *Miyazawa Kenji* 104; *Myths & Texts* 95, 104; 'North Beach' 95; 'Now India' 124; 'Out of the Soil and Rock' 90; 'Passage to More Than India' 98; *Regarding Wave* 96; *Riprap* 90, 93, 94, 104; 'Why Tribe?' 100; bibliography of 104
Solomon, Carl 82, 84
Solotaroff, Theodore, on Rosenfeld 11-12, 220, 221, 222, 223
'Something for the touts, the nuns, the grocery clerks, and you...' (Bukowski) 170-1
Sorrentino, Gilbert 25, 81, 233
Spain 65, 67
Spector, Herman 59
'St Agnes Eve' (Fearing) 57-8
Starting Out in the Thirties (Kazin) 178-9
'The State of the Nation' (Patchen) 79
Sterling, George 153
Stern, Sally 125
Stevens, Wallace 74
'Stompin 'the Sweet Swingin Sphere:' Celebrating Lord Buckley' (Treger) 144
'Strawberry Season' (Caldwell) 54
'Street Corner College' (Patchen) 79
Strike! (Vorse) 52
Sullivan, Ed 138-9
The Sun Also Rises (Hemingway) 43
Swank (magazine) 144-5, 227
Sward, Robert 163
TASS, news agency 67
Tender is the Night (Scott Fitzgerald) 43
'There were Hoofbeats at Sunset' (Montgomery) 149-50

They Keep Riding Down All The Time
   (Patchen) 80
Thirteen American Poets 168
This Kind of Bird Flies Backwards (di
   Prima) 119
Thomas, Norman 77
Timbouctou Press 124
The Times, Caldwell's obituary 48
To An Early Grave (Markfield) 225
'To Aunt Rose' (Ginsberg) 131
To Make My Bread (Lumpkin) 52
Tobacco Road (Caldwell) 47, 51, 52
Tocqueville, Alexis de 185
Tomlinson, Charles 156
Totem Press 121
Town (magazine) 122
The Town And The City 83, 84
Trager, Oliver 144
transition (magazine) 48
Trilby (Du Maurier) 31
Trilling, Diana 135
Troia: Mexican Memoirs (Bremser) 117
Trotskyists 192, 213, 218, 219
Turnbull, Gael 157, 158, 162
'Two Teachers – Nuts, Two Human
   Beings!' (Krim) 229-30, 234
Types from City Streets (Hapgood) 36
Ulewicz, Laura 126
Union Square (Halper) 59-60
*Village: As It Happened Through A Fifteen
   Year Period* (McAlmon) 46
'The Village Beat Scene: Summer 1960'
   (Polsky) 201-2
'Village Life' (Burns) 17, 18
The Village Voice 228
'Voices' (Bukowski) 172
Views of a Nearsighted Cannoneer (Krim)
   228, 234
'Villanelle of Marvellous Winds'
   (Fearing) 57
Volunteer for Liberty 67
Vorse, Mary Heaton 52
Wakoski, Diane 121

Wald, Alan 219, 221
Waldman, Anne 125-6
A Walk on the Wild Side (Algren) 185-6
A Walker in the City (Kazin) 177, 178
Walton, Eda Lou 211
Wang, David Raphael 163
Webb, Jon Edgar and Louise 125, 163
Weiss, Ruth 125
Welch, Lew 91:
   parents 105-6 (mother 109, 111,
   113); Reed College 106-7;
   emotional conflicts 107, 111;
   marriage and career 108; and Jack
   Kerouac 105, 108-9, 110;
   autobiographical novel (1959) 109-
   10; Big Sur 111-112; radio
   interview, with Snyder and Whalen
   112; and Magda Cregg 112, 113;
   death 114; works: 'After Anacreon'
   103, 110; 'Hermit Poems' 112;
   'How I Work as a Poet' 112;
   'Language is Speech' 112; *Ring of
   Bone* 112, 113; *Wobbly Rock* 110;
   bibliography of 115
Western literary tradition 99-100
Whalen, Philip 91, 93, 108, 110, 112, 124
'What's *This* Cat's Story?' (Krim) 221,
   228, 233
White Shroud (Ginsberg) 134
'Who was John Peale Bishop?' (Carroll)
   164
'Why Tribe?' (Snyder) 100
Wieseltier, Leon 200
'Wild Flower' (Caldwell) 55
Wild Hawthorn Press 164
Williams, Jonathan 77
Williams, William Carlos 26, 40-1, 74,
   107
Wobblies (Industrial Workers of the
   World) 95
Wobbly Rock (Welch) 110
'Wolfie' (Rosenfeld) 224
women writers 116-128

Women of the Beat Generation 128
Woodcock, George 75
Word Alchemy (Kandel) 123
Workers' Party 219
World of our Fathers (Howe) 197-8
Writing Was Everything (Kazin) 176-7,
    186, 187
Yeah (magazine) 121
Yugen (magazine) 121, 125
Zephaniah, Benjamin 130